A JOINT ENTERPRISE

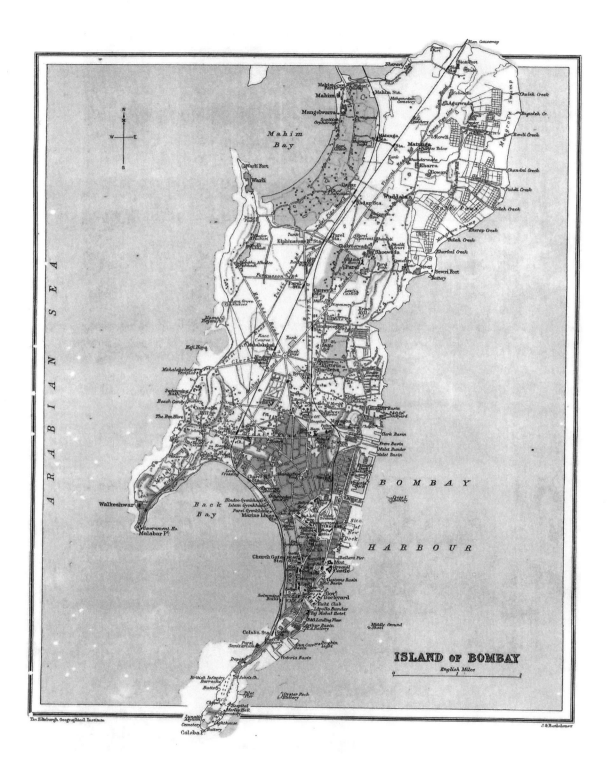

ISLAND OF BOMBAY

English Miles

ARABIAN SEA

Mahim Bay

BOMBAY HARBOUR

The Edinburgh Geographical Institute

J.G.Bartholomew

A JOINT ENTERPRISE

Indian Elites and the Making of British Bombay

Preeti Chopra

University of Minnesota Press
Minneapolis
London

The University of Minnesota Press appreciates funding to support the publication of this book. A subvention for this publication has been awarded through a competitive grant from the University of Wisconsin–Madison Provost's Office and the Graduate School; Graduate School funding has been provided by the Wisconsin Alumni Research Foundation (WARF) with income generated by patents filed through WARF by University of Wisconsin–Madison faculty and staff. Additional funding was provided by the Center for South Asia, University of Wisconsin–Madison.

Frontispiece: Island of Bombay, 1909, plan. From *The Gazetteer of Bombay City and Island,* volume 1, compiled by S. M. Edwardes (Bombay: Times Press, 1909).

Published by the University of Minnesota Press
111 Third Avenue South, Suite 290
Minneapolis, MN 55401-2520
http://www.upress.umn.edu

Library of Congress Cataloging-in-Publication Data

Chopra, Preeti.
    A joint enterprise : Indian elites and the making of British Bombay / Preeti Chopra.
        p.   cm.
    Includes bibliographical references and index.
    ISBN 978-0-8166-7036-9 (hc : alk. paper) — ISBN 978-0-8166-7037-6 (pb : alk. paper)
    1. Architecture and society—India—Bombay—History—19th century.
2. Architecture and society—India—Bombay—History—20th century.   3. Social ecology—India—Bombay.   4. Colonial cities—India—Bombay.   5. Bombay (India)—Buildings, structures, etc.   6. Bombay (India)—Social conditions.
I. Title.   II. Title: Indian elites and the making of British Bombay.
    NA2543.S6C49   2011
    720.954'79209034—dc22   2010047979

Printed in the United States of America on acid-free paper

The University of Minnesota is an equal-opportunity educator and employer.

18 17 16 15 14 13 12 11   10 9 8 7 6 5 4 3 2 1

To my parents,
Major General Uttam Chand Chopra,
PVSM (Retd.), and Mrs. Kushal Chopra

FIGURE 2.2. William Emerson, Arthur Crawford Market, Bombay, 1865–71, view of the west and northwest frontage of the fruit and vegetable markets, showing the center hall with three main gateways. Towering overhead is a clock tower. The Crawford Market was named after its founder, Arthur Crawford, municipal commissioner of the city from 1865 to 1871, and constructed on a prominent corner site at the junction of Hornby Road and Carnac Road. Photograph by author, 1999.

Napier advised such native gentlemen: "Discharge your Madras architect, and take a *mistry* from some remote part of the Mofussil where the traditions of the fathers are still preserved. Determine to have a national house, but such a house as an Indian gentleman should inhabit under an honest Government, in an age of peace, justice, and learning, a house in which the light of heaven and reason and freedom can penetrate."[31] Napier was sympathetic and respectful of the traditional domestic architecture produced by Hindus. Since Napier goes on to defend the Indo-Saracenic style in his lecture, it is useful to pause here and examine that defense in greater detail. Despite his respect for Indian traditions, Napier's position toward natives was condescending. Although critical of the architecture produced by architects for the wealthy and educated native, he seemed to think that members of the colonial elite, such as he, could judge and oversee the production of an appropriate style that melded Indic details and European styles—the Indo-Saracenic—that would not show a "confusion of taste."[32] This is quite different from the position taken by

Contents

Author's Note

This text uses both the words "native" and "Indian" to refer to non-Europeans, the latter term coming to play as nationalist themes resonate more strongly in the narrative. The choice of the term "native" needs some explanation, as Raymond Williams in *Keywords* (1983) shows that it can be used both pejoratively and in a positive sense. As Williams points out, "It was particularly common as a term for 'non-Europeans' in the period of colonialism and imperialism, but it was also used of the inhabitants of various countries and regions of Britain and North America, and (in a sense synonymous with the disparaging use of 'locals') of the inhabitants of a place in which some superior person had settled. Yet all the time, alongside this use, 'native' remained a very positive word when applied to one's own place or person" (215).

In Bombay, "native" was used both disparagingly and positively. Members of the colonial regime commonly referred to non-Europeans as "natives," but it cannot be assumed that every use of this term by Europeans was necessarily negative. Bombay's local inhabitants also used "native" when referring to themselves as a collectivity and before they saw themselves as "Indians." This term allowed them to see themselves as part of a larger community beyond their specific caste and religious affiliations. The term was used in a positive sense by "natives" unless a specific group, such as the Parsis at the end of the nineteenth century, no longer wanted to be included in the category of "native" and thus found the term pejorative. As Williams notes, the word "indigenous" has often replaced "native."

I chose to retain the term "native," as it is ubiquitous in colonial records, used self-referentially by the local population, and even deployed in the name of institutions. My use of "native" retains traces of the flavor of colonial records and the ambiguity of identity under colonialism.

Introduction

REGENT'S PARK IN LONDON is home to a drinking fountain, a structure that might draw little attention to itself except that it was paid for by a well-known nineteenth-century philanthropist from Bombay (Figure I.1). The Gothic fountain's sculptural features reveal the connection between Britain and its empire. Each side of the basin has a triangular pediment. The sculpted visage of Sir Cowasji Jehangir Readymoney, the fountain's donor, is flanked on one side by the face of a European lady and on the other by a European gentleman (Figure I.2). Beneath each of the four pediments is an arcuated frame. These contain a dedication stone, a coat of arms, a lion with a palm tree, and a horned Indian buffalo with a palm tree. Even without the dedication and portrait of Jehangir, the animals and vegetation suggest a tropical empire beyond Britain. Although the dedication plaque displays the gratitude of a loyal subject of the empire who benefited from colonial rule by being given imperial honors and a knighthood (1872), the similar location and detail of the sculptured medallion portraits suggests equality, not subservience, to the British worthies.

The dedication stone points to the history of the fountain's construction and its continued upkeep as a piece of Britain's heritage. The plaque announces that the fountain was raised by the Metropolitan Drinking Fountain and Cattle Trough Association and was gifted by Sir Cowasji Jehangir, who was a Companion of the Star of India, a chivalric order founded by Queen Victoria. Jehangir is described as a "wealthy Parsee gentleman of Bombay"; the gift was given "as a token of gratitude to the people of England for the protection enjoyed

FIGURE I.1. Fountain gifted by Sir Cowasji Jehangir and erected by the Metropolitan Drinking Fountain and Cattle Trough Association. Inaugurated in 1869, Regent's Park, London. Photograph by author, 2007.

by him and his Parsee fellow countrymen under British rule in India." Princess Mary, Duchess of Teck, inaugurated the fountain in 1869. Jehangir was knighted by the Queen in 1872, the second Parsi to receive such an honor. The dedication gives prominence to Jehangir's community—the Parsis. The Parsis, followers of the Zoroastrian religion, settled in India from Persia in the eighth or tenth century. They forged a close and beneficial relationship with the British, who encouraged them to think of themselves as distinct from the natives of India. The dedication articulates this community's self-consciousness by noting that this gift was made by a Parsi who, along with his fellow community members, had "enjoyed" the "protection" of British rule in India. The most prominent philanthropists in nineteenth-century Bombay were from the Parsi community. It often seems as if the Parsis, rather than the British, built British Bombay.

Described admiringly as the "Peabody of the East," Sir Cowasji Jehangir Readymoney (1812–78) was one of the most prominent Bombay philanthropists of his time. This tradition is continued by his family, making encounters with the Jehangir family name part of everyday experience. From an early start as a godown (warehouse) keeper, Jehangir gradually built a fortune, large sums of which he used in founding public institutions in Bombay and the Bombay Presidency—the province of which Bombay was the capital—and donating large amounts to public charities.[1] In the 1860s, Bombay Governor Sir Bartle

FIGURE I.2. Detail showing Sir Cowasji Jehangir's sculpted portrait above the dedication plaque on one side of the fountain. A sculpted portrait of an anonymous male figure above a sculptural panel with a lion and a palm tree in the background are carved on a second side. Photograph by author, 2007.

Frere's call was to construct a new Bombay; Jehangir was one of many wealthy men who responded to this call by pouring money into institutions, monuments, and other structures for the public-at-large. These philanthropists, a multiethnic and multireligious elite, gave their names to buildings and institutions; these names—Jehangir, Jeejeebhoy, Sassoon, Premchand Raichand, Gokuldas Tejpal, Cama, and Wadia, to name just a few—have a continuing impact on people's lives. While these native philanthropists constructed institutions for the benefit of their own communities, the new shared public landscape inaugurated by Governor Frere was marked by institutions for all members of Bombay's public.

From the second half of the nineteenth century, all of Bombay's citizens would have encountered institutions that Indian philanthropists helped found. Jehangir's philanthropic contributions in Bombay, for example, helped construct the educational and medical infrastructure of Bombay, the provisions of services (drinking water), and a public garden. In 1865, he encouraged female education by funding the Sir Cowasji Jehangir Readymoney School at Khetwadi.[2] Students graduating from Elphinstone College, one of the major new institutions for higher education at that time, would have spent years in the building paid for by Jehangir (see Figure 3.5). Students from the University of Bombay would have had their convocation ceremonies in the Sir Cowasji Jehangir Hall (1869–1874/University Convocation Hall) and gazed at his statue that graces the garden (see Figures 2.13, 2.14).[3] Individuals with vision problems could take advantage of the Sir Cowasji Jehangir Ophthalmic Hospital (1865) in Byculla, an independent building in the Jamsetjee Jeejeebhoy Hospital complex (see Figure 4.6). Those residents of the Bombay Presidency in need of mental assistance had the lunatic asylum established by Jehangir in Hyderabad, Sind. Residents of the Mahim section of Bombay and surrounding areas enjoyed the Sir Cowasji Jehangir Garden at Mori Road (1876). After 1865, Bombay's citizens drank water in one of the forty drinking fountains Jehangir raised in various areas of the city (see Figure 2.12).[4] One might say that by constructing a drinking fountain in London, Jehangir was leaving his philanthropic signature on the very center of British imperial power, just as he had across Bombay.

These projects were constructed by Jehangir and the colonial government in one manifestation of what I call the "joint enterprise," partnerships in which the philanthropist and colonial government shared costs and responsibilities in the making of a public realm in Bombay. Post-1860s Bombay was the product of scores of partnerships between native philanthropists and the colonial government. By joint partnership, Indians created a new landscape that supported the everyday lives of the city's cosmopolitan public, creating a new imagined community of Bombay's citizens.[5]

A JOINT ENTERPRISE: AN OVERVIEW

What is a colonial city? Two decades of careful scholarship have made it clear that cities are key to any understanding of the historical processes of colonialism, but this scholarship has also made it evident that we still do not really know how colonial cities came into being and operated, nor what their role was in the historical sociology of colonialism. Colonial cities are too often thought to be the products of the singular visions and needs of the colonial regimes that founded them, even though local inhabitants played a major role in shaping urban design and form. This book is a corrective to that distortion, concentrating on the role played by native communities in the physical transformation of the urban fabric of Bombay from 1854 through 1918. Though grounded in close attention to historical evidence in one place at one time, this study has broad ramifications for some of the most difficult issues currently being debated in the humanities and social sciences, including definitions of the public sphere, the multiple forms of collective agency, the significance of colonialism, the intersection of liberal exclusion and Indian practices of differentiation, and the relationship between religion and colonialism.[6] I argue that British Bombay was envisioned and built jointly by colonial rulers and Indian and European mercantile and industrial elites to serve their various interests. Key to understanding this urban history is seeing that the colonial city was the location for a range of new social spaces, such as the public realm, and new social practices, including important philanthropy by native elites.

The dates of this study encompass the years "of uncontested British supremacy."[7] The first textile mill was founded in Bombay in 1854, while the major physical transformations of Bombay, which included investments in infrastructure and public buildings, took place before 1918 and the end of World War I (Figure I.3). In 1864, the population of the city was 816,562; by 1911, it had risen to 979,445. The slow growth was due to the bubonic plague that first struck Bombay in 1896 and is not reflective of the continued vitality of the city. During this period of modernization, the old and new were juxtaposed. In Bombay, as elsewhere in India, this gave birth to various movements for social reform.

The joint enterprise that forged British Bombay was an intentional cooperation in several main ways. First, the colonial government and Indian and European mercantile and industrial elites shaped the city to serve their different interests, constructing an urban infrastructure conducive to economic and industrial entrepreneurs from both communities in the city as well as the colonial state (Figure I.4). Second, European and Indian engineers, architects, and artists collaborated to design the city, while Indian laborers and craftsmen left their mark on the designs they executed. Finally, Indian philanthropists entered

FIGURE I.3. India United Mills No. 1, a textile mill in Parel, Bombay. The large mills with prominent chimneys erected after 1854 transformed the landscape of Bombay. Photograph by author, 2006.

into partnerships with the colonial regime to found and finance institutions for the general public.

This joint enterprise of interest, design, labor, and financing produced the distinctive landscape of British Bombay. Public companies responded early to governor Frere's call by expanding the physical infrastructure and provision of services to the city. Large workshops were opened in Parel by the railway companies. The P. and O. Company embarked on the transformation of the Mazagon dock so as to make it the biggest and best timber slip in the city. In 1862, the Bombay Gas Company constructed a plant and successfully illuminated a section of the town with gaslight in October 1866.[8] In the second half of the nineteenth century, urban design schemes were centered near the Fort, the nucleus of the colonial settlement, which still possesses some of the finest Gothic Revival buildings in the world. Indian philanthropists helped underwrite many of these buildings, and Indians and British collaborated on the design of many of these structures. A good example of this partnership is the grand Victoria Terminus designed by Frederick William Stevens. It uses Indic details from the students of the Bombay School of Art, under the supervision of decorative-painting teacher John Griffiths, while the architectural decoration was carved by native craftsmen (see Figures 1.10, 1.12, 2.1, 2.7, 6.12).[9] Although the meaning of the Gothic Revival architectural style has been studied in the context

FIGURE I.4. Drawing of a visit of the Viceroy of India to the Sassoon Dock, Colaba, Bombay. The dock, opened in 1875, was constructed by Messrs. D. Sassoon and Company and purchased by the government for the Port Trustees in 1879. Courtesy Bhau Daji Lad Sangrahalaya, Bombay.

of Europe, no attention has been paid to how this architecture would have been read by a local population in the colonial world. As an analysis of their debates in architectural journals shows, finding the appropriate Anglo-Indian architectural style to represent "empire" was a matter of considerable anxiety for European architects and engineers. In the design and construction of these Gothic Revival buildings, European architects and engineers were assisted by native engineers. Although native engineers have been generally ignored by architectural historians, an exploration of one successful but anonymous native engineer reveals that he was an intentional actor, not simply a functionary, in designing the joint public realm of British Bombay (see Figure 3.1).

This joint public realm also functioned as a religious landscape for a publicly secular regime; commemorative spaces made reference to a civil religion in which mortal heroes and royalty replaced gods.[10] British and local commemorative and religious practices intersected, for example, in Bombay's Victoria and Albert Museum and the Victoria Gardens, where British royals were commemorated along with local philanthropists (see Figures 6.17, 6.18). Conversely, the secular British regime was also forced to accommodate a popular historical Muslim shrine whose devotees transformed a secular public space into a religious one, an example that reminds us that neither the colonial government nor the native elite could entirely control the current or future use or meanings of the spaces they produced (see Figure 6.21). The joint public realm celebrated the Indian making of British Bombay while acknowledging the role the British played even as it displayed the limits of colonial elites to shape the imagined community emerging in Bombay.

CHARITY AND PHILANTHROPY

As Raymond Williams shows in *Keywords,* words mean different things over time and reflect changed social and cultural understandings. "Charity," which came into the English language in the twelfth century, has meant many things: from "Christian love," to, in the seventeenth century, the idea of charity "as an institution." Originating in the eighteenth century and of immense significance to the practice of charity in colonial Bombay is the "specialization of charity to the *deserving poor* (not neighbourly love, but reward for approved social conduct)." Here, as Williams points out, charity was meant to uphold the bourgeois political economy in the sense of maintaining the need for wage labor.[11] Much like the earlier meanings of "charity," the meanings of "philanthropy" as "love of mankind" also shows the importance of feeling. However, philanthropy's concern with more concrete results is revealed in definitions such as "the disposition or active effort to promote the happiness and well-being of others," and "practical benevolence, now especially as expressed by the generous donation of money to good causes."[12]

After 1858, when India came directly under the British monarchy, the colonial regime increasingly looked to direct private native philanthropy toward projects the state saw as useful, such as schools and hospitals. They did not want the wealthy native elite to expend sums on feeding Brahmans, for example, whom they did not see as the deserving poor. Although Indians continued to feed Brahmans, pay *zakat,* and build fine temples and mosques, the Indian elite, particularly in Bombay, quickly learned that only by combining British ways of exhibiting charity in specific colonial projects would they be rewarded by the honors and titles they sought.[13]

The charity and philanthropy at the heart of joint enterprise in the building of colonial Bombay raises at least three questions. First, was this tradition of philanthropy new or are there precolonial examples of philanthropy or charity in South Asia? Second, was precolonial charity only directed toward religious ends or are there examples of nonreligious uses to which charity was put? Third, was charity that was directed toward the religious arena useless? Two brief examples from South Asia's precolonial past will suffice to show that philanthropy did not originate with the British and that all charity was not directed toward religious ends. Much of it was directed toward what the British would call useful ends even if they had a religious component.

Most of the public infrastructure—serving religious, economic, and other ends—in the city of Shahjahanabad founded in 1639 by the Mughal emperor Shahjahan (r. 1628–58) was constructed under the patronage of his family members, particularly by his daughters and wives. Shahjahan's daughter Jahanara Begum's numerous building projects in the city included the construction of the city's main thoroughfare Chandni Chowk (Silver or Moonlight Square), a *sarai* (inn), a hammam (public bath), and gardens, including the largest garden in the city, Sahibabad (Abode of the Master). High-ranking Mughal women also constructed mosques and other institutions in the city. One could argue that these noble Mughal women were philanthropists; their donations could be described as "practical benevolence."

Hindu temples in medieval South India often served economic functions. By concentrating on the shrine of Srî Venkateśvara in what is currently the southern Indian state of Andhra Pradesh, Burton Stein reveals the economic function of this southern temple in the medieval period of the late fifteenth and early sixteenth centuries. Land and other endowments were made to the temple. These cannot be seen as philanthropic donations since the donor was giving money so that temple rituals for the well-being of the donor or donor's family were performed. Temples were under the efficient secular management of the temple trustees, who invested money endowments in irrigation projects in rural areas. The produce that was generated helped provide employment to a number of temple functionaries. The economy of the town of Tirupati as well as the surrounding countryside was tied to the temple. This was not a unique arrangement; many South Indian temples used money endowments for irrigation projects and the development of the countryside.[14]

Such examples from precolonial India can be broadly categorized as examples of state patronage of useful projects, while in colonial India individual philanthropists collaborated with the state to create a public infrastructure. In contrast, in precolonial India, native elites were primarily involved in creating communal institutions at the neighborhood level. Although Jahanara Begum and the other women from the Mughal royal family are remembered for their individual donations, it is difficult to divorce them from the state. As high-ranking members of the royal family, they were part of the state that constructed the city. Burton Stein shows that temples became "indispensable because of the widely shared South Indian conception that authoritative human leaders (kings both large and small, imperial and local) and the deities installed in temples *share sovereignty*."[15] Here, the secular temple management, acting for the state where the kings and deities shared sovereignty, disbursed the funds effectively to create an infrastructure of wells and tanks in the temple's rural hinterland. In the precolonial examples, the state was the central provider of services and created the physical, religious, and economic infrastructure of the city and its surroundings. In contrast, in colonial Bombay, wealthy native businessmen who did not represent the state were philanthropists who worked with the colonial state to create institutions for the common public and are hence remembered for their individual contributions to the construction of British Bombay.

While these are examples of what the British regime would call useful charities, were charitable acts that resulted in feeding Brahmans, paying *zakat,* and building temples and mosques useless? Drawing on Mark Liechty's work on Nepal, I contend that they were not. Individuals participated in the religious arena for worldly and other-worldly gains and to retain membership in a community.[16] Bombay's native businessmen were caught between two worlds—the public religious arena of their respective communities and the secular public realm promoted by the colonial state. Those who participated in Bombay's joint enterprise continued to participate in what Liechty calls the "public religious arena" of their communities.

Although the colonial government in Bombay promoted philanthropy in this city based on long-standing practices in England, the parallels and contrasts between Indian and English philanthropy have not been explored. Charity has a long history in England, going back to the immense outpouring of wealth that flowed into Tudor charities and helped tackle many social ills. Private charity in England pointed the way to state action, which followed philanthropic efforts; in colonial Bombay, however, private charity did not in most instances point the way to state action.[17] Unlike in England, the native wealthy elite were the heads or leading members of their religious and ethnic communities. The colonial government considered them to be not only the leading representatives of their community but also those responsible for the welfare of their individual communities. As native philanthropists balanced the needs of their own communities and those of the colonial government, a new imagined community came into being, which allowed one to see a common public and a new common good, the good of the public-at-large.

THE PUBLIC AND THE JOINT PUBLIC REALM

Since the 1860s, the colonial government and wealthy native philanthropists founded institutions and built infrastructure to aid the emerging capitalistic development, but in so doing they also created a new public realm. My idea of the public realm is distinct from a conventional notion of the public sphere; I see the latter as an ideal type that needs to be more historically grounded. The work of the political philosopher Jürgen Habermas has dominated the discourse on the bourgeois public sphere. This public sphere is conceived of as an independent sphere that negotiates relations between the private realm (civil society and the realm of commodity relations) and the "sphere of public authority" (the state) and is able to hold the state accountable by the use of publicity. In theory, this is a democratic space that all citizens could inhabit and where public discourse takes place. Habermas sees the public sphere as an arena of discursive relations independent of the state and the economy, where private people come together as a public to discuss matters of common interest. In this idealized model, social and economic inequalities of status and interests are put aside in the effort to determine the common good.[18] The public realm in Bombay resulted from the dialogue and negotiations between the colonial government and the native elite. Although it was critical to the creation of a common public in Bombay, it was not the same as the public sphere. Distinct from concrete and imagined ethnic, religious, racial, and class enclaves, this joint public realm was a spatial arena that was, in theory, owned by and open to all of Bombay's citizens and helped in the construction of an imagined common public.

The creation of secular public institutions where people of all castes, religions, and races would interact at a more intimate level was a new phenomenon. The actions of the colonial government, however, were contradictory: it promoted the establishment of common public institutions and spaces, yet the British maintained their own separate institutions. The British encouraged Indians to shed caste prejudices; however, their practices of counting and separating (in the census operations and quotas, for example) fostered or created hard divisions in various Indian communities.[19] By examining hospitals and lunatic asylums, I show that this resulted in a fragmented public realm where the colonial government and native philanthropists tried to create special provisions for their own communities.

Ironically, despite the fractures in the public landscape of the city, the joint public realm fostered the sense of an Indian identity. While Europeans maintained a distance from the native population through exclusive and racially segregated clubs and hospitals, natives of varied classes, castes, and religions were forced to share space in hospitals and educational institutions. The jointly built landscape of civic institutions was appropriated by nationalists in the early twentieth century who argued for hiring native expertise to run medical and other institutions paid for by Indian philanthropists. Nationalists later argued that institutions founded by native philanthropists should be run by native expertise.

The joint public realm was a landscape of contradictions. It was both a fractured landscape that distinguished communities from one another as well as a cohesive landscape that brought people from diverse ethnicities, races, and religions together. At the same time, race and religion were the major fault lines running through this fractured landscape. Like Swati Chattopadhyay's study of Calcutta, this analysis of Bombay does not subscribe to the model of the dual city of colonialism, which sees race as central in organizing the city into a spatially segregated black town and white town.[20] The dual city was a colonial fantasy and obscured the hybrid realities of the daily lives of the colonizers.[21] Furthermore, in Bombay, race was a criterion used in the creation of intermediary groups between the British and native population—most notably, the Parsis, Baghdadi Jews, and Armenians, thereby further blurring boundaries. Native populations increasingly considered themselves members of multiple publics, each one larger and enclosing the former: the community/caste public, the religious public, as well as a member of the native public. However, Parsis were not always able to see themselves as part of the larger native public; at the same time, they were not considered to be Europeans. As Parsis were major philanthropists in Bombay, this community self-perception had spatial consequences, as seen particularly in the city's hospitals and lunatic asylums. Religion, the second fault line running through this fractured landscape, was far more unexpected and subtle, especially since religion was supposed to have no place in the joint public realm.

RELIGION AND SECULARISM

Even though the joint public realm—a spatial arena produced by joint enterprise—was putatively secular, religion continued to permeate it. By "secularization as a process," I mean what Peter Berger has described as "the process by which sectors of society and culture are removed from the domination of religious institutions and symbols."[22] Religious categories, the "civil religion" of the Freemasonry brotherhood, religious rituals, and religious spaces, continued to be relevant in the new secular public landscape.

The British had no problem accommodating religious communities in separate spaces in secular public institutions or visually dissecting South Asia's architectural heritage along religious lines. However, they were unwilling to allow religious rituals at these same sites. Nevertheless, the colonial government had no objection to Masonic rituals at foundation-stone-laying ceremonies at these sites, ceremonies that encouraged loyalty to the British monarch and the empire and helped to provide the foundation for the creation of a shared "civil religion." Even as practices of shared popular religion were being eroded in South Asia, a new civil religion was being forged that encouraged reverence of the British monarchy and empire.[23]

Knitting members of the European and Indian elite together was a brotherhood forged through the secretive bonds of Freemasonry. This brotherhood did not include all the Indian and European elite, but the social networks of its members extended far beyond Masonic lodges to include a large number of the elite. The role of Freemasonry in the joint enterprise lay in fostering an interracial, multireligious, and intercultural brotherhood; the encouragement of philanthropy toward projects that served the public good; and the formation of a "civil religion."

Modernizing Bombay required a clear separation between the religious and secular domains of the city. Religious structures standing in the way of modernization projects—such as new roads and railway stations—were demolished, and the sacred arena of gods and goddesses had to be contained within clearly demarcated and known boundaries.

However, the new public landscape in colonial Bombay was only secular on the surface. The statues of British worthies were the sites of the colonial regime's new civil religion, where the cult of remembrance flourished (see Figure 6.14). Indian philanthropists who contributed toward the foundations of these institutions were quick to raise their own statues hoping to be deities of this new era (see Figure 6.1). While Indians who encountered early statues of British worthies thought them to be those of gods, the colonial regime transformed Indian cave sites into on-site museums. Such monuments became sites of secular worship. Both British and Indian populations contributed to the continuance of religion, often in new guises and new forms, in the secular landscape of the joint public realm.

THE DESIGN OF THE BOOK

Chapter 1, "A Joint Enterprise," establishes the concept that Bombay was built and controlled jointly by the colonial rulers and the Indian and European mercantile and industrial elite to serve the interests of these classes and the commerce of the city. Arguing against the popular notion that a colonial city is the product of the singular vision of the colonial regime, I build on recent literature that shows how a variety of colonial cities resulted as much from contributions of local populations as from contributions of the colonial regime or settlers.[24] The objective is to demonstrate the operation of the joint enterprise and to introduce readers to Bombay by discussing the urbanization of the city and important phases of its growth.

Drawing on the work of Pierre Bourdieu's *Distinction,* chapter 2, "Anglo-Indian Architecture and the Meaning of Its Styles," argues that ongoing debates in the city over the appropriate format for Anglo-Indian civic architecture hinged on the maintenance of distance between the rulers and the ruled.[25] Drawing on Bourdieu's ideas on the importance of codes in analyzing a work of art and Dell Upton's distinction between style and mode, I address how the local population of Bombay understood its new public arena.[26] By focusing on the meaning of colonial architecture for its European designers and the local population, this chapter is central in underlining the importance of the local context to arrive at an accurate understanding of what was at stake in contemporary debates over architectural style.

Bombay's Victorian architecture was built by both British and Indian architects, engineers, and craftsmen. However, the role played by Indian architects and engineers in the making of British Bombay has been largely ignored. Chapter 3, "The Biography of an Unknown Native Engineer," examines the role of Indian architect and engineer Khan Bahadur Muncherji C. Murzban. This is a rare in-depth study of a native professional at a time when architecture itself—even in Britain—was just beginning the process of professionalization.

Focusing on hospitals and lunatic asylums, chapter 4, "Dividing Practices in Bombay's Hospitals and Lunatic Asylums," shows how European racial prejudices and the nineteenth-century obsession with counting, sorting, and separating met its counterpart in Indian prejudices of ritual pollution and local interests to create a divided public realm. In the case of the Parsis, philanthropy also became a means of altering their racial status.

Chapter 5, "An Unforeseen Landscape of Contradictions," examines the unforeseen contradictions of the joint public realm by focusing on the creation of government-run and jointly funded public institutions. Interestingly, the very success of the joint enterprise in Bombay made the British increasingly redundant.

Chapter 6, "Of Gods and Mortal Heroes: Conundrums of the Secular Landscape of Colonial Bombay," takes up the issue of the role of religion in the putatively secular public landscape produced by the joint enterprise. This concluding chapter shows that neither the British nor the Indian elite could contain or control the meanings ascribed to this landscape.

1 A Joint Enterprise

ON 5 MARCH 1839, five prominent native business-
men of Bombay proposed a scheme to the government that would cost over
two hundred thousand rupees, a huge sum in those days. The scheme consisted
of the building of a wharf and basin at the Cooly Bunder (dock) for the landing
of grain, and the extension of this wharf as far as the Bori Bunder for the landing of cotton or any other merchandise. In their letter the merchants added,

> We doubt not that considering the importance of the undertaking to the
> interest of a large portion of the community; and the expense that will be
> involved in the completion of it, upwards of two lacs of Rupees—as also
> the improvement it will confer upon the island of Bombay—*an improve-
> ment the furtherance of which we have always understood it to be a particular
> object of attention to the Government of this Presidency to have effected through
> private enterprise,* our humble request will be favorably taken into consider-
> ation by the Honorable the Governor in Council.[1]

In other words, business leaders understood that the colonial government believed that private enterprise would play an integral role in the development of
the city.

This chapter explores the city that was built and controlled jointly by the
colonial rulers and the Indian and European mercantile and industrial elite to
serve the interests of these classes and especially their interests in the commerce
of the city. In this city, the government and capitalists worked together to develop the city through projects that were mutually beneficial. Especially since

the 1860s the government, with the help of the philanthropic individuals of the capitalist class, created institutions to form the new public realm and built infrastructure to aid the capitalistic development that was emerging. These institutions included hospitals, educational institutions, asylums, and dispensaries for the use of the public at large. The joint partnership between the government and financial elite dominated the direction of urban planning and local government, but by the 1920s the control of the upper classes was under attack.

My argument that the building of colonial Bombay was a joint enterprise of the colonial regime and Indians stands in contrast to that of Anthony D. King, who credits European imperialism and colonialism alone with the creation of colonial cities.[2] King sees global influences at work in colonial cities, but in Bombay as well as elsewhere these influences were met head on by local influences and politics, which were equally determinant forces in the making of colonial cities. As the opening anecdote of this chapter indicates, in Bombay, taxpayers, landlords, and intellectuals, as well as industrialists and merchants who were involved in the global commodity exchange, were influential actors in molding urban-planning policies conducive to their agendas, demonstrating the ways, as geographer Jane Jacobs has argued, that global and local already inhabit one another.[3]

Gyan Prakash and Douglas Haynes recognize that in unequal power relations there is both dominance and resistance and "struggle is constantly being conditioned by the structures of social and political power." While acknowledging the importance of what James Scott calls "everyday forms of resistance," Prakash and Haynes argue for the need to look at both extraordinary and everyday resistance. Of particular significance is their argument that resistance is not always overt and conscious. They define resistance "as those behaviours and cultural practices by subordinate groups that contest hegemonic formations, that threaten to unravel the strategies of domination; 'consciousness' need not be essential to its constitution."[4] In Bombay, both ordinary and privileged sections of Indian society undercut colonial and elite projects by challenging the government in court or by bargaining with the government through contestatory acts that were not always overt or conscious. Although the cooperation of the native elite and colonial government was central to the operation of the joint enterprise, the native elite did not simply follow the government's directions. Instead, cooperation, the negotiation of unequal power relations, domination, and resistance were all features of the complex relationship that made the city of Bombay and shaped a range of more specific social processes: from migration—both from the hinterland to the city and within the city itself—to commerce and industry, urban design schemes, and the partnership between government and private enterprise.

THE CITY AS PALIMPSEST

Cities are in a continuous state of transformation and are comparable to a palimpsest: a text or a parchment that has been written on, erased, and written on again. The local elite played a complex and multifaceted role in city design, and by doing so they constructed, erased, and transformed the city. As landowners they made deals with the government. As men of business they acted as advisers, partners, or investors in schemes. As men of wealth, they built wells, tanks, and religious, educational, and medical institutions. They influenced the course of development and opposed government schemes if they negatively affected their interests. A city is made up of multiple layers, making this exercise of digging up the past an archaeology of the city. When talking of layers, I mean the erasures and writing that make the city a palimpsest—in this case, the destruction and construction of buildings, open spaces, and the city infrastructure—that characterized a certain era (Figure 1.1).

Negotiating the Best Deal: Native Landholders and the Width of Roads

Large landholders in Bombay concretely shaped the city in making deals with the government when the government needed to acquire lands in their possession. By the mid-nineteenth century, most of the land in Bombay was in the hands of Indians. This was the case with *foras* lands, which were in the hands of numerous tenants, some of which were required by the government for building roads and other public amenities. Sir Michael Westropp, the judge in one key case, derived *foras* from the Portuguese word *fora*, meaning "outside," to indicate the rent or revenue obtained from outlying lands.[5] Roads from the Fort traversing the Flats, or *foras* lands, between Malabar Hill and Parel, were generally known as "*Foras* Roads."[6] In 1805, *foras* land had a specific meaning as was shown by Advocate-General Thriepland of Bombay while arguing a specific case in Bombay: "It is called *foras*, . . . a Portuguese expression, the meaning of which is rent, but which in this island denotes the rent in particular which is paid by a cultivator or person permitted to occupy ground for the purpose of improving it, but without any lease or other grant by which he can maintain possession during the continuation of the term."[7]

It is significant that Thriepland discusses the understanding of the term *foras* in Bombay as the rent paid by a cultivator or person allowed "to occupy ground for the purpose of improving it" but without a formal lease or legal document. Apart from immovable objects such as houses, hedges, and fences, ownership of land in England could be acquired through repeatedly employing it for

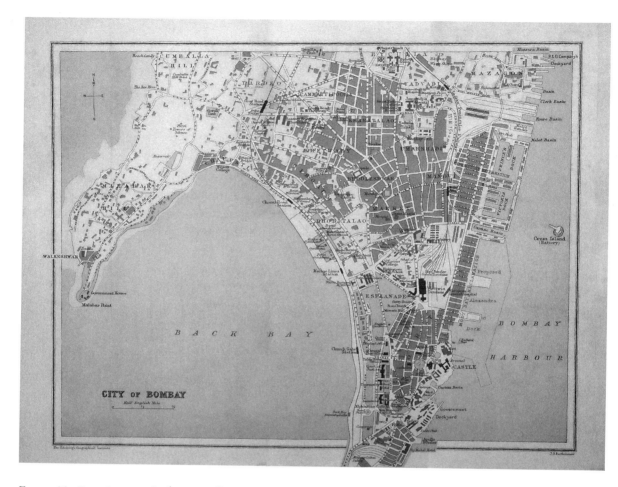

FIGURE 1.1. City of
Bombay, 1909, plan.
From *The Gazetteer
of Bombay City
and Island,* vol. 2,
frontispiece.

agriculture or for pastoral use, both of which activities were seen as improvements in the seventeenth and eighteenth centuries.[8]

Although the government owned the land, in practice the rent-paying tenants sold and disposed of it as they wished, treating it as their property. In 1841, the government took some pieces of land near the racecourse for stacking hay without compensating the occupants; the assumption was that it was government property. A memorial signed by over seven hundred persons was sent to the government in which they claimed their title to the lands. In his opinion, Advocate-General LeMesorier warned the government that if the memorialists entered into litigation, they would be successful in establishing their title to the lands, which many had held, directly or through their ancestors, for twenty, forty, sixty years or more. Based on this report the government issued an order on 4 April 1844 observing that the history of the origin of *foras* lands established the government's proprietary right over such lands. However, because of various circumstances the occupants were led to view this land as their inheritance. The governor did not wish to take all *foras* lands, but only to reserve those pieces of land that were going to be required for works of public utility in the future, while conceding the rest of the land to the current tenants on some scheme of tenure.[9]

In 1847, William Acland, the East India Company's solicitor, met with the major holders of *foras* land in Bombay, including Dadabhoy Pestonjee, Jagannath Shankarshet, and Bomanjee Hormusjee. Copies of the plans were handed out showing the various *foras* grounds and the projected roads. Acland explained to them that the holders of the *foras* ground needed to reach an agreement among themselves for compensating the holders of the ground that was to be made over to the government, free from all claims, because it was required for roads and so on. After this the government was prepared to draw up legal documents confirming the tenure of the landholders. The landholders conveyed to Acland that rather than having their rights being declared by a legislative act, they preferred this course of action, as each landholder would have his own deed of confirmation of title.[10] Acland thought he had come to a satisfactory arrangement with the landholders, but he found this was not the case. Enclosing a letter from the three landholders, he advised the government to take swift action as buildings and other improvements were rising in the *foras* lands. The advocate general assured him that it would be possible to deal with the whole matter by a legislative act if necessary. The act could provide for a committee with the powers to ensure that landholders whose lands were taken from them for public purposes were fairly compensated by other landholders.[11] In short, if the landholders did not make a deal, the government could threaten them with a legislative act.

The letter from the three principal landholders to Acland addressed the question of the width of the proposed roads. They argued that the sixty-foot breadth requirement of the new roads seemed excessive to them since Grant and Bellasis roads, which were major public thoroughfares, were approximately forty feet wide. The proposed roads, on the other hand, were unlikely to be used except by the occasional foot passenger or vehicle for pleasure or recreation. Furthermore, even a forty-foot-wide road would require a sacrifice of a large portion of their respective lands, large sums of money, and a loss of time and trouble spent in persuading people to agree to the proposed project. If the sixty-foot width included twenty feet for the drains, then they opposed the proposal on the grounds that the drains, with their stagnant water and "noxious effluvia," were themselves objectionable. They pointed out that the island abounded in examples of such problematic sewers, and the "tainted atmosphere" could only be remedied by constructing covered sewers.[12] The government was ready to restrict the width of the road to forty feet, if the landholders completed the arrangements for the settlement of this long-standing issue by giving a definite date for effecting the transfer of the required land to the government. If not, a legislative enactment would be used to deal with the matter.[13] By threatening to use a legislative act, the government was able to make a deal with the major landholders regarding the width of the proposed roads. However, the major landholders could not fulfill their commitment to the deal, as a small minority of landholders opposed the conditions.[14] Finally, a few leading *forasdars,* or landholders, applied to the government to pass an act empowering it to take possession of the required land and to appoint a commission to determine the amount of compensation and to collect ratable contributions for a fund.[15]

Although the government's desire to build broad roads may have been influenced in part by policies emanating from England, it had to adjust to the local circumstances of Bombay, where Indians controlled most of the land. Since the principal landholders were unable to fulfill their part of the deal, it is not clear whether the government agreed to let the proposed roads be forty feet wide instead of sixty feet. However, the government recognized that compromise with the native elite was necessary to arrive at mutually beneficial solutions so necessary to the further improvement and building of Bombay. In this example, the businessmen were not engaged in conscious acts of resistance toward the colonial regime, but as property owners they were simply ensuring that they got the best out of this deal. Doing business with the government led them to appropriate colonial discourses on sanitation—as the discussion on the drains shows—for their own purposes. By criticizing the drains in the city, the landholders hoped to make an argument against the proposed twenty-foot drains, thereby allowing them to hold on to more of the *foras* lands instead of turning these over to the government and be responsible for paying less compensation to those who had lost their land since less land would have been lost. Men of property in Bombay were preoccupied with making money, and they did not let colonialism stand in the way.

Early Philanthropy and the Erasure of a Landscape of Wells and Tanks

With a few notable exceptions, most of the early philanthropic efforts in Bombay were directed toward the building of wells and tanks for the use of the general public. Not merely sources of water supply, these water sources with their platforms, steps, shrines, and trees formed part of the cultural landscape of Bombay. They were the foci of daily rituals, spaces of public interaction, and public spaces that shaped the neighborhoods around them creating a multifocal urban landscape in Bombay.

COMMENCEMENT OF THE RESERVOIR, IN THE VALLEY OF VEHAR, ISLAND OF SALSETTE.—(SEE NEXT PAGE.)

Bombay had long suffered from a shortage of clean water, and the government and public in the 1850s were keenly aware that contaminated drinking water led to the death of thousands from cholera. The construction of the Vehar reservoir in 1850 was the first attempt to tackle the water problem on a large scale (Figure 1.2).[16] A series of schemes followed, but each proved insufficient to meet the needs of the growing population. Water from Vehar was first introduced to the city in 1859, but people only began to get water at their door in 1864.[17] In 1879, the Tulsi works were completed; the Bhandarwada and Malabar Hill reservoirs were constructed in 1884. In 1889–90, Tomlinson's water works in the Powai Valley was begun. The Tansa water works, a major project, was initiated in 1885 and opened in 1891–92.[18]

The relatively small sums of money required for the construction of tanks and wells allowed many wealthy citizens to participate in acts of charity (Figure 1.3). Several of the wells and tanks built by native philanthropists became famous landmarks in the city. Sir Dinshaw E. Wacha noted with approval that "Hindus and Mahomedans of the first half of the nineteenth century vied with each other to supply this great necessity of life to the masses in the town by the construction of large tanks."[19] It was Framji Cowasji, a Parsi citizen of Bombay, who was the first to think of redirecting water from its original source to the

FIGURE 1.2. Drawing showing the commencement of the reservoir in the valley of Vehar on the Island of Salsette. Work on the Vehar Lake and Water Works started in 1856. Courtesy Bhau Daji Lad Sangrahalaya, Bombay.

FIGURE 1.3. Parsi well near the Esplanade *maidan,* Bombay, late nineteenth century. Courtesy Bhau Daji Lad Sangrahalaya, Bombay.

place where it was most needed. In 1837, he got the freehold lease of the Powai estate. The Cowasji Patel Tank in the native town was widely used by the local population and was built around 1780.[20] In 1846, the level of water in the tank fell. Cowasji conceived of overcoming this deficiency by supplying it with water from a nearby *oart* (coconut garden) known as Mugbhat.[21] Three wells were sunk here and water was conveyed to the tank through steam machinery that cost thirty thousand rupees. Using an aqueduct, he conveyed water from Cowasji Patel Tank to two tanks at Duncan Road that were colloquially referred to as Do Tanki (Two Tanks). Cowasji came to an arrangement with the government regarding the rents and revenues of his Powai estate, and in return promised to ensure an adequate supply of water to the two tanks.[22] Suslaji Subanji, a Muslim, constructed the Do Tanki in 1826 and presented them to the public.[23]

Tanks and the roads that featured them were named after their benefactors. Thus we find that these tanks also gave their names to various roads and localities. Framji Cowasji reconstructed the tank known as Dhobi Talao and subsequently renamed it Framji Cowasji Tank in 1839. This tank was used by *dhobis* for washing clothes until they moved to two wells on the northwest corner of the Esplanade some years before this tank was filled in.[24] The Babula Tank was constructed in 1849, and there is a Babula Tank Road. The tank on the Esplanade known as the Nakhoda Tank, constructed in 1856, was paid for by Muhammad Ali Roghay, a prominent Konkani Muslim businessman.[25] The Cowasji Patel Tank, built by a Parsi gentleman by the same name, has given its name to the Cowasji Patel Tank Road. Colonel George A. Laughton's maps of Bombay in the early 1870s, based on a survey conducted between 1865 and 1872, show the town and island to be studded with tanks, while municipal maps of the early twentieth century reveal thousands of wells (Figure 1.4).

In the mid-nineteenth century, two wells in the Fort area were so famous "as to be a household word in every family." Their names were Ganbava and Ramlal. Ganbava was located at the eastern end of a street with that name, where Borah Bazaar Street crossed it. Men, women, and children would crowd around the well from morning to evening. Often, fights would break out, presumably as people jostled for their turn to fill their vessels with water. At the height of summer people would come there as early as one in the morning to fill their "chatties" with water. The Ramlal well, constructed by a wealthy Marwari, was located in the southern part of the *maidan*. It is buried into the outer wall of the High Court near the judge's entrance gate facing the Oval, revealing a plaque, which details its origins.[26]

The building of wells and tanks for the public was seen as an act of public good by the government. Donors were not averse to reminding the government about these good acts when asking for its favor. One example is the application for a grant of land on Malabar Hill by Bomanjee Jamsetjee Moollah and his partners in 1850. Moollah was building a bungalow on his land and requested the government to allot him two adjacent waste plots of land to convert into a compound with a garden and carriageway. In his application he mentioned that he and his partners had spent over three thousand rupees in sinking a well in the neighborhood, which provided all the gentlemen living in that area "good water." In light of the "heavy expenses" incurred by his firm, he hoped the government, "as a slight remuneration," would waive the rent of these additional pieces of land. The collector, in his report to the secretary to government, stated that the applicant planned to sink another well for the use of the public, marked D on the plan, at a cost of thousands of rupees. Citing these acts of public benevolence, the collector urged the government to grant Moollah the spots A and B, at the same ground rent as paid by other holders of government land. The government refused this request as there was a police *chowky* (check post) on one of the spots and because it did not want to encourage building in a locality that it considered overcrowded.[27]

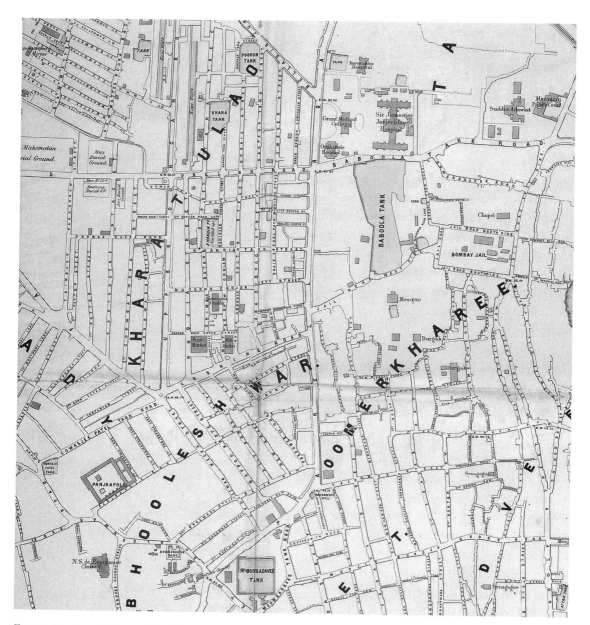

FIGURE 1.4. Detail of map of the Island of Bombay, enlarged from Colonel George A. Laughton's survey map, 1882. Note the numerous tanks, including the Baboola Tank adjacent to the Bombay jail, the Moombadavee Tank at the center bottom, and the smaller Khara and Poorum tanks near the top of the plan. Copyright The British Library Board. Maps 186 v.4.

Donors of wells protested as the destruction of the ramparts in the 1860s resulted in the removal of the wells and thus erased a landscape created by philanthropic efforts. The new area opened up by the removal of the ramparts provided an open terrain for the exercise of a new era of philanthropy on the burial ground of the old. In 1863, several donors wrote to the government asking for reparations. Dinshaw and Nusserwanjee Manockjee Petit gently reminded the government that in 1854 and 1855 their father was granted permission by the government to sink two wells, one on each side of the bridge that led to the Fort from the Church Gate. Over and above the cost of the wells, their father incurred considerable expenses for the alteration of the palisades and other associated costs. Now they found that these "works of charity which our father had erected, and which he, no doubt, believed would have remained for many years as mementos of his liberality and public spirit, are to be destroyed." The Petits clarified that this was not a complaint, but an inescapable result of the great public improvements carried out by the government. Referring to a similar concession made to a Goculdass Lilladhur in regard to a well he had sunk on the Bombay Green, they said that they would be happy to augment the compensation the government was going to give for these wells. The money would be used toward the construction of a well or a fountain in Elphinstone Circle or Frere town that would help perpetuate their father's memory.[28]

Alarmed by the possibility of paying compensation to these founders of wells and setting a precedent, the government referred the matter to the solicitor to government, who said that the founders of wells had no legal claim to compensation. In 1864, a government resolution stated that since it had supplied the inhabitants of Bombay with "ample" supplies of water, these charities had ceased to exist and the government had to remove them to prevent them from becoming a public nuisance. The government did not admit the right of the donors to compensation, but stated that it would honor the memory of the charity of those who had sunk wells at a time of great need by asking the Rampart Removal Committee to preserve the inscriptions on all wells and suggest a way of permanently commemorating these public acts of charity.[29] I know of no memorial to these wells. However, it points to a larger issue of the ownership by government of wells, tanks, and institutions dedicated to the public. There are other examples, at a later date, of the government changing the use of an institution to something quite different from that for which it was originally endowed.

Wells were closed not only because they were in the way of modern improvements but also to ensure that Bombay's inhabitants used Vehar water and compensated the municipality for these improvements. This is quite clear in the protest made by Sayad Amadudin Sanaf Sayad Shah Jehan Rafai and other Muslim inhabitants of Bombay who petitioned the government in 1880 and

1881, asking them to exempt mosques from the new water rates since these rates were against their religion. In their 1881 memorial, the petitioners elaborated in some detail how this violated Muslim law. In their petitions, they also emphasized that they now no longer had wells and tanks of their own because they had been filled in since the introduction of Vehar water. In their 1881 memorial, they petitioned the government to reconsider their memorandum no. 3457, dated 17 November 1880, a response to their earlier memorial which stated that the "Government sees no reason why a distinction should be drawn between Mahomedan and other places of worship."

The memorialists were attempting to resist the policies of the municipality by appealing to a higher authority, namely, the government. Their use of a signed petition reveals the adaptation by the native citizenry of colonial British procedures. In applying water dues to all areas of the city, the municipal authorities, using the logic of capitalism, assumed that the city was a neutral grid. Referring to the government's tolerance of various faiths, the petitioners attempted to remind the government of their responsibilities as protectors of religious practices and refuted the logic of universality by contrasting it to the logic of the particular, in this case, of Muslim law. The government replied that they could not interfere in the matter and the use of water supplied by the municipality was optional. If its use was considered to be against their religion, then, they were told, they should find other sources of supply.[30]

In 1911, Dr. Bentley's final report on the malaria epidemic of 1907 and 1908 correlated the high incidence of malaria with high numbers of domestic wells. The municipality-led campaign that followed resulted in the closure of most of the wells and tanks in the city of Bombay in the second decade of the twentieth century despite major opposition from the public on grounds of inadequacy of municipal supply of water and religious concerns. All wells, not just domestic wells and tanks, were targeted.[31] The municipality's water supply was insufficient throughout the second half of the nineteenth century and the early decades of the twentieth century. In 1914, members of the public petitioned the government against the closure of wells; they argued that wells were used to make up for the inadequacy of the water supplied by the municipality.[32] The filling in of tanks and wells by December 1917 created 28.01 acres of open spaces and implied the complete transformation of the landscape of the city.[33] A visit to Banganga Tank or an old print of the Framji Cowasji Tank with buildings around it brings to mind the impoverishment of the landscape and the removal of gathering places and ritual sites that resulted from the sealing of these tanks (Figure 1.5; see also Figure 6.7).[34] A plaque at the latter site reminds us of its previous existence, but the memory of most tanks persists only in the names they have left to localities and roads (Figure 1.6).

FIGURE 1.5. Banganga Tank, Walkeshwar, Bombay, view of tank framed by the *deepstambhas*, or lamp pillars. Photograph by author, 1999.

FIGURE 1.6. Plaque commemorating the Framji Cowasji Tank on the boundary wall of the Framji Cowasji Institute, Dhobi Talao, Bombay. Photograph by author, 1999.

Although this early philanthropy was characterized by relatively simple structures—wells and tanks—the partnership of philanthropists with government, characteristic of the joint enterprise, was considerably more complex, as were the institutions that were founded as a result of this partnership. The basic elements of the partnership were set in place by Sir Jamsetjee Jeejeebhoy and the colonial government and would be the model followed in subsequent arrangements made by native philanthropists and the colonial government.

An Ideal Type of a Philanthropist: A Portrait of Sir Jamsetjee Jeejeebhoy, the First Baronet, and an Early Partnership in Public Buildings

Sir Jamsetjee Jeejeebhoy (1783–1859), a man of prodigious wealth renowned for his charities, was the first Indian knight and baronet and the first Indian philanthropist to build public institutions in Bombay in partnership with the British (Figure 1.7; see also Figure 6.1). Jeejeebhoy, in his charitable activities, partnership with the British in the building of the joint public realm, and as a leader of the Parsi community, could serve as an "ideal type," in the Weberian sense, for other leading nineteenth-century philanthropists of Bombay.[35]

Born in Bombay to a Parsi family, Jeejeebhoy was the youngest child of a poor weaver. The family was forced by circumstances to return to their native town of Navsari in Gujarat. There Jeejeebhoy lived until the age of sixteen, when he returned to Bombay. He was largely unschooled, and it was on his return to Bombay that he picked up the rudiments of bookkeeping, Gujarati,

FIGURE 1.7. Sir Jamsetjee Jeejeebhoy (1783–1859), portrait of the first baronet. Courtesy Bhau Daji Lad Sangrahalaya, Bombay.

and a little English. In Bombay, he worked for his uncle selling bottles, but later he built his fortune in the China trade exporting opium and cotton.

Jeejeebhoy's name is synonymous with charity, and he spent approximately two and a half million rupees on various kinds of charities. Bombay's first native general hospital and school of art bear his name (see Figures 4.6, 4.7, 5.1, 5.3, 5.4). It was in recognition of his charities that he received a knighthood in 1842 and a baronetcy in 1858.[36] His charities for the benefit of his own Parsi community as well as for the general public included public buildings and public works, such as the building of bridges in Poona (now Pune) and over the Thana Creek. Jeejeebhoy's charities were not restricted to Bombay but covered other areas in the Bombay Presidency and abroad, such as his subscription in 1846 to the Ireland Famine Fund.[37]

An early charitable institution funded by Jeejeebhoy displays the partnership between a native elite and the government and was perhaps a model for subsequent partnerships in the creation of public buildings. In 1844, Jeejeebhoy submitted a plan to the government with the offer to build a new and more appropriate *dharamshala* on Bellasis Road to replace the existing building, which was insufficient to meet the needs of its users. A *dharamshala* is a philanthropic institution that might be a rest house for travelers and pilgrims, or an almshouse. Its construction is an act of religious merit. The *dharamshala* was run by the District Benevolent Society of Bombay, an institution that had its origin in Bombay after a visit to the city by Dr. Turner, Bishop of Calcutta, in January 1830. Turner suggested the adoption of a plan to relieve the poor of the city, based on one that had been successfully followed in Madras and Calcutta in recent years. In 1838, the government stepped forward with a monthly grant of three hundred rupees to aid the running of the institution, which helped the poor, sick, maimed, and blind of every religion by offering them shelter, food, and medical attention. Between 1 June 1837 and 31 December 1839, the society had helped five hundred and twenty people. Pointing to the large number of people the society had aided, and its inadequate funds, Jeejeebhoy offered to increase the society's income by giving the government a sum of fifty thousand rupees if the government agreed to double its monthly contribution to the institution.[38] The government accepted his offer, and the new building became known as Sir Jamsetjee Jeejeebhoy Dhurrumsalla.

Jeejeebhoy made some very specific points about the intentions behind his donation and the agreement he thought he had with the government regarding this public building. He thought that he had made arrangements for this building to be kept in repair by the government as a public building for the District Benevolent Society, so that it would not be a drain on the funds of the society. In 1847, he was surprised to find that this was not the case and asked the government to reconsider its decision. He stated that his original intentions behind building this *dharamshala* were to facilitate and extend the functions of the society and give it some permanence, "and to identify it with the Government of the Country." The building was to be built entirely from funds donated by Jeejeebhoy in a "substantial" manner, based on "plans prepared by the Officers of Government, and under their Superintendence, in the same manner, in all respects, as any other Public building would be." He reminded the government of his letter to Secretary Escombe, dated 15 May 1844, stating, "*On the completion of the Building I propose to make it over to Government for the* DISTRICT BENEVOLENT SOCIETY." Clearly, he added, if his intention was to hand over the building to the society, he would not have asked for the intervention of the government.[39] The government responded favorably to his request that the *dharamshala* be kept in trust for charitable purposes by the government and that it would be kept in repair as a public building. As such the Sir Jamsetjee Jejeebhoy Dhurrumsalla became a government building.[40] After the 1860s, there were many opportunities for such partnerships, as numerous public buildings were raised in Bombay through the collaboration of native philanthropists and the government.

Wealth and Architectural Pretension after the 1860s

An unrelated and distant event—the American Civil War that raged between 1861 and 1865—was to have an electrifying effect on the fortunes of Bombay. Cut off from its cotton supplies from America, England imported cotton from India, which was funneled for export through the port of Bombay. Within two years, as prices rose, firms and individuals in Bombay made unprecedented profits. At this point, all sorts of wise and unwise schemes were formulated and led to imprudent speculation. Share prices rose to great heights, bearing no relation to their actual value. The cessation of hostilities in America and consequent availability of their cotton to English markets resulted in a crash in the Bombay markets where banks collapsed and fortunes were lost.

The twin forces of speculation and philanthropy, based on the large fortunes that had been built during this time, transformed the face of Bombay after the 1860s. One sound speculative scheme, the Back Bay scheme, aimed at the reclamation of 1,500 acres of land along Back Bay, fell victim to the collapse of the Asiatic Bank in 1865. Only a portion of the land was reclaimed, and through an odd twist of fate the government received all of it free of cost.[41] Another reclamation company, the Elphinstone Land and Press Company, formed for reclaiming land along the foreshore of the harbor, was very successful in developing its property, which was later transferred to the government.[42] Bombay's first colonial urban design scheme—the Elphinstone Circle scheme—inaugurated this era.

The Elphinstone Circle Development

The Elphinstone Circle was Bombay's first major urban design scheme. Located in the heart of the fortified city, between the native and European sections, the development formalized and beautified the most important public arena in

FIGURE 1.8. Elphinstone Circle Garden, Bombay, 1869–72. In the foreground is the ornamental fountain at the center of the garden. It appears that temporary shelters have been erected over the statues of Marquis Cornwallis and Marquis Wellesley, probably to protect them against the monsoon rains. In the background to the left and beyond the garden the spire of St. Thomas Cathedral can be seen and, to the right, a part of one of the crescents that make up the circle. The photograph was most likely taken from the steps of the Town Hall. Courtesy Bhau Daji Lad Sangrahalaya, Bombay.

the city. This was "the old dirty and dusty Cotton Green" that was surrounded by some of the most important institutions of the city including the Town Hall and St. Thomas Cathedral (Figure 1.8; also see Figures 6.10, 6.14).[43] Central to the impact of this scheme were the fort walls, which were pulled down as the circle rose from the ground. This destruction sounded the death knell of the old center, the Green, as it opened a new arena for public buildings along the *maidan*, shifting the heart of the city outward to a new frontier between the Fort and the "native town" (see Figure 1.1).

Charles Forjett authored the scheme for Elphinstone Circle. Forjett, a Eurasian, grew up in India and was superintendent of police in Bombay from 1855 to 1863. A legendary figure in Bombay's history, he became famous for his role in suppressing the Indian Mutiny, also known as India's First War of Independence, and for his facility in assuming native disguises. A member of the Board of Conservancy (1845–58), he later became one of the triumvirate of municipal commissioners, established by Act XXV of 1858. These commissioners controlled the entire sanitation and improvement of Bombay until 1865, when a full-time municipal commissioner and the body corporate of the Justices replaced them. In 1861, Forjett conceived of the scheme for Elphinstone Circle and received full support from the governors of Bombay, Lord Elphinstone, and Sir Bartle Frere. The municipal commissioners bought the land and made a considerable profit by dividing it into building lots, which were sold to English and Indian firms.[44] By 1865, Elphinstone Circle was almost completed.[45] Colonel Laughton's plan of the Circle in 1870 shows the occupants at that time.[46]

A letter from a clerk in the municipal commissioners' office conveyed the municipal commissioners' proposal to the government to convert the green into a circle, to be named the Victoria Circle, in 1861.[47] The proposed plan was practical from a real estate point of view and incorporated architectural uniformity and urban design in its schemata. The buildings were adapted to the commercial enterprises they were to house by ensuring that maximum frontage was given to each block and that the lateral fronts were as valuable as those fronting the green. The commissioners were of the opinion that the design should have "some degree of architectural nicety, which will harmonize with the Town Hall," particularly the buildings facing the green. Accordingly, building elevations would be prepared in advance so that the purchasers of land would be aware of "their responsibility in this respect." The commissioners suggested that the crescents they proposed erecting on each side of the green could be named after the largest private investors in the scheme.[48] The government approved, but the royal associations were removed. In a government memorandum, Colonel Turner suggested that it should be stipulated that "the frontage of the new crescents be of an uniform and ornamental style of architecture."[49] The government left it to the municipal commissioners to name the crescents and new streets after prominent Bombay merchants or the main owners of the crescents, and at least one of the buildings is named after an Indian merchant.[50]

The government later ratified two resolutions passed at a meeting held on 14 February 1862 at the offices of Messrs. Ritchie Steuart & Company and attended by the representatives of all who had agreed to buy land on the Bombay Green. The first resolution passed was that the government would be requested to name the whole circle Elphinstone as a tribute to the former governor of Bombay. The second resolution passed was that the participants would notify the municipal commissioners that those attending the meeting would prefer that the proposed buildings be three stories instead of two stories in height. Furthermore, the ground floor should be made as high as possible, and each story should have a minimum interior height of fourteen feet. Although it is left unsaid, one might deduce that the addition of an extra story would bring greater profits to those investing in the land. It is a commentary on the influence of the investors that their recommendations were carried out. Not only was the circle named Elphinstone Circle (now Horniman Circle), the

FIGURE 1.9. Elphinstone (now Horniman) Circle, Bombay, circa 1864–66. James Scott, chief engineer to the Elphinstone Land Reclamation Company, designed the frontages of the buildings that make up the circle. Courtesy Bhau Daji Lad Sangrahalaya, Bombay.

final buildings were more than three stories high (Figure 1.9). Focusing on the Town Hall with its enormous Doric columns and impressive flight of steps, the scheme consisted of a circus around a central garden with a fountain, surrounded by ornamental iron railings imported from England. The Italianate facades of the buildings were controlled to create a "uniform and ornamental style of architecture."

The native public adapted to the new circle, which replaced the *chakri* or circle where children played. The fountain was erected on the exact spot where a well of spring water existed and was named after the well's donor. The well was a spot where passersby—cotton and opium brokers, clerks, and strangers—quenched their thirst. The old tamarind tree, where "groups of all kinds of men" gathered at noon or in the afternoon to rest and refresh themselves in the 1850s, was not cut down and in 1920 was frequented by men on a daily basis between noon and four o'clock.[51]

The circle, a new innovation in Bombay, was a time-tested urban design solution in England. In 1764 John Wood the Younger completed the Circus begun by his father John Wood and in 1769 built the Royal Crescent in the small town of Bath in England. In eighteenth-century England, going to "take the waters" at the hot springs in Bath was part of the social calendar. Wood, who was at the same time architect, artist, builder, and speculator, built Bath for the "new bourgeois society." In the Royal Crescent built by his son, we find thirty standardized houses fused together in the shape of an "open ellipse" to form a unified whole. Men such as Wood, who combined the qualities of builder, artist, and speculator, built Bath and many of London's squares and crescents on speculation, and yet their architecture reflected a disciplined working of a "vigorous tradition."[52]

Like Bath, Elphinstone Circle was built on speculation and was conceived and built at a time when speculators in Bombay had acquired unprecedented amounts of wealth. Unlike Bath, where one man encapsulated the roles of builder, artist, and speculator, in colonial Bombay this scheme was a partnership between government and private enterprise in a mutually beneficial speculative enterprise. In 1864, grateful purchasers of sites in the new Circle, "among whom are numbered the leading members of the commercial community of Bombay," requested that the government allow them to give Forjett a sum of money equivalent to 2.5 percent on the value of the land purchased as a token of their appreciation of his work in Bombay and particularly for his role in the Elphinstone Circle development. A government official referred to the scheme as a "great public improvement."[53]

In its classical architecture, the Elphinstone Circle was a less restrained relative of the Town Hall and the Mint building in its vicinity. The new buildings beyond the Fort were to adopt the more dynamic architecture of the sculptured Gothic style. The almost flat-bearded male face that became the recurring keystone of the colonnaded arcade of the Circle was to give way, in the new Gothic buildings, to molded surfaces and exuberant three-dimensional sculptures. The new architecture was to draw one's gaze up toward the sky; and in the Victoria Terminus, strange unheavenly creatures seem caught, frozen in motion, in the act of leaping forth from the roof of the building into the sky (Figure 1.10).

Throwing Down the Fort Walls: The Creation of a New Arena for Philanthropy

The cotton boom encouraged the colonial government, under the leadership of Governor Sir Bartle Frere (1862–67), to embark on the long-contemplated project of throwing down the fort walls, no longer necessary for military purposes, and divide a part of the plain into allotments of ground for building. In 1861, a committee was appointed by the city to examine the issue of land and fortification. It decided to remove the walls and derive profits from the land so freed.[54] By the 1860s, land for building purposes was in short supply and Frere

FIGURE 1.10. Frederick William Stevens, Victoria Terminus, Bombay, 1878–87, detail. A gargoyle in the form of an animal figure seems to leap out from the building. Photograph by author, 2005.

received large sums of purchase money from those who bid for the allotments. These moneys, combined with sums received from the government, were collected in a special fund for the construction of public buildings in Bombay.[55] The style and architectural features of the buildings in the Esplanade were regulated to create some urban design uniformity even though it would be several decades before all the buildings were constructed.[56] The fall of the fort walls opened up the plain, creating a new public arena for government offices and public institutions. The regime of collecting funds for the latter signaled a new era of philanthropy.

The city was transformed in multiple ways after the 1860s. The map of the island was reshaped and the city's physical appearance was transformed by improvements that can be categorized under three major headings: (1) reclamations; (2) communications, through the extension and improvement of the road system; and (3) public buildings.[57] The Municipal Corporation, founded in 1865, became a major player in directing municipal, sanitary, and other improvements in the city.

The creation of "New Bombay" caused Edwin Arnold to exclaim in 1886, after a long absence from India, that "I left Bombay a town of warehouses and offices; I find her a city of parks and palaces."[58] These new buildings, based on designs by architects from Britain, were "to be of the highest character architecturally" and to produce an "artistic effect," in keeping with Bombay's prosperity, high population, and geographical situation. Work on Frere's meticulously planned scheme for this new arena began while he was in Bombay and was continued by his successors. Facing the sea in one grand sweep were the Government Secretariat (1867–74), the University Library and Clock Tower (1869–78), the Convocation Hall (1869–74), the High Court (1871–78), the Electric Telegraph Department (1871–74), and the Post Office (1869–72), all based on variations of the Gothic style—French, Venetian, and Early English (Figure 1.11). Buildings in similar styles, predominantly Gothic, were built in other parts of the city, including Elphinstone College (1871, see Figure 2.4) and the Victoria and Albert Museum (1862–72, see Figure 6.15) on Parel Road, Elphinstone High School, Sir Jamsetjee Jeejeebhoy School of Art (1857), Gokuldas Tejpal Hospital (1870–74), the Sailors' Home (1872–76), and many others.[59] In the 1870s and 1880s, many more Gothic buildings were erected in

FIGURE 1.11. The Secretariat, University Buildings, and High Court, Bombay, circa 1880s. To the right is the Secretariat, designed by Colonel Henry St. Clair Wilkins, 1867–74. Left of that is the University Senate/Convocation Hall, 1869–74; the University Library; and Rajabai Clock Tower, 1869–78, all designed by Sir George Gilbert Scott. Barely perceptible in the far distance is the High Court, 1871–78, designed by Colonel J. A. Fuller. The Oval *maidan* with a riding track on the outside edge foregrounds this ensemble of buildings. Courtesy Phillips Antiques, Bombay.

FIGURE 1.12. Frederick William Stevens, Great Indian Peninsular Railway Victoria Terminus and Administrative Offices, Bombay, 1878–87. The administrative buildings form three sides of a square, enclosing a garden whose entrance gates are guarded by a huge lion and tiger carved in stone. A massive figure of Progress (which can be seen from afar) crowns the huge dome. Sculptural groups representing engineering, commerce, and agriculture surmount the principal gables of the building, and a life-size statue of Queen-Empress Victoria stands in front of the central facade. A horse-drawn tramway, introduced to the city in 1874 by Stearns and Kittredge, can also be seen in the photograph. Photograph by Clifton & Company, circa 1880s. Courtesy Phillips Antiques, Bombay.

Bombay, generally in the triangle bounded by Cruickshank Road, Carnac Road, and Hornby Road. Perhaps the finest Victorian Gothic building in India is the Victoria Terminus (1878–87), located north of the Fort (Figure 1.12). The historian Philip Davies observed that in a relatively short period of time, Bombay became the proud possessor of some of the finest Gothic Revival buildings in the world and also came to resemble Victorian London.[60]

Although there were continuities with the past, this new era was distinguished by several new features. Wells and tanks had been spread throughout the city and were acting as centers that attracted institutions—schools, *dharamshalas,* religious institutions—and activities around them. Dispensaries and schools were spread around the city, like wells and tanks. However, they did not act as foci for other activities. These institutions created a new public realm, in theory open to all, in contrast to the wells, some of which could not be used by particular castes or religious groups. The major institutions were grouped in specific locations—between the Fort and the native town, along the Parel Road, and later around the Government House, Parel. Self-conscious about the artistic effect of their architecture, they were designed and located along main roads, to be seen and admired.

The government and the predominantly Indian philanthropists financed the construction of this colonial Bombay. Most public buildings were built with substantial help from philanthropists and through public subscriptions, thereby ushering a new era in philanthropy in the creation of a shared public domain of Bombay. Whereas philanthropy before the 1860s primarily dedicated itself to the building of wells and tanks, after the 1860s, institutions for the instruction or practice of Western educational and scientific techniques—schools, colleges, the university, hospitals, and dispensaries—became the objects of the philanthropy. Wells and tanks required smaller outlays of money compared to most institutions, and many moneyed people of all religious groups participated in the building of this landscape. Smaller projects, such as dispensaries, did allow a larger group of people to participate after the 1860s, but a relatively small group of families were builders of larger institutions, built in partnership with the government and designed by architects from Britain.

Until 1918, these major philanthropists were predominantly from wealthy minority communities such as Parsis and the Baghdadi Jews. They were rewarded with high titles. For reasons that are not entirely obvious, Hindus and Muslim philanthropists were not major players until about the turn of the century. By 1913, the British government had made eight men from the Bombay Presidency baronets. The Parsi baronets were Sir Jamsetjee Jeejeebhoy (1858), Sir Dinshaw Manockjee Petit (1890), and Sir (Jehangir) Cowasjee Jehangir (1908). Three Baghdadi Jewish baronets were created from the Sassoon family, Sir Albert Abdullah Sassoon (1880) of Kensington Gore, and Sir Jacob Elias Sassoon (1909) and Sir Sassoon (Jacob) David (1911), both of Bombay. Sir Currimbhoy Ebrahim (1910) was the Muslim representative and Sir Chinubhai Madhowlal (Runchorelal), the adopted grandson of the founder of the Ahmedabad textile industry, the Hindu representative.[61] The names of these baronets and other titled luminaries were associated with most of the public buildings of Bombay.

The Plague and Sanitizing the City after 1896

In September 1896, the bubonic plague first struck Bombay; soon after, it spread to all parts of the presidency. Only after the passing of the Epidemic Diseases Act in February 1897 were a number of public health policies enforced to control the epidemic. The plague resulted in the flight of a panicked population and great losses in commerce and industry, forcing the authorities to the realization that sanitary reform could not be ignored in the creation of a modern trading and industrial city. A board of trustees, created for the improvement of Bombay City, began work in November 1898 armed with great powers for clearing unsanitary areas and laying out new streets.

Even though the government's policies of displacement and reclamation were primarily geared toward the promotion of public sanitation and social welfare, in actual practice the policies of the trust were directed toward creating an aesthetically beautiful Bombay. Although landlords ruled in the corporation, commercial magnates and industrialists dominated the trust, which led to an imposition of their vision on Bombay. By 1918, little had been done to remove slums, and the government had earned the anger of both merchants and landlords.[62]

The activities of the City of Bombay Improvement Trust were to shape the future growth of the city decisively for many decades. After 1898, the great powers allotted to the trust enabled the colonial authorities to penetrate and destroy localities, displace people and erect sanitary structures within the native town, and plan for the extension of the city in the northward direction.

The constitution and powers of the trust resembled those of the Port Trust and were based on the model of the Glasgow City Improvement Trust. The trust was responsible for (1) the laying of new roads, (2) improving crowded localities, (3) reclaiming further lands, (4) constructing sanitary dwellings for the poor, and (5) providing accommodation for the police.[63] The trust's road projects linked the city through a network of roads to ensure the smooth flow of goods, including important arteries such as Mohammedali Road, and east-west ventilation schemes such as Princess Street and Sandhurst Road.[64]

Although its activities were based on the Glasgow model, the Bombay Improvement Trust had to deal with the local reaction to its projects. Forced acquisitions, demolitions, and displacements brought about by the trust's schemes affected many lives, and opposition by landlords and tenants took the form of thousands of petitions and court cases.[65] People who lost their homes often spurned the trust's suggestion of alternative accommodation, when it was offered, to reside close to their former place of residence forming a ring of congestion around the original zone of demolition. The trust's improvement strategies of "slum patching," by the construction of a few *chawls* (a building type that is often four to five stories in height and has numerous single-room tenements) and thoroughfares, took place in an environment in which the municipality continued to control the city's bylaws and supervise the general sanitary administration of the city (Figure 1.13). Great though its powers were, the trust felt itself hampered

FIGURE 1.13. *Chawl* building constructed by the City of Bombay Improvement Trust, Bombay, early twentieth century. Photograph by author, 2006.

by its inadequate funds and powers to bring about sufficient change. Its critics were equally unimpressed by the results of the trust's activities and in about 1917 began an agitation for the transference of the trust to the municipality. Engaged in a public debate of mutual recrimination, the Municipal Corporation accused the trust of neglecting the overcrowded and unsanitary areas of the city, while the trust pointed out that the municipality had neglected to change its bylaws and been unable to control building operations.[66] The trust's demolition activities and rebuilding activities dispossessed a significant section of the population who were not rehoused (Figure 1.14).[67]

DIVIDING THE CITY

In the twentieth century, the Bombay elite, through their institutions, continued to play a decisive role in shaping Bombay as primarily responsive to their needs and interests. By 1907, there was a housing crisis in Bombay faced by all classes, from the wealthy to clerks and others of lesser means. The housing shortage had resulted in an increase in rents in recent years that threatened to make Bombay a more expensive place to live than London. The government saw this as a time to tackle the issue of the development of Bombay in a more comprehensive manner.[68]

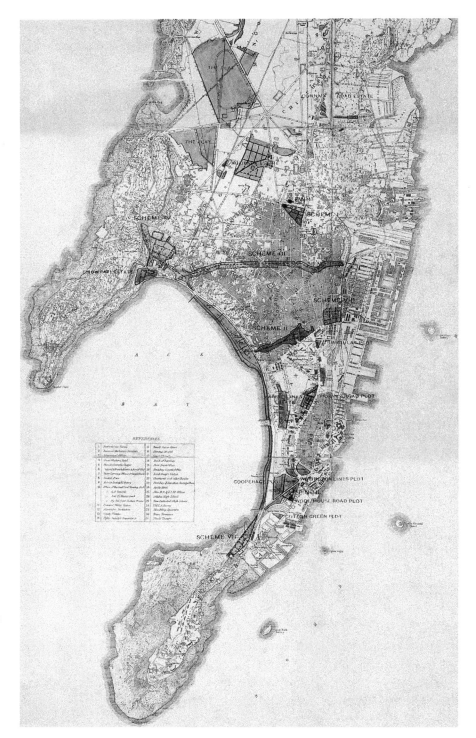

FIGURE 1.14. Lower half of Island of Bombay, 1902–3 plan showing various Bombay Improvement Trust schemes. From *Administration Report of the Municipal Commissioner for the City of Bombay, 1902–1903.*

On 9 December 1907, the government sent a questionnaire to certain Bombay institutions, asking them to respond to questions relating to (1) segregation of areas by income groups, (2) coordinating and improving the various channels of communication, and (3) the best means of traveling for the population displaced.[69]

The institutions that responded represented the elite of the city: the City of Bombay Improvement Trust, the Municipal Corporation, the chamber of commerce, the Millowners' Association, the Bombay Port Trust, the G.I.P. and B.B. & C.I. Railway Companies, the Bombay Presidency Association, the Indian Merchants' Chamber, and the Bombay Native Piece Goods Merchants' Association. The last-named institution is the only one that gave its unsolicited opinion on the subject. Headquartered in the premises of the Sheth Mulji Jetha's Cloth Market Hall in the heart of the native town, it represented the interests of the business groups who did not have Western business associations or a Western lifestyle.[70]

Each institution replied according to its own interests, and based on these responses, the government proceeded in 1909 with a policy that would be implemented in Bombay over the next twenty years. It was recommended to reserve the western shores for the accommodation of the wealthy. Two of the alternatives considered were rejected: (1) Mahim Woods for being too distant and (2) Worli, as the atmosphere had been polluted by sewage disposal schemes. The reclamation of Back Bay was seen as the only solution for providing additional accommodation for this class, and a decision was made to transfer the reclamation rights from the Bombay Improvement Trust to the government. No particular localities were reserved for the middle classes since it was assumed that they would move into the areas vacated by the upper classes and to the northern area, which was being developed for those who could afford it. Laborers and factory workers would continue to live near their place of work as their long hours of work demanded and as they would be unable to bear transportation costs.[71] Significantly, one of the questions raised was regarding the possibility of cheap trains or tramways for workers that would allow them to be accommodated in the undeveloped areas of the island. The question was whether the workers would be able to pay adequate rent and transportation costs to be able to give a reasonable rate of return on the investment on accommodation projects.[72] Such a policy would require employers to adequately compensate their workers, and it was not in their interests to do so. The only institution in favor of workmen's trains or trams was the chamber of commerce.[73] Far from simply responding to orders emitting from London, the heart of the empire, Bombay was shaped by local forces that were dominated by an industrial and mercantile elite. High government officials and the commercial elite shared a common interest in fostering the capitalistic development of the island and for dividing the city, reserving its best spaces for their own use.

CONCLUSION

Colonial Bombay was made jointly by Indians and the colonial regime. Particularly in the second half of the nineteenth century, the colonial regime and the Indian and European financial and mercantile elite cooperated in creating an infrastructure—for commerce, but also institutions for the public good—that was conducive to the commerce and well-being of the city. Indian philanthropists played an important role in financing educational and medical institutions in particular for the use of the public at large. In doing so, the joint enterprise resulted in the creation of a new public arena for all of Bombay's citizens. In contrast to exclusive community spaces, this was a landscape that was open to and, in principle, owned by all of Bombay's citizens. In spaces such as these, they could imagine themselves as not only members of their individual community but forge new identities as citizens of Bombay. These identities of fragmentation and cohesion were produced in the community and public landscapes of Bombay.

Amid a landscape populated by public buildings, predominantly in the Gothic Revival style, the product of a partnership of British colonial and Indian financial and technical expertise, Bombay's citizenry could join together in an arena that reminded many of Victorian London but also showcased the Indian making of British Bombay. Thus the joint enterprise resulted in a joint public realm that not only was partially underwritten by Indian philanthropists but was built by native and European expertise. The construction of Bombay was a product of the joint enterprise that called on European architects, engineers, sculptors, artists, and also Indian engineers, artists, craftsmen, and other functionaries to design and construct British Bombay. The joint enterprise led to native participation—financial, technical, and artistic—in the creation of British Bombay and by doing so infused this landscape with new meanings. This is addressed in chapter 2, on the question of the appropriate style for Anglo-Indian architecture and the significance of Gothic Revival architecture, and chapter 3, which focuses on the exemplary role of a single native engineer's contribution to the building of British Bombay.

2 Anglo-Indian Architecture and the Meaning of Its Styles

MOST SCHOLARS OF THE ARCHITECTURE of the British Empire focus on the question, how was empire represented in its architecture? Buildings and architectural style were of particular importance in the Victorian era because, as the architectural historian Mark Crinson notes, "to build was to create meaning"—yet the meanings ascribed to style were contested.[1]

The meaning of architectural style and the appropriate style for empire were hotly debated in colonial India. In 1920, John Begg (1866–1937), consulting architect to the government of India from 1908 until 1921, observed that there were two schools of opinion on how to build in India. The first school made the case that the British should take the Romans as their model and plant British architecture as well as British notions of justice, law, culture, and order not only as improvements but also to reflect the brilliance of the empire, while civic architecture should reflect all these qualities to the Indians. In contrast, the second school maintained that there was a living tradition in Indian architecture that needed to be nurtured and sustained by curbing outside influences and that the carriers of this living tradition, Indian craftsmen, native architects, or master builders—*mistris* and *stapathis*—needed to be patronized. Begg tentatively named the two schools "the Roman school" and "the 'swadeshi' school" respectively; the architectural historian Philip Davies would later call them "the aesthetic imperialists" and the "native revivalists."[2]

Thomas R. Metcalf's insightful analysis of Indo-Saracenic architecture in India shows that the debates and divisions between various schools of thought were considerably more nuanced than such binary oppositions allow. While acknowledging that the British drew on classical European forms to represent empire as they had long done in Europe, Metcalf shows that the revolt of 1857 brought a change of heart. After this period the British sought to project themselves as legitimate successors to the Mughals—in other words as indigenous rather than foreign rulers. Such a reworking of the ideology of empire required a new architecture, the Indo-Saracenic architecture that was at once European but at the same time linked to India's past through its mastery of Indic detail.[3] Builders of the Indo-Saracenic style do not fit neatly into either of Davies's categories. It was, after all, not just a question of style but of how to build, and "native revivalists" did not necessarily approve of Indo-Saracenic architects since they, rather than native craftsmen, retained control of the design and construction process. This chapter shows that the meaning of architectural style was far less fixed than Metcalf's account would have it. Metcalf's focus on imperial ideology obscures the varied applications of the Indo-Saracenic style, which was not simply deployed or even commonly understood by its practitioners to show that the British were legitimate successors of the Mughals. It was also used in Bombay, for example, to mark a break between the practice of architects and engineers.

After India became part of the British Empire, many architects and officials were critical of the architectural style of previous British forces in India. The attempt to find an appropriate Anglo-Indian style remained a concern for officials and architects until independence in 1947 and spanned a continuum from Classical, Gothic Revival, and Indo-Saracenic styles to those who rejected the control of buildings by architects or engineers in favor of the native *mistris,* who would, on their own, develop a style that reflected the synthesis of Indic traditions and European forms.

The styles that emerged or remained dominant after 1857 and the meaning of these styles were influenced by local conditions. At least for its architects, the Indo-Saracenic of Madras did not have the same meaning as the Indo-Saracenic of Bombay. Apart from the Indo-Saracenic, were there other ways of showing that the British were indigenous rather than foreign rulers? Sir Bartle Frere, who promoted the use of the Gothic Revival in Bombay, spoke in 1870 of the development in that city of what he hoped would become "an indigenous school of Anglo-Indian architecture, as extensive and as distinct as the pure Hindu and Mahometan schools of former days," a statement that makes one question the exclusive claims made on behalf of the Indo-Saracenic.[4] And yet, once again, despite the focus on imperial ideology, we are left with the fact that if the British sought to portray themselves as indigenous rulers, then their hybrid architecture would be seen as a reflection of their contradictory reality. How could the ruler be simultaneously indigenous and yet remain "British to the backbone"?[5] Discussions on the subject of the appropriate Anglo-Indian style did not address how architects could stylistically portray the Raj as the legitimate successor to the Mughals. Instead, as I show, the discussions were about aesthetics and, directly or indirectly, about the maintenance of distance between the ruler and the ruled. Debates about style, usually directed to an audience in England, focused on assurance that the hybridity seen in colonial architecture was the sole intellectual product of British architects, who combined European forms with universal principles in Indic design, rather than the aesthetic fruit of the intermingling of races, which was from the intermixture of the ruler and the ruled. At the same time, the claim for universal principles was an attempt to assure the British who used or worked in these hybrid spaces that they were not really hybrid subjects.

The engagement with imperial styles and ideologies has allowed for an almost exclusive focus on British professionals (architects, engineers, teachers in schools of art, sculptors), who, as representatives of empire, are thought to represent it in their architecture. Their buildings and debates are more or less well documented, allowing historians to adequately reconstruct events from that period. Although it is evident that Europeans who participated in or followed these or similar debates received some version of the intended message of colonial civic architecture, it is important to ask, even if a full answer is not possible, what message was received by most Indians who did not follow these debates. In other words, underlying the focus on imperial ideology and the agenda of British architects is the premise that architecture relays some ideas of the designer—it is "a maker study."[6] Accordingly, we must consider what meaning or what ideas of the designer are being communicated. Dell Upton argues, "We need to look beyond economic incentive and social communication" to see how people begin to "fuse their surroundings into a meaningful whole."[7]

This chapter, then, highlights this neglected imaginative act in the particular case of Bombay's architectural surroundings. While retaining a focus on architecture and the creation of meaning, this chapter also considers race, status, and professional rivalries in its examination of Bombay during the period roughly between the second half of the nineteenth century and World War I, a period when most of Bombay's public institutions were founded and the city's image as a Gothic Revival capital was established.

In Bombay, the Gothic Revival style, rather than Indo-Saracenic, defined empire after 1857. Examining the Victorian city that architects, engineers, and craftsmen helped to construct with the collaboration of native philanthropists and the colonial government, I argue that the imperial styles—particularly Gothic Revival—of Bombay reflected this joint partnership and the new public arena they created rather than simply the virtues of the colonial regime. In my analysis of the discussions on style conducted by the colonial elite and my interpretation of the built environment, I show what Bombay's Gothic Revival architecture meant to the colonial elite and its native population more generally.

PROFESSIONAL DISTINCTIONS AND RIVALRIES

Rather than embark on a survey of Bombay's Victorian architecture, which has been adequately described by various authors, I focus on British architects, engineers, and sculptors who were involved in the construction of colonial Bombay's public buildings. I investigate the tensions between and within these groups, much of which revolved around differing notions of who should control the design and construction of buildings in terms of professional expertise, training, and race. I develop the quick, general observations made by Gavin Stamp, the architectural historian, about the public buildings constructed under Sir Bartle Frere's governorship (1862–67) and later. First, a large number of them were a result of local philanthropy. In particular, he highlighted the role played by the Parsi community. Second, these buildings were built by the Public Works Department (PWD) of the government of India. Designed by government architects, their construction was overseen by European architects/engineers, but Indian craftsmen and masons actually built the structures. Finally, most of these structures were in the Gothic Revival style. The architects who designed Bombay's buildings were generally in government service or from the Royal Engineers. Buildings were constructed under the supervision of a resident royal engineer and an assistant engineer, who was generally an Indian.[8]

The tensions between and within groups were ideological but also had to do with negotiating issues of status. These groups include the European engineers—military and civil—and architects, many of whom worked for the PWD. By the beginning of the twentieth century, architects asserted their right to control building design and construction, reflecting the growing authority of the profession of architecture. British teachers at the Sir Jamsetjee Jeejeebhoy School of Art and Industry (henceforth, Sir J. J. School of Art) in Bombay, who were engaged in nurturing Indian craft traditions, constituted a group of their own. All the members of these groups are of British origin.

Tensions between the military and civil engineers and architects who constructed Bombay's buildings were long-standing. In 1854, the PWD was put into place under the central government.[9] The *Builder* took up the issue of the PWD in an editorial in 1868 calling for a reform of the department highlighting the high-handed manner in which the military engineers treated the civil engineers.[10] The tensions between the military and civil engineers over issues of status reveal the difficulties in moving from a culture of conquest to a culture of governance.

What was the work of engineers in the PWD in India? Begg described them as men who had until the closure of the Royal Indian Engineering College at Cooper's Hill been "specially selected and specially trained for their work." However, he clarified that they were not "trained as specialists." In fact their work was diverse and "embracing many kinds of specialism" including architectural work, railway projects, work on irrigation, and so on. The men were encouraged to be generalists rather than specialists so that they could deal with the diverse projects they had to tackle in India.[11]

The relationship between architects and engineers was also not free of friction. T. Roger Smith, an architect from Britain who won a competition for the design of the European Hospital, visited Bombay in 1864 when the government of Bombay decided to construct the building based on his plans. Relating his experience to an audience at the general meeting of the Royal Institute of British Architects (R.I.B.A.) on 27 April 1868, Smith spoke disparagingly of the PWD, a department under the control of the military engineers "and the great evil which, in that case, the architect has to fear, and if possible to guard against, is his work being wholly or in part modified, set aside, or superseded."[12] At that time in Britain, architects had begun to distinguish themselves from other professions who also dealt with building. Architects construed themselves as artists whose particular responsibility was not simply to raise a building but to produce "works of art." Smith went on to say "that of us is expected, indeed, not merely a work of skill, but also a work of art." Since architects made buildings into works of art, it was intolerable for architects, like Smith, to find that his designs in India were transformed by and under the control of engineers of the PWD who produced buildings that were, as he puts it, "serviceable as structures."[13]

The PWD and its engineers were also not admired by John Lockwood Kipling, an artist, scholar, and professor of architectural sculpture at the Sir J. J. School of Art in Bombay from 1865 to 1874, and principal of the Mayo School of Art in Lahore between 1875 and 1893. Nor was it admired by his intellectual successors, men such as A. K. Coomaraswamy (1877–1947), the Sri Lankan–born scholar of Indian art and aesthetic philosophy who became immersed in the end phase of the Arts and Crafts movement in England between 1905 and 1907, and Ernest B. Havell, who taught at the Madras School of Art from 1884 to 1895 and was the principal of the Calcutta School of Art between 1896 and 1905. Committed to maintaining Indian craft and building traditions, these thinkers might even be considered anti-imperial. In an essay on contemporary

Indian architecture written in 1884 or 1886, Kipling characterized much of the architecture built by Europeans in India as ugly but at the same time impressive to the "native eye" because they were built by the colonial elite:

> To the native eye the striking facts of modern India are things that many Europeans take as a matter of course—improved roads and bridges, railways with their miraculous straightness and truth of line, and their substantial buildings, our military cantonments in long monotonous lines, and our civil stations. These, though occasionally ugly enough, are imposing. . . . And they have the prestige of authority.[14]

Both Smith and Kipling thought little of the buildings produced by the PWD, although they took issue for different reasons. Smith argued that architects, who as artists, brought art into buildings, should control the building process rather than engineers. Kipling took issue with the PWD for helping to destroy native building traditions because engineers rather than *mistris* were patronized by both government and the educated Indians. Furthermore, Kipling thought the architecture of the PWD was a bad model, but "to the native eye" colonial architecture was seen as beautiful since it was associated with the technological achievements of colonial rule, and even though "devoid of architectural pretension" it represented the landscape of the rulers that natives desired to emulate. This was equally true of the *mistri,* the "native builder and architect," who were impressed by this and saw no reason for not emulating European architectural styles, and educated Indians, for whom "foreign styles stand for enlightenment and progress."[15]

The PWD remained under the control and domination of engineers until the end of the nineteenth century, but the new century brought changes. In 1901, Begg was appointed as an architect by the government of Bombay.[16] His experience with the PWD was not unlike Smith's experience almost four decades earlier: Begg faced an uphill battle in getting the engineers to understand the work of an architect and respect the work they did.[17]

Begg's struggle to define the position of the architect in Bombay was part of the larger struggle in England as the profession sought to define itself.[18] Rising levels of popular education and the growth of architectural journalism in the nineteenth century encouraged the public's interest in architecture. Architectural competitions for national projects became matters of public interest, and debate and comment on these issues appeared in the daily press and a number of journals, as well as specialized architectural periodicals, the most important of which was the *Builder,* which began in 1842.[19] As Dell Upton points out, to be seen as architects, "professionals must present themselves as a recognizable, predictable body."[20] To do this architects collated varied pieces of architectural knowledge into a theory, created professional bodies, and increasingly tried to standardize the education of the architect.[21]

In England in the second half of the nineteenth century, the debate over the role of craftsmen had not gone away. Colonialism brought the debate over the role of craftsmen to the fore in India. Mahrukh Tarapor has demonstrated how Kipling was a leading promoter of the Arts and Crafts ideas of William Morris in India. Morris also influenced Frederick Salmon Growse who, in his attempts to create an indigenous style in his building projects as a district officer of the Indian Civil Service, tried to "combine rather than fuse Hindu and Islamic forms, while exploiting as fully as possible local craft traditions."[22] Although architects would gain greater control over building design by the beginning of the twentieth century, the question of the role of the Indian craft tradition in fostering a genuine indigenous architectural tradition for modern India persisted.

THE CORRECT ANGLO-INDIAN STYLE

In his well-known article on style, Meyer Schapiro defines style as "the constant form—and sometimes the constant elements, qualities, and expression—in the art of an individual or group."[23] After 1857, the search for an appropriate architectural style was related to three issues. First, architectural style was intimately related to issues of conquest and colonization. The variety of styles revealed differences in ideas of how India should be ruled and the relationship between the rulers and the ruled. At the same time, the use of a term like "Indo-Saracenic" to define a style that sought to unite British and Indic forms disguises the differences in ideology between, for instance, Growse's and Begg's desire to use this style.

Second, the search for an appropriate architectural style by those constructing official architecture was intimately connected to issues of maintaining distance between the rulers and ruled. There were those who believed that it was impossible to produce architecture of quality that melded British and Indic forms unless it was a product of the intermixture of these two societies. On the other hand, others saw this as an intellectual exercise where an understanding of universal principles would allow for a distinguished architectural marriage of European and Indic forms without compromising the distance to be maintained between the rulers and the ruled.

Third, after 1857, the governors of Bombay and Madras were active promoters of a suitable Anglo-Indian style for their capital cities. Because of their important foundational roles, Gothic Revival would come to represent Bombay, while in Madras, Indo-Saracenic would reign. These styles that came to dominate these cities were also memorials to their early promoters whose patronage encouraged some styles and discouraged others. However, each city had a different local culture that would also influence the meaning of the style.

Sir Bartle E. Frere and Bombay's Indigenous School of Anglo-Indian Architecture

In 1870, Sir Bartle E. Frere gave a lecture on the subject of modern architecture in western India. He observed that when England came to have a mighty empire with its wonderful architecture, architecture in England was going through a low phase. As a result, nothing of consequence had been built by earlier generations of the British in India before 1857. Contrasting London's architecture, as one that grew out of the expression of free people, to architecture in cities such as Paris that was produced by despotic regimes, Frere implied that the former was superior:

> We were very apt to decry our own City of London as inferior to the capital cities of the despotic powers of Europe, but in London was to be seen the impress of an architecture that grows from within—an architecture that expresses what the people think, and feel, and mean, and not what they are told to think, feel, or mean, as was too often the case in despotic capitals of Europe.[24]

Frere immediately turned to the subject of India when "the Empire came under British rule" and to the status of Bombay when R. W. Crawford was Chairman of Justices. Crawford's many reforms brought water and drains to the city, while Henry Conybeare, influenced by Sir Gilbert Scott's earlier designs, designed the Afghan Memorial Church of St. John the Evangelist and thus "erected the first church worthy of the name in India."[25] Frere seemed to imply that the more liberal regime put in place after India came under the Crown was foundational to the transformation of Bombay, both in creating infrastructure for its citizens and beautiful architecture.

Frere concluded by talking about the importance of Parsi and other native philanthropists "and on the influence which their munificence has had on the architecture of the great cities of the Empire." Furthermore, he talked about the work of W. Paris, Morrisey (most likely a reference to G. T. Molecey, who worked with Paris and was assistant to James Trubshawe), and William Emerson, who were tracing the footsteps of James Trubshawe "in endeavouring to found what he believed to be an indigenous school of Anglo-Indian architecture, as extensive and as distinct as the pure Hindu and Mahometan schools of former days."[26] It is difficult to know whether Frere thought that native philanthropy contributed to the making of an "indigenous school of Anglo-Indian architecture," and thus because of this local connection it was, like London, "an architecture that grows from within." Nor do we know whether he meant that it was indigenous because it incorporated indigenous decorative details or flourishes. However, what is definite is that Bombay's Gothic Revival architecture was the "indigenous school of Anglo-Indian architecture." Although the Indo-Saracenic style has been privileged in discussions of how the British sought to portray themselves as indigenous rulers after 1857, Frere's self-conscious reference to the development of an indigenous Anglo-Indian school similar to Muslim and other traditions shows that Bombay's Gothic Revival architecture was also a style that sought to portray its colonial rulers as indigenous.

Talking about Frederick William Stevens's (1848–1900) Victoria Terminus constructed between 1878 and 1887, Davies argues, "The stylistic experiments of Fuller and Wilkins, Trubshawe and Emerson to find a form of High Victorian Gothic architecture adapted to the climatic extremes of Bombay, here find their resolution in a supreme expression of controlled composition" (Figure 2.1; also see Figure 1.12).[27] It seems that the indigenous school of Anglo-Indian architecture had certainly arrived with this building.

However, climate was not the only influence. There were earlier attempts to marry indigenous details or references to a Gothic building. For example, William Emerson's Crawford Market, based on a twelfth-century Gothic, has bas-reliefs above its entrance by John Lockwood Kipling that show an "Imperial ideal—strong-limbed Indian peasants thriving under a beneficent Imperial sun" (Figures 2.2 and 2.3).[28] Kipling's close and sympathetic attention to Indians was revealed in these bas-reliefs. Its prominent location would have been visible to all who entered or passed by this building on its prominent corner site. James Trubshawe of the Rampart Removal Committee, who was brought to India by Frere to make a plan for civic improvements, designed the Elphinstone College (opened in 1871) building opposite the Victoria Gardens. Davies described it as being "distinguished by a lofty central tower with a projecting canopied balcony. This appears to have been extended at a later date into an elaborate two-storey affair, reminiscent more of the ornately carved galleried facades of local Gujarati houses, than the architectural spirit of mediaeval Italy" (Figure 2.4).[29] The carvings executed by Kipling and native sculptors trained at the Sir J. J. School of Art and the eclectic range of influences—such as the Gujarati-style balcony—married to Gothic architecture in buildings

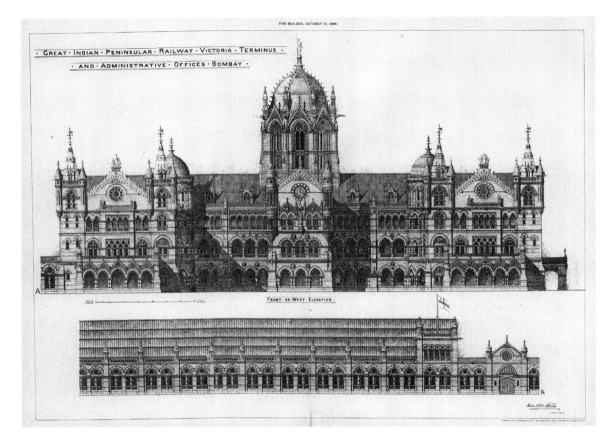

· GREAT · INDIAN · PENINSULAR · RAILWAY · VICTORIA · TERMINUS ·
· AND · ADMINISTRATIVE · OFFICES · BOMBAY ·

· FRONT · OR · WEST · ELEVATION ·

FIGURE 2.1. Frederick William Stevens, Great Indian Peninsular Railway Victoria Terminus and Administrative Offices, Bombay, 1878–87, architectural drawing of west (and front) elevation. From *Builder* 55 (July–December 1888).

underwritten by native philanthropists created Bombay's "indigenous school of Anglo-Indian architecture."

Lord Napier and the Indo-Saracenic in Madras

South of Bombay in Madras a different approach to the correct Anglo-Indian style was emerging. In a lecture delivered in India in 1870, Lord Napier discussed modern architecture in India and briefly discussed the four styles of architecture that currently existed in India: the Hindu or Brahmanical, the Muslim, the European Classical, and the European Medieval. Needless to say, the Indian styles were based on the two broad religious divisions in India, while the styles from "Europe," not simply Great Britain, were characterized by the period. Napier praised Hindu domestic architecture and was critical of the path chosen by wealthy and educated natives who "imitate the arts of strangers whom, in this respect, he might be competent to teach," leading to "corruption and confusion of taste" producing buildings where "the Hindu and European styles and ornament are all jumbled and piled together."[30]

FIGURE 2.3. Arthur
Crawford Market,
Bombay, 1865–71,
detail of arched com-
partment with bas-
relief carved by John
Lockwood Kipling.
The main entrance of
the market consisted
of three entrance
gateways with a
clock tower. Each
gateway was divided
by a column, and the
arched compartments
above were to contain
sculptured panels
depicting scenes
from everyday life.
Kipling completed
only two of these
panels before he left
Bombay. Photograph
by author, 1999.

Kipling, also sympathetic to native traditions, who felt that the *mistri* or work-
man could forge an appropriate style that assimilated "foreign elements" into
Indian forms:

> If the design of the future buildings of India, which means also the design
> principles of most of the minor arts, could be expected to remain in his [the
> Indian craftsman] hands, it might be left to him with the certainty that in
> some way, at present unforeseen, foreign elements would be absorbed and
> transfused as before into something rich and strange.[33]

Napier was critical of the confusion of English cities where older styles of
architecture resided next to various modern styles and argued for uniformity in
cityscape that could be achieved by using the same style for sacred and secular
architecture.[34] More important, Napier argued that northern European nations
required only one style since all had the same religion. Although England and
other countries of Germanic religion could have one style, this was not possible in India "where for centuries two peoples, sharply opposed in religion and
distinct in many other respects, have occupied the soil, and where a third race
and a third religion have recently been planted in artistic antagonism with the
others."[35] In short, style was related to religion, and while it is well known that
the British analyzed Indian architecture by racial and religious categories, in

FIGURE 2.4. James Trubshawe, Elphinstone College, Byculla, Bombay, opened in 1871. View of the college building with its tall central tower and projecting roofed balconies at two levels, one above the other. The balconies are reminiscent of the intricately carved galleries of Gujarati houses. In 1890 the college was moved to a new location on the Esplanade. This building, now a hospital, still stands across from what were known as the Victoria Memorial Gardens. Courtesy Bhau Daji Lad Sangrahalaya, Bombay.

Napier's lecture we see a clear articulation of Christian also as a religious category and European Classical and European Medieval as Christian styles.

Napier argued that the English had simply reproduced the fashions followed at home in India, using one style of architecture for their domestic and work life and another for worship. Napier condemned both, saying, "If the Classic houses are bad, the Gothic churches are worse."[36] Arguing in favor of one style for both public and private architecture, Napier suggested that the Muslim style of architecture was the most suitable for secular public buildings and also, he felt, for the domestic architecture of Europeans in India. But this immediately raised the question: if the Muslim style of architecture reflected Islam, how could Napier argue that it be used by Europeans, who were Christians?

Napier did this by emptying Muslim architecture of any Islamic content, first, by arguing for its deployment for European purposes by the erasure of signifiers of Islam such as calligraphy; second, by freeing it from any nation or faith; and third, by converting it into architecture that was "spiritual and universal":

> There is nothing in that style incompatible with our habits and beliefs. It allows no images, it uses no symbolic ornaments, it possesses nothing that essentially fixes it to any particular nationality or particular faith. The florid calligraphic inscriptions in the Persian and Arabic characters, which occupy in this order of art the place of pictorial representations, can be dispensed with, or supplanted by the superficial linear combinations which are equally sanctioned. The rest is mere form and colour—Mussulman art is essentially spiritual and universal.[37]

Napier clearly felt that this explanation was insufficient to persuade Christian Europeans to live in homes or worship in spaces whose style was associated with a different religion. The question was "Where, then, is the method of reconciliation between native and Christian art? To what point of approximation can the European advance? The history of art supplies an expedient. It contains a style which is at once Oriental and Christian."[38] Looking back into the history of art, Napier found that under Muslims, Roman architecture was transformed into Saracenic while Christians in the east reworked that same Roman architecture to create what was generally called Byzantine. Both styles shared "a certain family likeness" and the "dome constitutes a capital point of union." According to Napier, "The Byzantine style seems to offer the best architectural type for Christianity in India, a type sufficiently distinct, yet most in harmony with one capital section of the ancient monuments of the country."[39] With an argument for the use of Byzantine for the architecture of places of worship, Napier concluded his lecture with a plea to the government of India to consider using Muslim forms "as the official style of architecture" because "very little study would render them familiar to English and native builders. They would be found, after a short experience, to be cheaper than the present forms, and far superior, with reference to shade, coolness, ventilation, convenience, and beauty to all that we see around us."[40] As an example of this style, Napier referenced the use of Muslim style for the building of the Revenue Board Buildings in Madras, designed by the architect Robert Fellowes Chisholm (1840–1915) (Figure 2.5).[41]

Napier's argument for the appropriate official style of architecture in India made no mention of using the "Muslim style" so that the British would be seen as heirs of the Mughals. His argument rested on aesthetics, and he was critical of the way in which European styles had been applied in India.

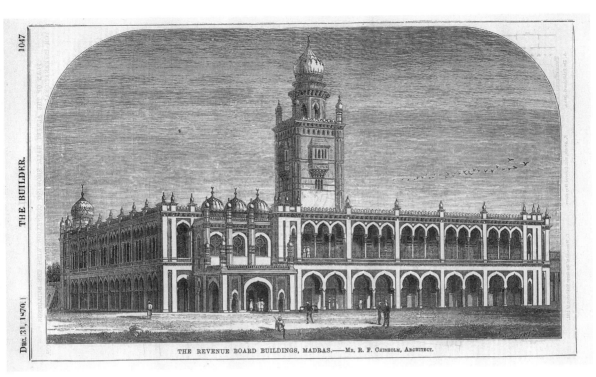

THE REVENUE BOARD BUILDINGS, MADRAS.——Mr. R. F. CHISHOLM, ARCHITECT.

FIGURE 2.5. Robert Fellowes Chisholm, Revenue Board Buildings, Madras, completed in 1871. Chisholm drew on Islamic architecture in the design of this building, which is an early demonstration of the Indo-Saracenic style. The view shows a low, two-story, rectangular building with arcades running along the facades at both levels. Dominating and overlooking the complex is a tall central tower with projecting balconies, corner spirelets topped by domes, a machicolated parapet, and an onion-shaped dome capping the tower. From *Builder* 28 (January–June 1870).

He admired Muslim architecture, saying, "The Mussulmans should never adopt anything from any foreign source whatever. They possess a perfect style, which can only be debased by alliance."[42] For Napier, different religions produced different architectural styles. In arguing for the use of Muslim styles for European domestic and official architecture, Napier divested Muslim style of its Islamic references (such as calligraphy) and freed it from its fetters of nation or religion by pointing to its universal principles. Napier's argument was necessary to assure the British that this architecture would not undermine or erode their Christian and British identities, since the underlying principles were universal and not Muslim.

In 1870, the government of Madras made a decision to expand the Chepauk Palace into a set of offices for the Revenue Board. Giving the commission to Chisholm, Lord Napier instructed him to create a design that was sympathetic to the existing buildings. According to Davies, the project created enough of a stir for Napier to make an extensive argument for or defense of this style in the *Builder* for 1870. Davies argues, "Napier was an enthusiastic advocate of native styles and his influence was instrumental in transforming Madras from a classical city into a magnificent Indo-British metropolis."[43] Indo-Saracenic architecture was used to produce a coherent landscape of public buildings along the Madras waterfront.[44] Unlike Bombay, most of Madras's public buildings were government constructions, and while its Indo-Saracenic architecture obviously referenced India's architectural past, Bombay's Gothic Revival buildings perceptibly reflected a style that was initially contemporaneous with the prevailing style in England. Whereas Madras's public buildings were a creation of the colonial regime, in Bombay the statues and medallions of native philanthropists and government officials were visually seen on and in buildings as they created a joint public realm.

Napier's views were not universally accepted. In a lecture given in 1873, T. Roger Smith contrasted the methods employed by the Romans and Muslims when they occupied new territory. Whereas Romans carried their architectural style to the territory with very little change, Muslim conquerors in India assimilated many features of the art of India into their architecture. The reason for this, according to Smith, was that Muslims settled among a population whose civilization was of an equivalent level. Speaking positively of the Gothic Revival architecture rising in Bombay, Smith argued in favor of employing European architecture for buildings used by Europeans in India and against the suggestion made in a lecture on architecture by Lord Napier where the gentleman concluded that the government of India should consider using Muslim styles "as the official style of architecture."[45] Persuasively arguing against the Indo-Saracenic, Smith claimed:

> In occupying India we have not become colonists: we have remained conquerors. We have not sought to divest ourselves of our national habits, or manners, dress, or laws, even when convenience would have been consulted by so doing. . . . Let us, then, for consistency's sake be European in our art; for art, if it be true, is an expression of national individuality more intense and more truthful than custom, fashion, or government.[46]

In other words, it made little sense to design in the Indo-Saracenic style when Englishmen remained "British to the backbone" in every other way in India.[47]

Smith also argued that by remaining conquerors and not colonists, or in other words, by remaining outsiders who did not live and intermarry the locals, it was impossible to design a building of high quality for Europeans that was not European, because the best art was national art. Smith observed, "True art is a very national affair, tinged most strongly by the national peculiarities of the time, the place, and the people among whom the artist learns his art and gets his inspiration."[48] These issues were to come to the fore in Bombay in the last decades of the nineteenth century.

The Builder *and the Work of F. W. Stevens and R. F. Chisholm in Bombay*

In an editorial in 1888, the *Builder* noted that there were two opposing theories of Anglo-Indian architecture, or in other words, architecture as practiced by the English in India. One theory advocated "adopting or assimilating native styles" and was illustrated by the prize-winning design by the architect Chisholm for the proposed Municipal Offices Buildings in Bombay (Figure 2.6).[49] Even though the design won first place, it was abandoned for reasons that seemed clearly unfair but unknown. The second theory of Anglo-Indian architecture

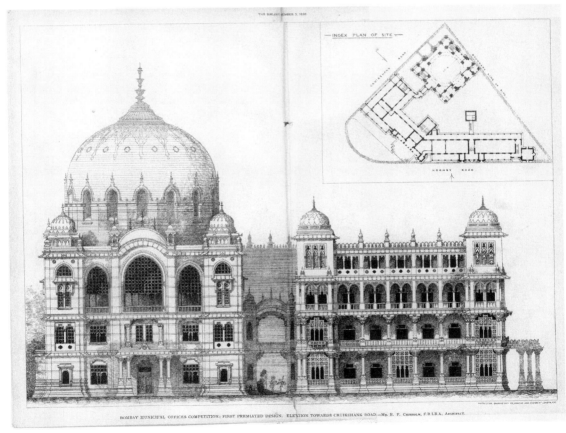

FIGURE 2.6. Robert Fellowes Chisholm, Municipal Offices Buildings, Bombay, plan and elevation toward Cruickshank Road from Chisholm's competition entry drawings, circa 1888. Capped by a massive central dome, and clearly drawing on Indic stylistic elements, Chisholm's design effectively responds to the triangular site. Despite winning the competition, this design was not selected for the construction of this building. From *Builder* 55 (July–December 1888).

was to transpose European forms to India with minor changes; the example given in the *Builder* was of Stevens's Victoria Terminus of the Great Indian Peninsular Railway, recently built in 1878–87.[50]

The *Builder* believed that the Victoria Terminus was an example of the theory of "European forms with special local treatment" and praised Stevens for incorporating native vegetative detail and encouraging the ability and tastes of native craftsmen (Figure 2.7; also see Figures 1.12 and 2.1).[51] However, it regretted that such a monumental and expensive building was "erected in a style so devoid of artistic refinement and reserve."[52] Many in Bombay were ecstatic about the building, thereby giving the *Builder* an opportunity to mock the tastes of the Anglo-Indian community as a whole, which it characterized as being "in a very provincial stage" where people customarily believed second-rate work to be the finest of the period.[53] Pierre Bourdieu has argued, "Taste classifies, and it classifies the classifier. Social subjects, classified by their clas-

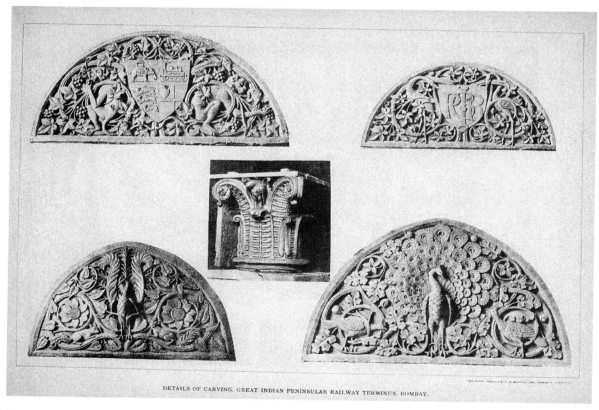

DETAILS OF CARVING, GREAT INDIAN PENINSULAR RAILWAY TERMINUS, BOMBAY.

FIGURE 2.7. Great Indian Peninsular Railway Victoria Terminus and Administrative Offices, Bombay, 1878–87, details of carving. Note the vegetative detail and carvings of peacocks and monkeys, representative of the Indian natural environment. The majority of models for this decorative work were executed by students of Mr. Gomez at the J. J. School of Art and by native craftsmen under the superintendence of John Griffiths. From *Builder* 51 (July–December 1886).

sifications, distinguish themselves by the distinctions they make, between the beautiful and the ugly, the distinguished and the vulgar, in which their position in the objective classifications is expressed or betrayed."[54] The *Builder* saw itself as an arbiter of taste, and by characterizing Anglo-Indian taste as provincial, the *Builder* was clearly passing a judgment thereby in the games of status, marking Anglo-Indians as inferior.[55]

But there is another reason for the *Builder*'s unease with the Victoria Terminus. Ian Baucom argues that with its Gothic Revival frame and "Kipling's tropical plants and animals" as details:

> The terminus seems to be at once the factory of Englishness that John Ruskin, T. Roger Smith, and Governor Frere intended it to be, *and* to be a monument to the imperial production of hybrid identities, *and* to be a space in which the colonial state reveals its capacity to collect and exhibit alterity. The same object produces all of these readings—not in sequence, but simultaneously.[56]

The *Builder* seems aware of the terminus as a producer of hybrid identities. The imperial collection of Indic details in encyclopedias such as Swinton Jacob's six-volume *Jeypore Portfolio of Architectural Details* in 1890 showed their mastery over India's past. But the lack of restraint in the Victoria Terminus, which the *Builder* saw as "devoid of artistic refinement and reserve," reveals that the mastery over India was illusory. Rather than expressing unease, the enthusiastic response of the Anglo-Indians to the Terminus revealed them to be hybrid subjects.

The *Builder* had earlier criticized Chisholm's design for the Municipal Buildings by noting, "Though there is a general Oriental look about the design, the European hand is everywhere obvious, and thus there is a sense of incongruity and incompleteness; the building has an Oriental aspect without Oriental feeling."[57] Chisholm denied this declaring, "It would be utterly humiliating if those conclusions were well founded, if thirty years of almost continuous exile in India, and a close study and practice, for many years, of Indian art, should result in producing nothing more than a European building dressed with Indian details!"[58] He submitted a photograph of the palace at Sircage (probably Sarkhej) that had a Classical feeling to prove his point. Chisholm also noted that he had no illustrations of European buildings when he designed this building while journeying on ship. Although the *Builder* agreed that the Indian palace at Sircage did indeed have a Classical feeling, they reiterated that Chisholm's design had a "European feeling" because he had been a European architect, and traces of that could not have left him.[59] In this they echoed Smith's sentiments that an artist represented his national background and training. Most notably, the

Builder showed a refusal to acknowledge Chisholm's claim that he was transformed by his experience of India, that he was a hybrid subject.

The *Builder* had an opinion about the correct way of working toward an appropriate Anglo-Indian style. This lay somewhere closer to the second theory of Anglo-Indian design:

> The great point is, that a modification of the style in regard to the climate and associations of India should be set about on an intellectual basis, as a piece of artistic development; a task which requires high artistic culture, and cannot be undertaken extempore by engineers or others who have given no study to architecture as an art.[60]

Just as its colonial rulers' adaptation to the "climate and associations of India" was necessary but admitted of no hybridization, similarly the use of Indic elements as intellectual exercise showed that despite appearances, the product was not a hybrid but a taming of Indic details in a Western framework.[61]

The *Builder* saw itself as the arbiter of taste, thereby allowing the journal—representing the architectural establishment in Britain—to have a final say in delivering damning judgments on colonials as well as British architects practicing there. Its insistence on the maintenance of European standards of taste reflected not only a fear of erosion of these standards but also an assurance that the British back home could continue to read, analyze, interpret, and judge the architecture of Empire in the original and not in translation.[62] In the case of Chisholm, he sent the photograph of the Indian palace because he felt that the *Builder* did not have the complete code to understand his design for the Municipal Buildings. Although not admitting to any such lack, for the *Builder* the correct way to build in India was to have mastery of the codes, which also implied that the boundaries between the rulers and those they ruled over had not been breached.

John Begg and the Appropriate Anglo-Indian Style

But the question of the appropriate architectural style did not go away, just as the question of the purpose of British rule had not. In a lecture he gave at R.I.B.A. in 1920, Begg, consulting architect to the government of India, observed that British architects practicing in India needed "to agree on a definite architectural policy" because the lack of it prevented their dispersed architectural works "from becoming a genuine 'movement.'" Begg argued that this was "a controversial point" and voiced his disagreement with the two schools of opinion on how to build in India. Parting company with the Roman school, he argued that unlike the Roman Empire, the British conquest of India was commercial and possibly cultural rather than a military conquest, and the purpose of British rule was not merely to retain India but to aid India so that she would be able to learn how to govern herself. Thus any architecture that expressed the idea of the conquest of a superior over inferior race would defeat the purpose of British rule. He found the *swadeshi* school to be equally unsuitable, as it would be a problem for modern India to find that it had no architects, for the native craftsmen were undemanding folk who did not understand modern life and their knowledge of business was basic.[63] Begg's stated position was between these two schools, as he outlined below:

> Let the architect take to India all of his real principles, all of his technical skill both in design and execution, all the essence of his training, *but nothing more.* There let him set himself to a new pupilage, and study India's indigenous forms and expressions into his consciousness, until, without abandoning one essential of his earlier training, he can, as it were, not only speak, but also think architecturally in an indigenous manner. Then, and not till then, let him tackle the problems of design for specific conditions, and he will find he can arrive at a solution at once indigenous and architecturally sound, modern and vital.[64]

According to Begg, British architects in India needed to pave the way for Indian architects of the future, and thus every piece of architecture needed to be judged by the questions: "How will this fit in with the scheme of the future? Does it contribute anything to the carrying on of India's architectural tradition, or does it not?"[65] Like the opinion of the editorial in the *Builder,* Begg was arguing that finding the appropriate style was an intellectual endeavor. Begg upheld the idea that "the principles of art are universal, and it is these that give us our common meeting-ground in architecture."[66] Thus in studying India's ancient architecture—such as that in Ahmedabad, Champanir, Bijapur—sites that Begg had studied and was inspired by, one could "find materials from the still living tradition" for use in modern Indian buildings.[67] What Begg seemed to be suggesting was that it was not mere copying, but a search for universal principles of art that would guide the British architect in producing a modern building that expressed a living tradition.

Begg's position on the appropriate "architectural expression" to be used in India was tied to his position on the purpose of empire, which was to train Indians to govern themselves.[68] It was a paternalistic position but it helped clarify his position on the role of British architects in India:

> A living tradition of craftsmanship and design still exists in India in a somewhat feeble state of vitality; and our aim should be to keep that alive, to

foster it and give it a new lease of life. In it are the germs of India's future architecture, an indigenous architecture by indigenous architects. The métier of the British architect now should be to act foster-mother to the infant growth.[69]

Begg's position was also a political position. He saw the first school—the Roman—as similar "to autocracy, to military imperialism," while he compared the *swadeshi* school to "bolshevism." His own vision, a middle way but not a compromise, was "rather on the lines of a sane democracy."[70]

Begg's use of the term *swadeshi* to characterize one school of thought is significant. Bernard S. Cohn has argued that there were two sources for the ideology of the *swadeshi* movement in Bengal from 1903–8. Although the movement had many goals, it argued for the boycott of European manufactured goods to be replaced by indigenously produced items. This movement was influenced both by Europeans, who were persuaded by the Arts and Crafts movement in Britain as well as their insights from their period of stay in India, and by early Indian nationalists, who argued that government policies contributed to the continuing poverty of India.[71] Begg's reference to *swadeshi* acknowledges the significance of this anticolonial movement and of the influence of this school of thought on the *swadeshi* movement. At the same time he evades its critique of colonialism, its argument for indigenously produced items, by referring to them as Bolsheviks. Instead he sees himself as a leader in helping give birth to an indigenous architecture in the future. Begg seemed to see an independent India in the horizon and exhibited a desire to leave a positive legacy of colonial rule.

The search for an appropriate Anglo-Indian style and the diversity of solutions suggests that there was no agreement on how to rule India. At the same time, those who designed public buildings or governed did share some common concerns for what was appropriate for official architecture. First, there was a common agreement that it was the European architect or engineer and not the Indian craftsman who should build official architecture. Kipling, Havell, and others who disagreed with this position were marginalized. Second, it was commonly accepted that the colonial government with its architects, and not native patrons or Indian craftsmen, should take the lead in exploring ways of melding indigenous and European forms. Third, although the appropriate Anglo-Indian style was widely debated, it was a given that all structures had to be adapted to the local climate and, if indigenous details were used, the buildings still had to be fundamentally European. The meaning of Anglo-Indian style in India— whether Classical, Gothic Revival, or Indo-Saracenic—was about the negotiation of the relationship between the ruler and the ruled, it was about the maintenance of distance. The use of Indic detail was an acknowledgment of the necessity to articulate some relationship between the British and the populations they ruled over. However, restraint was necessary both in personal behavior and architectural style. Stevens had been criticized by the *Builder* because the Victoria Terminus showed an excess, a lack of restraint; it could be too easily enjoyed, and it chastised the Anglo-Indian population for applauding it. By drawing on India's past *as an intellectual exercise,* one could even build in the Indo-Saracenic and yet remain "British to the backbone." Napier and Begg's attitude toward an appreciation of Indian architecture and the *Builder*'s endorsement of the correct way to build is close to the ideal of the Kantian aesthetic, which is opposed to popular taste.[72]

The abstraction of universal principles from Indian architecture allowed the British to maintain a distance from it, which was also meant to signify its distance from Indians. An appropriate Anglo-Indian style would use Indic details but in such a way that "it demands respect, the distance which allows it to keep its distance" and not as something that could easily be enjoyed.[73] Taste was used in the colonial context to police racial boundaries through the critique of architectural design. The distinctions drawn were not simply between social classes, but between the rulers and the races they ruled over.

INDO-SARACENIC AND THE TRIUMPH OF ARCHITECTS

Chisholm's Indo-Saracenic design for the Municipal Buildings was never built. Stevens, rather than Chisholm, got the commission in 1888 to design and build the Municipal Buildings (1888–93). In this and increasingly in the Church Gate Station (1894–96) designed for the Bombay, Baroda, and Central Indian Railway, Stevens tried to marry the Venetian Gothic with the Indo-Saracenic, the latter effect created mainly through the shape of the domes. John Adams's Anjuman-i-Islam School (1890–92) was constructed in the Saracenic style, whose architectural references would have been considered appropriate for an educational institution for Muslims. Thus the Indo-Saracenic style really came to Bombay with Begg's design for the new General Post Office (1903–9), and was followed by George Wittet's Prince of Wales Museum (1905–37) and the Gateway of India. As Metcalf notes, these structures in the Indo-Saracenic style were built at a time when the style itself was at the end of its reign as a leading style and so had little impact on Bombay.[74]

Metcalf argues that the Indo-Saracenic did not meet with success in Bombay, which as a port city controlled the bulk of trade with Europe after the opening of the Suez Canal in 1869. Furthermore, Bombay was unique in that a large number of the city's major institutions were partially or wholly funded by Indian philanthropists—usually Parsis and Baghdadi Jews. These small minorities conceived of themselves somewhat as outsiders in India, were loyal to the colonial regime, and became anglicized. They wanted to appear modern by adopting the English language and modes of dressing, and also by surrounding themselves by things European. Thus the Indo-Saracenic was hardly attractive to them and not surprisingly, "Not just the British, but the city's Indian residents as well, made of Bombay a Gothic city."[75]

This is a persuasive argument that gives Indians agency in their rejection of or indifference to Indo-Saracenic, but it becomes less persuasive when one realizes that Bombay was not an exception; even Calcutta was indifferent to Indo-Saracenic, and in each of the three major cities—Bombay, Calcutta, and Madras—a particular style reigned supreme.[76] James Ransome thought he would have an opportunity to do something new when he went to India in 1902 as consulting architect to the government of India. Ransome recalled his "disappointment when I found that in India the desire was for entire purity of style. Here, in England, we were striving after originality when there was but little opportunity, except by slow evolution. In India, where ingenuity was required more than anything, we were forcing purity of style. I was told to make Calcutta Classic, Bombay Gothic, Madras Saracenic, Rangoon was to be Renaissance, and English cottages were to be dotted about all over the plains of India."[77]

The "purity of style" in each of these cities makes one question whether the Indo-Saracenic style truly expressed the idea espoused by Metcalf of the "British Raj as legitimately Indian, while at the same time constructing a modern India of railways, colleges, and law courts."[78] For a particular style of architecture to have an impact, one needs to see the reiteration of a style in many buildings. If Calcutta and Bombay, the most modern of Indian cities, were not dressed in the Indo-Saracenic, then did Madras's Indo-Saracenic apparel represent the city as provincial or traditional? In fact the Raj was more successful in persuading the Indian princes to adopt the Indo-Saracenic, a style both embodying the past and modern future, which perfectly suited the way the Raj wanted to mold the princes of India.[79]

The deployment of Indo-Saracenic in Bombay was significant, but not necessarily for representing imperial ideology. Both the General Post Office (GPO) and the Prince of Wales Museum were located in and around the Fort, near the city's Victorian Gothic architecture (Figure 2.8). While the former was a government building, the construction for the museum was partially supported through local native philanthropy. Located in the public arena where

Gothic Revival architecture built by the government and native philanthropists resulted in the creation of institutions and spaces for the public at large, these structures represented continuity with that tradition.

The break with the past was one of architectural style—from Gothic Revival to Indo-Saracenic—and in who controlled the design of public buildings—formerly engineers, but now architects. The post office, designed by Begg, represented a decisive break from the half-century tradition of Gothic Revival architecture in the city. The building's large dome drew on the architecture of Bijapur, which Begg was familiar with and admired. Undoubtedly, the building was an architectural challenge where Begg sought to blend the right mix of Indic and Western forms and details for a modern purpose. This building exemplified a middle way and a new way between the "Roman school" and the "*swadeshi* school" that he would discuss in a later lecture.[80] His decision to draw inspiration from Bijapur was praised by the *Building News*.[81] The large scale of the GPO with its massive dome and Indo-Saracenic details was a bold move by an architect who made his presence in the city felt through this structure. At the same time it was an object lesson to the engineers of the PWD of the work done by architects. This building was part of the struggle by Begg and other government architects to change the engineers' perception of the architect's role in building, and to wrest control from them of the design of government buildings:

FIGURE 2.8. John Begg, General Post Office, Bombay, 1903–9. Designed in the Indo-Saracenic style, the large central dome was inspired by the architecture of Bijapur. Photograph by author, 1999.

I found the Indian Public Works Department, Roads, and Buildings Branch (observe Roads first, Buildings second!), a department run by engineers, and therefore, largely *for* engineers. Thanks to Wittet (and others) we have changed all that somewhat. The architect is now better understood, and holds a fairly defined and honoured position. But he has had to fight for his position, to contest every foot of ground gained against the passive inertia, mingled, perhaps, with a certain amount of active jealousy, of a whole Department of Government, and the uninformed prejudice of the rest.[82]

Begg's successor George Wittet (1878–1926), who worked in Bombay for nineteen years until his untimely death in 1926, dominated the design of public architecture, taking charge of ninety-five major projects for the government of Bombay, including the design and planning of the Ballard Estate, as well as forty-four projects for Messrs. Tata and Company.[83]

Begg and Wittet developed a close relationship. In 1904, when Wittet came to India from England to work as Begg's assistant, the GPO was under construction. Wittet was alarmed by the Indo-Saracenic-styled GPO and reportedly exclaimed: "Why has Begg gone in for *that* stuff? Why hasn't he done a good Renaissance building?" On hearing of this Begg promptly sent Wittet on a fortnight's tour to Bijapur "where," according to Begg, "the best of the old work is to be found."[84] Wittet returned convinced of the architectural grandeur of Bijapur, and apparently the results of his conversion were seen in his design for the Prince of Wales Museum, except that his *original* design, for which Wittet won the competition in 1908, was *not* Indo-Saracenic.[85] While Wittet seemed to be attempting to find his own style, the controlling committee and government, who, according to Begg, were infatuated by his new GPO building, insisted on making Wittet rethink his museum elevations so that they would echo the style of the GPO. The committee would likely have included influential natives, and far from discouraging the Indo-Saracenic, Wittet was forced to use this style (Figure 2.9).

The Gateway of India drew on the architecture of Ahmedabad and marked the spot where the king-emperor George V and Queen Mary first stepped on land in India in 1911 (Figure 2.10). Apart from the inscriptions that remind the viewer of the royal visit, this of all the Indo-Saracenic structures would have made some natives see the Raj as indigenous. This link would be made more insistently through the temporary civic decorations designed by Wittet in the Saracenic style for the royal visit and not the permanent memorial.[86] Rather than in permanent architecture, it is in the temporary Saracenic architecture of durbars and street decoration for royal visits such as this that the Raj came closest to projecting an image of themselves as indigenous rulers.

FIGURE 2.9. George Wittet, the Prince of Wales Museum, Bombay, 1905–37, photograph circa 1920s. The foundation stone of the building was laid in 1905 by George V when he was still the Prince of Wales. The plan of the building called for three blocks to be laid out in a quadrangle. The central block was completed in 1914 and one of the wings in 1937. The photograph shows the central block with its large central dome. In the middle ground is the Wellington Fountain, erected in 1865 to memorialize the duke's visits to Bombay in 1801 and 1804. Courtesy Phillips Antiques, Bombay.

After the Gateway of India, Wittet did not use the Indo-Saracenic style again.[87] So what purpose did the Indo-Saracenic serve in Bombay? Architecturally speaking, it served as a transitional phase as architects Begg and Wittet wrested control from engineers of the architecture of the Bombay Presidency. With Wittet fully in charge until his death in 1926, the public architecture in the presidency reflected the style he developed and ended the era of Gothic Revival in Bombay. Neither style reflected a change in government policy. By the early decades of the twentieth century, the era of the joint partnership came to an end in India, and so it is Wittet's architecture that represented its final decades.

FIGURE 2.10. George Wittet, Gateway of India, Apollo Bunder, Bombay, 1924. The gateway was built to commemorate the visit of King George V and Queen Mary in December 1911. The stylistic elements were drawn from the architecture of sixteenth-century Gujarat. The gateway served as a reception hall and consisted of three domed spaces: a central hall with massive arches that formed the gateway, flanked by side halls that could accommodate up to six hundred people. Photograph by author, 2002.

THE GOTHIC REVIVAL IN BOMBAY AND NATIVE RESPONSE

Even though much of Bombay's public architecture was in the Gothic Revival style, Bombay's earliest architecturally prominent buildings were located in the Fort and were neoclassical in design.[88] However, Bombay's first Gothic Revival building, the Afghan Memorial Church of St. John the Evangelist (1847 to approximately 1858), was located south of the Fort, at Colaba, and constructed well before Gothic became the leading style in Britain and Bombay in the 1860s.

Gothic began to be used for modern buildings around 1840 due to the efforts of A. W. N. Pugin and the Cambridge Camden Society (the "Ecclesiologists"), "who both argued for Gothic not only because of romantic and national associations and because it was a rational manner of building, but also because it was the only true architectural expression of a Christian society."[89] In Britain, leading church architects—Pugin, Scott, Butterfield, Street—therefore took the lead in propagating the Gothic Revival style.[90] Designed by Henry Conybeare, perhaps with the design involvement of Anthony Salvin and J. M. Derick, and consecrated in 1858, the Afghan Memorial Church was not the first Gothic church in India, but as Davies observed, "Historically it is most important[,] for it was the first church erected in India along the lines laid down by the Ecclesiological Society, embodying the new principles of Gothic architecture advanced by Pugin."[91] It is unlikely that the native public knew or cared about the architectural significance of the Afghan Memorial Church.

Apart from Sir Bartle Frere's active encouragement of the use of the Gothic Revival style in Bombay in the 1860s, Stamp points to two reasons for its success in Bombay. First, one could find good stone of different colors for construction, allowing for the solid construction desired by Gothicists as well as polychromatic detailing by the use of stones of contrasting colors. Second, Gothic Revival required dynamic architectural sculpture and decoration. This became possible when John Lockwood Kipling was hired as a professor of architectural sculpture at the Bombay School of Art in 1865.[92]

It was under the supervision of Kipling that students at the Bombay School began to make marble, stone, and plaster decorations for many of the public buildings that were coming up in Bombay and Poona. As Mahrukh Tarapor has noted, "Their decorations were particularly noteworthy for introducing natural forms into much architectural ornament in India's official edifices, an innovation."[93] Colonel H. St. Clair Wilkins (1828–96), A. D. C. to the Queen and architect of the Bombay Secretariat (1867–74) and the Public Works Secretariat/Offices (1869–72), wrote to Kipling to congratulate him on introducing the "artistic sculpture of natural objects" to India and making it now possible for the architect to realize the sculptural elements in his architectural design such as carved capitals.[94] In other words, Kipling and teacher of decorative painting John Griffiths (1838–1918) and their Indian students were necessary for the success of Bombay's Gothic Revival. Griffiths, for example, led a group of students in the decoration of the High Court and Victoria Terminus buildings. Architectural details, including carved capitals, gargoyles, and corbels for the High Court, were made by four students. For the General Hospital, four large heads depicting four distinct races of India were prepared. Partha Mitter notes, "In the decoration of public buildings in Bombay under Kipling, students enjoyed giving 'play to the grotesque and the fanciful common to Indian and Mediaeval art'" (see Figure 1.10).[95] It is likely that students from the Sir J. J. School of Art would have been proud of their contribution to Bombay's public architecture, as would have other members of the public who were aware of their work.

How did Bombay's public respond to its Gothic Revival architectural style? In his reminisces for the period between 1860 and 1875, Sir Dinshaw E. Wacha, a well-known Parsi figure in Bombay, was of the opinion that by and large none of Bombay's public buildings, including places of religious worship, had any architectural merit:

> Even to-day, after the Government led the way in 1864, and especially after 1870, to the construction of public edifices possessing some architectural pretensions, Bombay cannot boast of a single edifice which could rejoice the heart of Ruskin or Ferguson. The new structures—religious, educational, and others which have sprung into existence after the sixties, are of no striking or original design. Almost all proclaim their poverty so far.[96]

Wacha not only had an opinion on Bombay's Victorian architecture, but was also well informed enough to judge most of it harshly as well as the government for using the services of "architectural mediocrity."

However, Wacha was hardly representative of the majority of Bombay's public who would not have heard of Ruskin. Nor is it important whether Bombay's public uniformly found these buildings beautiful or not. The question is, by what means could Bombay's public respond to these buildings—not necessarily as interpreting the meaning of this style for the makers of these buildings, but as a public landscape they experienced, which consisted of buildings, free-standing sculptures, and open spaces? Upton has pointed out that the apparent order of our surroundings is a result of human structuring of our environment. This allows us to see similarities. However, for these to be noteworthy some kind of analysis as to its meaning is necessary. This can vary from person to person. "Effective social life requires that individual interpretations be knit together by a common ideology. An ideological interpretation succeeds when its assumptions or propositions are made to seem self-evident—when they are transformed into common sense. Then they appear to be neutral depictions of the natural. The interpretation achieves legitimacy, what Antonio Gramsci called 'hegemony.'" We can see how Bombay's citizens understood Bombay's Gothic Revival by looking for "commonsense understandings" of this environment.[97]

It is likely that the "artistic sculpture of natural objects" used on these buildings was important to the local population, not simply because of the so-called love of decoration of Indians, but because in its representational forms it was a visual language that the public could at least partially read, giving them access to this architecture with its alien style. Bourdieu's comments on the reading of a work of art are pertinent here, where he notes: "In a sense, one can say that the capacity to see *(voir)* is a function of the knowledge *(savoir)*, or concepts, that is, the words, that are available to name visible things, and which are, as it were, programmes for perception. A work of art has meaning and interest only for someone who possesses the cultural competence, that is, the code, into which it is encoded."[98] In other words, one needs a point of entry in order to comment on a work of art or architecture, and most of Bombay's population would have not known of or understood the significance of the Gothic Revival style as discussed in British journals and newspapers. In Bombay, the Gothic Revival style was an unscripted script whose meaning was grasped in terms of experiences or concepts familiar or relevant to the local population. Their limited or more likely complete lack of knowledge of the moral and intellectual meanings associated with architectural style freed them from the burden of translating and applying alien concepts to this style.

However, the concept that buildings could be embellished by sculpture was familiar to Indians. The surfaces of Bombay's Gothic Revival architecture were enlivened by sculptures of the natural world—peacocks, monkeys, and vegetation—that were familiar. Many would have recognized some of the faces on the medallions that were affixed to buildings, and others would have responded to human faces as well as sculpted groups like the castes in the university buildings (Figure 2.11; also see Figure 2.7). They would have also looked at the figures representing Queen Victoria or other virtues (see Figure 1.12). They may or may not have known what they represented, but they would have recognized them to be figures of women. The sculpture of animals, vegetation, and human forms inhabited Bombay's Gothic Revival architecture, and accompanied by fountains and statues in the surrounding or adjacent grounds, they made this into an inhabited landscape. The interaction of Bombay's public with parts of this landscape is clear in the names they gave, such as "Cowasji Cross" to the donor of the fountain that has a cross atop it at St. Thomas Cathedral, and to the ongoing ritual activity at many of the statues and to the desecration of others (Figure 2.12). It is not important that the recognition of the form of a woman or a bird is an engagement of the most basic kind. What is relevant is that the Gothic Revival allowed for many levels of engagement and analysis, even the most basic.

Even though style is commonly thought to represent an "underlying mental temperament," Upton points out that "much of its visual unity comes from generally accepted conventions." Furthermore:

> Style is pervasive. It provides a context, or system of common understanding, for the members of a society. To refer once more to linguistics, style resembles what sociolinguistics call a code: a concise, bonding body of implicitly understood assumptions that need not be rehearsed. Allusions suffice. . . . Style is in this sense consensual.[99]

FIGURE 2.11.
Sculpted portrait
medallion of Bai
Sakarbai Dinshaw
Petit, Bai Sakar-
bai Dinshaw Petit
Hospital for Animals,
Parel, Bombay,
opened 1882–84. Bai
Sakarbai was the wife
of Sir Dinshaw M.
Petit, who donated
land with a bunga-
low for the animal
hospital on the provi-
sion that the hospital
be named after his
wife. Photograph by
author, 2006.

For many of Bombay's engineers who designed its Gothic Revival architecture, the style was a convention they would become skilled at using; it continued to be used long after it ceased to be fashionable in England. For the users, the deployment of the Gothic Revival style for the new public buildings in the new public landscape helped to mark them out. For the historian, Bombay's Gothic Revival helped to unify a group of buildings for discussion. In Bombay, the Gothic Revival signified the consensus between native philanthropists and colonial officials on the need for and the aims underlying the new public land-scape for all of Bombay's citizens.

Apart from responding to sculptural decorations that were familiar, it was the context of Gothic Revival in Bombay that would provide its meaning to the native population. In Bombay, the Gothic Revival style was associated with secular public buildings. Pugin argued that Gothic was not only suitable for churches but for all architecture and was a way of building that allowed sculptors and builders alike to show their abilities. However, England itself had few preexisting examples of secular Gothic architecture.[100] In Bombay, the Gothic Revival style was overwhelmingly used and associated with secular architecture and for natives, who did not follow the columns of British architectural journals; the Gothic Revival may have reminded some of churches but did not have the same Christian associations or British national associations. Instead, it

FIGURE 2.12. Fountain in front of the St. Thomas Cathedral, Bombay, erected with the support of a contribution of Rs. 7,000 by Sir Cowasji Jehangir, circa 1860s. The Parsi community expressed its displeasure at their coreligionist's support of a Christian institution by giving the donor of the fountain the nickname "Cowasji Cross." Photograph by author, 2006.

represented the new public landscape for Bombay's citizens, funded by both the colonial regime and philanthropic natives. This public landscape included government offices and the Municipal Corporation, courts of justice, services such as postal services, railway stations, educational institutions, libraries, hospitals, and markets.

These were substantial public buildings that were palaces for the people and not some monarch. One gets a sense of the feeling of awe provoked by these buildings in the autobiography of the famous actress Durga Khote, a graduate of Bombay's prestigious Cathedral School, who wrote of her reaction to St. Xavier's College in the early 1920s:

> I entered St. Xavier's College after matriculating from Cathedral School. I simply could not take my eyes off that Victorian structure when I first entered it. It wasn't all that large. But its carved columns, long corridors, and tall church-like arches created an illusion of grandeur. The minute I stepped into the college, I began to feel grown-up.[101]

Despite the fact that the arches of St. Xavier's College reminded Khote of churches, European architectural styles were not seen as representative of a Christian style by Indians. If this were the case, they would not have been used for religious buildings such as mosques and temples. This does not mean that Indians were ignorant of the fact that their European rulers were Christians. Instead it means that these styles were divested of their religious associations and were seen to reflect being "grown-up," that is progress and modernization and the high status associated with the ruling power. On the other hand, India's British rulers, who divided India's architectural history into racial and religious categories, did see these styles as European and Christian, hence one of the reasons for their discomfort at their use by Indians. Similarly, the use of native styles—Hindu or Islamic—for Christian architecture was repugnant to them.[102]

In contrast to style, which is consensual, Upton suggests the term "mode," whose function is to distinguish:

> Artifactual modes serve not to unify but to distinguish. . . . Modes are limited, as well as limiting: by definition, they are small-scale phenomena standing highlighted against the background of style.[103]

Nineteenth-century Bombay was a cosmopolitan city with a wide variety of groups. With their distinct clothing, the modes of each group distinguished them from other groups. Each community dressed in a different way that signaled their affiliation, while at the same time they constructed their own religious and social institutions, forming distinct community landscapes. Before Frere's transformation of the city, the Classical architectural style of the British was the mode that distinguished their community landscape from that of other groups. Apart from the limited public use of the Town Hall, there was no genuine public arena (see Figure 6.10). The significance of Frere's transformation of Bombay was not simply stylistic, but lay in the creation of a common public landscape. This then made Bombay's Gothic Revival style significant as representing the consensus—the common ground for Bombay's citizens—and formed the backdrop to Bombay's multiple modes of life, architectural styles, and community landscapes. Used in buildings constructed in partnership with Bombay's native elite, this style was not simply the mode of the colonial regime or the British, but represented the consensus of the colonial and native ruling elite.

Bombay's new secular public buildings, funded in part by native philanthropists, enhanced their social standing. It was a way for native philanthropists to distinguish themselves from ordinary wealthy natives who were not philanthropists, not as wealthy, or those whose charity was exclusively directed inward toward their own community. Native philanthropists who were, visually or by name, associated with these buildings reflected the cosmopolitan character of Bombay's elite, while the buildings themselves were eclectic in origin and inspiration. The combination of native philanthropy and government support helped to produce or inflect the meaning of these buildings. Sir Gilbert Scott's University Library and Convocation Hall gives an idea of this. Scott himself never visited India and his design for the apsidal Convocation Hall "with an ecclesiastical air" is based on a French style from the fifteenth century.[104] Sir Cowasji Jehangir Readymoney, the famous Parsi businessman, helped finance this building, which was named after him. Jehangir's statue was first housed in the hall in 1876 but was later moved on a huge base to the front of the entrance to the Hall, which now forms the backdrop to his statue, reminding every visitor of this association (Figure 2.13). Premchand Raichand (1831–1906), a wealthy and well-known Jain, donated money for the University Library, whose substantial Rajabai Clock Tower is named after the memory of his mother. In 1894, a bronze bust of Sir George Birdwood, a leading exponent of the industrial arts of India, was placed in the hall of the University Library. Depicted in the pose of a lecturer, Birdwood wore a skull cap and a loose morning gown. In his hands he held a small bronze figure of Saraswati, the Hindu goddess of learning. The Rajabai Tower was based on Scott's interpretation of Giotto's campanile in Florence (Figure 2.14). The building is also famous for the eight-feet-high sculptured figures that stand around the octagonal carona that represent the castes of western India. Hovering above these figures as finials on each face are additional sets of caste figures. The building has a total

FIGURE 2.13. Sir Gilbert Scott, University Senate Hall, Bombay, 1869–74. Sir Cowasji Jehangir Readymoney contributed toward the costs of the convocation hall, which was named after him. In 1876 Jehangir's statue by Thomas Woolner was placed in the hall but was later moved to the front entrance of the building, where it still stands. Behind him is the arched entrance porch, and still farther back is the gable front of the hall with its large rose window. Bookending the front facade are spirelets that contain stone staircases and are capped by finials. Photograph by author, 2007.

of twenty-four such caste figures modeled by an Indian assistant engineer, Rao Bahadur Makund Ramchandra (Figure 2.15).[105] Davies points out: "Although the location and figures may be Indian, and the inspiration Italian, the building exudes all the ecclesiastical fervour of mid-nineteenth-century Oxbridge. From the chimes of this monumental landmark emanate the sounds of 'Home Sweet Home,' 'God Save the Queen,' and popular hymn tunes."[106] These buildings that used Italian and French Gothic detailing and had an ecclesiastical air nevertheless had Indian castes on the upper story of the University Library whose tower, named after a deceased Jain lady, emitted "popular hymn tunes" among other sounds. In short, the references were an eclectic mix.

The ecclesiastical flavor of these buildings may not have been evident to most Indians who had never visited Oxbridge. When Sir Cowasji Jehangir Readymoney, who had previously donated money toward the construction of the Afghan Church, paid for the cross and fountain in front of St. Thomas Cathedral, there was an uproar in the Parsi community, not because this was

a Gothic structure, but because these donations were directed by a Parsi to a Christian institution (see Figure 2.12).[107] A cosmopolitan city had an architecture that was not dominated by a style that, for Indians at least, had religious overtones. Since Gothic architecture drew on many sources, it was not tied to any one national community either, a fact certainly more evident to the British to whom these buildings would have been both familiar and unfamiliar, but possibly not to Indians.

One can discuss the sculpture of Indian castes on the Rajabai Tower as an illustration of the British obsession with documenting and characterizing India's tribes and castes and their concern with "types." Maclean's *Guide* certainly directed the European tourists' gaze to them and characterized some briefly:

> These figures, which have been modelled by Rao Bahadur Muckoond Ramchunder, the Assistant Engineer in charge of the work, and carved on the spot out of Porebunder stone, are very accurate representations of the peculiar types of face and dress which are noticeable amongst many of

FIGURE 2.14. Sir Gilbert Scott, University Senate Hall, 1869–74, and the University Library and Rajabai Clock Tower, 1869–78, Bombay, photograph circa early 1880s. The Back Bay can be seen in the background. Courtesy Phillips Antiques, Bombay.

FIGURE 2.15. Rajabai Clock Tower, part of the University Library and Clock Tower, 1869–78, detail. Assistant engineer Rao Bahadur Makund Ramchandra is thought to have sculpted twenty-four figures, each eight feet high, on the Rajabai Tower, representing various castes of Western India. Photograph by author, 2007.

the numerous castes included in the native communities of the Bombay Presidency. They are the mild Hindu; the shrewd Kutchi; the traditionally fierce Rajput, with his hand on the hilt of a huge *tulwar;* a praying Parsee, appropriately facing towards Back Bay, in which position so many Parsees are seen every day at their devotions; a sleek high-caste Brahman; a Memon; a Gujarati Bunia; a Ghogari Bunnia; a Maratha; and a Kathiawari.[108]

Indians looking at these figures may not have been conscious of their own documentation as types in a negative way. Whether Indians were flattered, curious, puzzled, or repulsed, they would have seen these representations of the public of western India crowning a section of a complex associated with the ruling regime and some leading members of the native community. Many may have known that an Indian carved them and taken pride in that fact. Indian caste groups on the exterior joined carved heads of Shakespeare and Homer on the interior staircase in being part of the very fabric of the University building. The Indian sculpture and details helped make Bombay's Gothic Revival indigenous.

Bombay's Gothic Revival architecture did not simply transform the visual public landscape of the city but housed new public institutions and spaces that fostered a period of accelerated change for the city's public. In a period of rapid change, Indians in Bombay had to constantly make decisions of what to keep and what to discard in a range of practices—from what to wear and when to wear it, to those that related to the spatial arena of the domestic realm.[109] Even though there was a wide variety of responses to change, the hybridity that resulted from the juxtaposition of the old and new were evident. The new institutions—colleges and universities, and hospitals—were clearly agents of change; and the statues, faces on medallions, and names of leading members of Bombay's native society on these buildings helped Bombay's native citizens accept them. The hybridity of the elite not only helped in making decisions about negotiating continuity and change, but made hybridity the norm or even something associated with the tastes of the elite. Jehangir stood before the Convocation Hall, a Gothic Revival building, in Parsi robes. At the same time, he had a title from the British, and his coat of arms, also from the British, were displayed in the hall along with those of past chancellors. Upton notes, "Modish artifacts that accorded with élite tastes and that were not available to everyone demonstrated native gentry familiarity with the aesthetic preferences of an international élite with whom they wished to be identified" and at the same time distinguished them from ordinary wealthy natives.[110] Since these buildings did not personally benefit the native philanthropists, nor were most of them for the exclusive use of their own communities to whom they were responsible, this philanthropy showed the innate nobility of the philanthropists and enhanced the status of these institutions. Occasionally, however, the motives of the philanthropists were suspect, such as Sir Cowasji Jehangir's donations to Christian foundations. In such cases they were often upbraided by the native press. The partnership between the colonial government and native philanthropists meant that these new institutions and the changes they would produce had the sanction of the local elite and were not seen as simply imposed by the colonial regime. The hybridity of Bombay's Victorian Gothic architecture was in keeping with the hybridity of the native public's lived reality where change was constant.

Even though most of Bombay's Victorian architecture was designed by engineers in the PWD or Royal Engineers, it is now commonly agreed that much of it was of high quality and showed a familiarity to buildings being constructed in England that were illustrated in the *Builder* and *Building News*.[111] Gothic Revival certainly meant copying from the past and from other examples, and this phenomenon was hardly unique to this revival. As Colonel H. St. Clair Wilkins (1828–96), Lieutenant-Colonel James Augustus Fuller (1828–1902) of the Royal Engineers, and the prestigious British architect Sir Gilbert Scott demonstrate, practitioners of the Gothic Revival in Bombay certainly copied from earlier precedents or from British models.[112] However, this copying of the frame (not necessarily the details) and the references were unidirectional. Even though Bombay came to have some of the finest Gothic Revival architecture in the world, it did not serve as a model for English architecture. What makes Bombay's Victorian architecture colonial is that in Britain, the heart of empire, it was assumed that the origin of Bombay's architecture was Britain and that the empire could only produce copies that were derivative.[113] It is not only architecture in the Gothic Revival style that is analyzed by reference to British precedents, but even Indo-Saracenic architecture.[114] For most scholars of imperial architecture, Britain is their point of reference, the source of the original. However, for Indians from Bombay or elsewhere, Bombay's concentration of Gothic Revival architecture distinguished Bombay from other Indian cities. If the Indians had traveled abroad, Bombay would be their point of reference; and when viewing the Gothic Revival architecture in Britain or Canada, they would be reminded of Bombay.

CONCLUSION

In Bombay, buildings were not exact copies of those in Britain but only seemed to reference them, thereby increasing the aura of the original for historians of British imperial architecture. However, even when buildings in India were explicitly copying designs from Britain such as Calcutta's Government House, whose plans were based on Keddleston Hall, the copy was not the same as the original. As Swati Chattopadhyay shows in this case, the adjustments made by the copy (the Government House in Calcutta), even if for reasons of climate, produced profoundly different social relations between the colonial elite and their native servants as compared to those between the British elite and their servants in Britain, illustrating the hybrid lived reality of the British in India.[115] Buildings designed for India—whether Classical, Gothic Revival, or Indo-Saracenic in style—were not simply copies of British buildings. Central to their production was the issue of finding the appropriate Anglo-Indian style for India, a style that calibrated the correct distance between colonizing elite and those they ruled. The intellectual underpinning of these spatially and stylistically hybrid buildings was vital in buttressing the denial that they reflected the hybrid realities of colonial life.

In his discussion of how to build in tropical climates, particularly India, T. Roger Smith outlined various points that the architect was required to keep in mind regarding the domestic arrangements—in other words, the plan as it has to do with climate, materials, sewage disposal, and also the large number of servants. Smith followed this by stating, "As far as I have seen it, most of our building work in the East is not creditable to our taste, though it bears witness to our energy and rigour. It is unmistakably European, but of a very bad type."[116] Discussions of style only avoided the issue that their spatial domestic arrangements were not British but a product of colonial conditions and that the British were surrounded by Indians in their domestic lives and also at work. Indians had to accept the accelerated rate of transformation in the second half of the nineteenth century; this would have helped them to embrace Bombay's Gothic Revival architecture. The British had a different problem. Despite the hybridity of their lives and the architecture that surrounded them, they had to remain "British to the backbone."

To return to the issue of meaning of architectural style, what did Gothic Revival architecture mean to Bombay's native inhabitants, particularly since the codes available to understand it were visual and contextual, drawn from their location in the city and people's experience of everyday life? The Gothic Revival was the face of the new public landscape, a product of the joint enterprise—the partnership between native elites and the colonial government. It was a secular public arena for all of Bombay's citizens, a meeting ground for people of all races, religions, and classes. It consisted of both open spaces and buildings that were substantial in size. At the same time these institutions represented new practices that Bombay's citizens would have to adapt to and learn, such as going to hospitals—practices that many were reluctant to accept. Many of these institutions had the backing of Bombay's native elite who signaled their acceptance of these new institutions and practices by helping to fund them. The

Gothic Revival as a European style may have been attractive to many of the educated native elite who saw these styles as symbols of progress. Many members of the public could also take pride and pleasure in the carvings executed on many buildings by Indians and also in the fact that Indian engineers worked or designed many of these buildings and Indian philanthropists funded many of them. Bombay's Gothic Revival came to symbolize the city itself. The Indo-Saracenic style was briefly used in public architecture, but since it was not accompanied by a change in policy it had no significant impact. Bombay's Gothic Revival architecture represented an era of the partnership between the colonial and native elite that resulted in a common public arena containing many institutions for the welfare of the public.

Discussions about style, about who should build, and about how to foster an indigenous tradition were not superficial, and taking an unpopular position took great courage and had consequences. Chisholm's defense of Indo-Saracenic was mocked by the *Builder*, which noted that the tastes of the educated and important native men was becoming more Europeanized, and the Europeanized Hindu would hardly care for a building in the Hindu revival style.[117] In other words, the *Builder* was letting Chisholm know that they did not think that he had an appreciative audience for his architecture. A member of the colonizing elite who claimed to be a hybrid subject or was dangerously in favor of Indian traditions was neither acceptable to the British at home nor to the Europeanized Indian elite. The *Builder* was not entirely wrong. The native students of the painter Griffiths were hired to copy all the wall paintings at Ajanta from 1872–75. While Griffiths himself greatly admired Ajanta, many of the students of the Sir J. J. School of Art, who had been convinced of the "implied inferiority of Indian art," refused, to make copies of the paintings. Threatened with expulsion, they still refused, seeing this exercise as "child's play."[118]

The building of Victorian Bombay was dominated by European engineers and architects working for the PWD. However, this is only part of the story. It was also built by Indian engineers. In the next chapter I examine the role of native engineers in constructing Victorian Bombay and focus particularly on the meteoric career of Khan Bahadur Muncherji Cowasji Murzban.

3 The Biography of an Unknown Native Engineer

IN MOST ARCHITECTURAL HISTORIES of Bombay, native engineers are either ignored or summarily dispatched because they are not seen to be the originator of ideas but, rather, functionaries who carried out orders.[1] But is this all they were? Macaulay's Minute (1835) articulated the aim to create through missionary education "a class of interpreters between us and the millions whom we govern—a class of persons Indian in blood and colour, but English in tastes, in opinions, in morals and in intellect," or as Homi Bhabha dubs them, "mimic men."[2] My work examines the role of one prominent Indian architect and engineer, Khan Bahadur Muncherji Cowasji Murzban (1839–1917), who belongs to this "class of interpreters" and might offer an example of a "mimic man" (Figure 3.1). How does one examine Murzban's role in the construction of colonial Bombay? Is Murzban an ideal type of "mimic man," someone who could imitate the architectural forms desired by the British in his designs and yet forge no independent path of his own? Or are there other, more revealing ways of analyzing the work of Murzban and others like him?

Murzban worked in the Public Works Department (PWD) from 1857 to 1893. He was appointed executive engineer, presidency, PWD in 1884 and retired from the government on 24 January 1893 after a thirty-six-year career in government service. In 1892, Murzban was appointed executive engineer of the Municipal Corporation of Bombay, a position he held for eleven years until his retirement in December 1903.[3] In a career in Bombay spanning almost half a century, Murzban was responsible for the design and/or supervision of construction of many of Bombay's public buildings.[4] Murzban became a member

FIGURE 3.1. Khan Bahadur Muncherji Cowasji Murzban (1839–1917), portrait photographs taken at various ages. From Murzban, *Leaves from the Life of Khan Bahadur Muncherji Cowasji Murzban*, 29.

of the Institute of Civil Engineers (C.I.E.) in 1896 and a fellow of the Royal Institute of British Architects (R.I.B.A.) in 1889. Commenting on the award of his fellowship by R.I.B.A., the influential daily, the *Times of India*, wrote on 16 July 1889: "This gentleman, who has earned quite an enviable reputation in Bombay, having been associated, in some capacity or other, with nearly every work of magnitude during the past ten years or so, has recently had the very high honour conferred upon him of election to the class of Fellows of the Royal Institute of British Architects—a distinction which, in these days of qualifying examinations, is given only to men of some distinction."[5] In 1881, he applied to the government for a plot of land in the Esplanade area so that he could build a house that was close to both his office and the buildings being constructed under his supervision in the vicinity. The government granted the plot to him, in this most prestigious area, on favorable terms. The house, named Gulestan, was completed by 1884 (Figures 3.2, 3.3).[6] I have been unable to locate the house. However, a road in the vicinity of the house continues to bear Murzban's name.

In contrast to the construction of native engineers as more or less anonymous intermediaries who got the job done, Murzban's son's life sketch of his father and grandfather represented his father's life as exemplary:[7]

> Muncherji's life furnishes an object-lesson in "Self-Help," he being one of those who have risen, from the lowest rung of the ladder of Government service, to the highest that was reachable at the period of his career as Executive Engineer, Presidency, terminating in a very well-earned pension.[8]

Although Murzban depicted his father's life as an "object-lesson in 'Self-Help,'" this chapter shows that Murzban's life also offers us object lessons on the possibilities and limits of a native engineer of his time.

Early in his career Murzban became a protégé of Sir Bartle Frere and was brought to Bombay by him in the 1860s to help him realize his dream of a new Bombay. Murzban was first appointed as assistant to the secretary to the Rampart Removal Committee in 1863. In my estimation there was no architect or engineer in the second half of the nineteenth century who could rival the length, depth, and diversity of Murzban's almost half-century involvement in the construction of colonial Bombay's public buildings and infrastructure. And yet Murzban is a relatively unexplored figure.[9]

Assistant engineers, who were usually natives, were often responsible for supervising the erection of buildings, so we usually only hear their names in passing. Vasudev Bapuji supervised the construction of the Secretariat, while assistant engineer Rao Bahadur Makund Ramchandra is thought to have done the sculptures on the Rajabai Tower that represent the various castes of Western India (see Figure 2.15).[10] Their names fleetingly appear in the pages of

FIGURE 3.2. M. C.
Murzban, Murzban's
house, Gulestan,
Esplanade, Bombay,
1884. From Murz-
ban, *Leaves from the
Life of Khan Bahadur
Muncherji Cowasji
Murzban*, 58.

Bombay's history and then they vanish, with the exception of Murzban, whose
professional association in an official capacity with Bombay lasted from 1863
to 1903, a time span far exceeding that of any other engineer and architect in
Bombay. Murzban's successful career as an engineer was unusual but might be
compared to figures such as the legendary Sir Ganga Ram, who worked for the
PWD in Lahore.[11]

This chapter seeks to revise the account of who built Bombay by introducing a new set of actors—Indian civil engineers who worked for the government and who also participated in the construction of major civic buildings
that represented the Raj. They have been long neglected not only because their
work and biographies are not well documented, but also because they have no
place in this narrative. Having no voice in most debates, it is not clear how one
can talk about such figures because one cannot know what their buildings were
trying to say, if anything. Here, I will focus on the career of one individual,
Murzban, and by "personalizing colonial rule," I hope to complicate its working
and experience.[12]

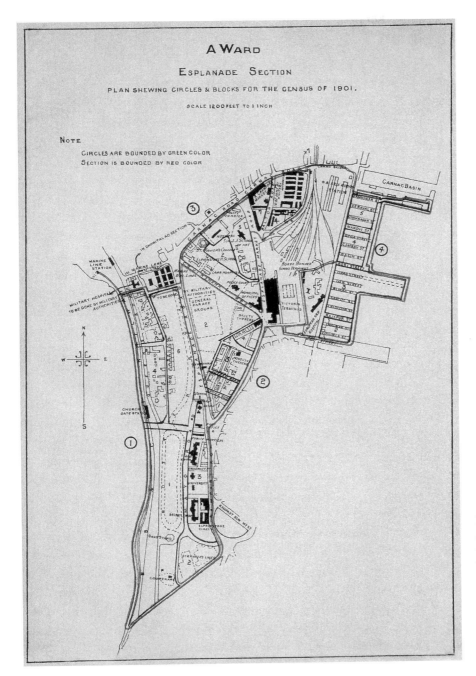

FIGURE 3.3. Plan of Esplanade section, 1901. Many buildings designed or built by M. C. Murzban are located in this section. From Edwardes, *Census of India—1901*, vol. 11, facing 76.

In his comparative study of urban space in colonial and postcolonial Africa, the cultural geographer Garth Andrew Myers introduced the idea of "verandahs of power," a phrase borrowed from Elspeth Huxley to conceptualize colonial power as a three-tiered structure. The upper tier was occupied by the colonial elite, replaced by the colonized elite in the postcolonial state. The second tier housed the colonized middle, while the third tier consisted of the urban majority.[13] This three-tiered model of colonial elite, colonized middle, and urban majority could certainly be complicated by the augmentation of additional verandahs. However, Myers's model is elegant in its simplicity and for drawing our attention to the colonized middle, whose members acted as intermediaries between the upper and lower levels. In India, the colonized middle was the "class of interpreters between" the Raj and "the millions" they ruled over.

Bombay's British engineers and architects belonged to the colonial elite and occupied the top verandah, whereas Bombay's native engineers represented the colonized middle. The engineering department of the Bombay PWD, for example, might have a handful of British officials at the top while most of the staff consisted of natives. A photograph of the officeholders in the Executive Engineer Presidency's Office, PWD from 1893, when Murzban was the executive engineer, seems to have possibly only a couple of European members and even that is not certain (Figure 3.4). It was this silent and usually invisible native majority that carried out most of the work in the construction of the public buildings and infrastructure of colonial Bombay. European and Indian engineers, architects, and artists collaborated with each other to design the city—its infrastructure, architecture, public sculpture. At the same time, the city was literally constructed by Indian laborers and craftsmen. This kind of collaboration in the design and construction of the city is the second sense in which Bombay was a joint enterprise.

Intermediaries such as Murzban did not come from specific racial groups, though in different eras certain castes and communities were more likely than others to acquire a Western education. Murzban was both representative of individuals of the middle verandah and was at the same time distinct from other native engineers in Bombay who were his contemporaries, not only because of his remarkably successful career but because of the extent of his multifaceted engagement with the city.[14] Undoubtedly, Murzban was a good engineer, but his rapid advancement can be attributed in part to his skill as an intermediary who interacted with powerful elites in a number of different forums. In his engineering career, he was aided in his rise by many British mentors who are mentioned in his biography. As a Freemason, Murzban would have met members of both the colonial and colonized elite. Murzban was a Parsi, as were the majority of Bombay's philanthropists during the second half of the nineteenth

FIGURE 3.4. Members of the Executive Engineer Presidency's Office, PWD, Bombay, photograph taken 11 February 1893. From Murzban, *Leaves from the Life of Khan Bahadur Muncherji Cowasji Murzban*, 82.

century, allowing him to act as an effective intermediary between them and the colonial elite. He also sat on the board or was a committee member of various charities through which he would have also come in touch with Parsi and other philanthropists. He hailed from a family that had a distinguished record of social reform in Bombay. On a professional basis, as the architect of many philanthropic institutions as well as some community institutions, Murzban had contacts with many powerful and wealthy Parsis. Furthermore, and most significantly, this interaction with Parsi philanthropists and his construction of public buildings allowed him to emerge as a philanthropist in his own right, as well as an organizer of philanthropy toward special projects, including hospitals and housing projects for the Parsi community. In the remarkable success he achieved in his official career, he can be compared to such other legendary figures as Sir Ganga Ram of Lahore, who was also a philanthropist, but Murzban emerges as a visionary in his nonofficial capacity—as a philanthropist and as a facilitator of philanthropy leading to the construction of institutions and housing colonies for the exclusive use of Parsis.

THE PLACE OF THE NATIVE ENGINEER

If British civil engineers complained of their inferior status in the PWD hierarchy, for Indian engineers just getting a job in the PWD was no mean achievement.[15]

European graduates were eligible for jobs in the Indian PWD apart from two positions that were annually reserved for subject citizens of the British Empire. While figures such as Bapuji, Ramchandra, and Murzban were appointed to the PWD before the foundation of the Royal Indian Engineering College or Cooper's Hill, England, it is likely that they would have had to compete with British civil engineers for positions in and subsequently for promotions within the PWD hierarchy.

Despite the many Victorian buildings he designed in Bombay, Murzban's neglect by Britain's architectural press did not simply reflect racial prejudice but disdain for the work of engineers in a general environment of limited interest in the empire. The lack of attention architectural works in the empire received was demonstrated in a lecture given by John Begg (1866–1937), consulting architect to the government of India from 1908 to 1921, on 22 April 1929, before the R.I.B.A. in London, where he poignantly observed while "testifying, here at the very centre of the arcane of British architecture [that it] has been said—I have said it once or twice myself—that only those at or within sight of the centre need hope to obtain adequate professional recognition."[16] Well-known colonial architects such as Begg were sensitive to professional neglect while military engineers received even less attention from architectural journals.[17]

Figures such as John Lockwood Kipling, the artist, scholar, and professor of architectural sculpture at the Sir J. J. School of Art in Bombay from 1865 to 1874, were also unsympathetic to the native engineer. As Kipling saw it, the classes of natives that were being educated in Western institutions were often the classes for whom foreign styles of architecture symbolized "enlightenment and progress."[18] He thought that native subordinates who worked at the PWD had only theoretical knowledge derived from books. Kipling cynically observed, "There are hundreds of them indeed, earning relatively large salaries, who are mere copyists and tracers," unlike the native craftsmen, trained from childhood, who had practical knowledge and were often proficient at several crafts. However, by the 1880s, well-trained men of the *mistri* class were not easily found and were especially difficult to find in the "official centres" of British India, "and when they are employed they are regarded as hands merely by overseers who, in an artistic sense, are their inferiors." According to Kipling, the English-educated Indian elite who were the native subordinates in the PWD were neither of nor sympathetic to the craft tradition and would only help in its demise.[19]

Kipling was also critical of the training at the Roorkee College of Engineering. He had no quibble with the training in engineering but highlighted the lack of an Oriental department in the college and noted, "Not a single native draughtsman turned out from this school has been taught the architecture of the country." Kipling pointedly and correctly observed that this was detrimental even from an engineering point of view. The knowledge and use of only European forms would require the import of crucial structural supports, such as iron girders, while dome forms evolved in the Hindu and Islamic traditions in India, "which are at once economical and architectural," were not used.[20]

Even though Indian engineers received no training in the architecture of India, it is possible that some of them sought to educate themselves on this subject. Murzban, for instance, toured North India in 1872 and South India in 1891. In 1873, he gave an illustrated lecture in Gujarati at the Gnyan Prasarak Mandli on "Architecture."[21] Yet it is unlikely that this self-education gave Murzban anything close to the understanding of the craftsmen's knowledge of the symbolic, ritual, social, and cultural aspects of design. His travels in India did not cause Murzban to experiment with Indic styles. Even if he had been interested in incorporating Indic forms in his architecture, as a "native" he would have known that he did not have the authority to experiment with architectural style in his official capacity. Rather than symbolizing his mastery of Indian tradition or the demonstration of an ideology, it would simply reveal him to be backward or traditional. Murzban designed few buildings in the 1870s and would have been mastering or copying Gothic architecture during this period. It is likely that he saw Western styles as modern and progressive and desired to emulate them. Even if Murzban had read A. W. N. Pugin and John Ruskin, it is difficult to see how he could have been sympathetic to their ideas, nor would the relationship of Gothic architecture to Christianity have been attractive to a Zoroastrian. The success of Murzban's entire education and career was predicated on the demise of the craftsmen's control of building. Western styles then may have meant very little, perhaps simply "enlightenment and progress," but as I will demonstrate, this vacuum in meaning would be filled over time as these buildings reflected very real transformations in social and cultural practices.

British architects wanted to wrest control of the building process from engineers while Kipling and others of his ilk wanted native builders to regain control of the building process. British military and civil engineers controlled the PWD, and the native engineer wanted a foot in the door. The native engineers of India were sympathetic to European styles, had rudimentary knowledge of Indian building traditions, represented castes that had benefited from British rule and education, and since they brought little that was "native" from their tradition to their work, the "native" in the native engineer expressed at least two things: his subaltern position in the colonial hierarchy and his ability to act as an intermediary between the rulers and those who worked on engineering projects.

What role did native engineers think they should play in the building process? In 1886, Queen Victoria's secretary of state requested the creation of a commission to reconsider the issue of admission of natives to the Covenanted Civil Service. Murzban was one of the witnesses, and in his evidence given in January 1887, he weighed the relative merits of native and European engineers:

> Khan Bahadur Muncherji Kavasji Murzban, Executive Engineer, considers that Natives are quite fit for service in the Engineering grade, but for some time there should be in that grade a fair proportion of Royal Engineers and British Civil Engineers. The former by their high education and military position give prestige to the Department, and the latter bring to it fresh knowledge acquired by visits to Europe. Such Engineers should be drawn from the profession at large and not taken fresh from College. Assistant Engineers should be posted to offices of Executive Engineers in charge of large works. Native Engineers are better than Europeans for checking scamping of work and fraud on the part of contractors. In the efficiency of their works there is not much difference. The European Engineer's education is superior.[22]

Murzban judiciously weighs the merits of both groups, noting that native engineers were far more capable of detecting the misdemeanors of contractors. Murzban describes how native engineers acted as intermediaries between the European engineer and the contractors (and his workers) in managing a practical situation, and suggests that native engineers had a greater ability to detect fraud and, although it is not mentioned directly, to deal with the contractor, use the right language, and ensure that things were done correctly. In judging that in "the efficiency of their works there is not much difference," he was concluding that despite their different strengths the European and native engineers were equal. Further, Murzban's language of "a fair proportion" of native and European engineers working together may be read to articulate a faith in the idea of the joint enterprise, that both European and native engineers (each with their own area of expertise) were necessary only "for some time," leaving unasserted the implication that in the future natives would be able to manage quite well independently.

ANGLO-INDIAN ARCHITECTURE AND ENGINEERS

Just as architects were concerned with Anglo-Indian architecture, so were engineers. And yet, each emerging profession had overlapping but different concerns: architects primarily with aesthetics and engineers with the physics of construction. Whereas architects were interested in the meaning of style as illustrated in the discussions covered in their professional journals, engineers were conscious of the style they used but their professional journals did not dwell on the meaning of style. According to Dell Upton, while style is thought to represent an "underlying mental temperament," it is more often a result of "accepted conventions arising from functional necessities" that helped to resolve certain technical problems.[23] At the same time, engineers measured their worth on their resolution of technical problems. In the second half of the nineteenth century, it was engineers rather than architects who designed most of Bombay's public architecture, and of the engineers, no one worked on a larger number of public buildings than did Murzban, who also designed many of them. Many of the engineers designed buildings that have subsequently been recognized to be architecturally successful. As a native engineer, Murzban has not received the same kind of attention. However, although some of the buildings he designed—such as the Sir Cowasji Jehangir Readymoney, Kt., building for Elphinstone College and the State Record Office (opened in 1889), a large part of which appears to have been designed by John Adams; and the Byramjee Jeejeebhoy Parsi Charitable Institution, Queen's Road (built in 1909)—are handsome and well-proportioned buildings, the purpose of this account is not to rehabilitate Murzban's reputation as an architect whose design talents have been wrongly overlooked (Figure 3.5). By aesthetic design standards, the plans, spaces, and details of most of his buildings are practical and ordinary, but as an engineer, Murzban valued his technical skills above aesthetics.

If architects had a sense of themselves as those who introduced art into the building process, engineers took pride in their ability to understand the science of building, talking about style but in a practical manner. In an article on Anglo-Indian building in the first issue of *Professional Papers on Indian Engineering*, the journal's editor, Major J. G. Medley, condemned the monotonous architecture of cantonments unflatteringly nicknamed "the Military Board style."[24] As the editor of this journal and the principal of Thomason College in Roorkee, his views are fairly typical of the engineering profession. Medley's critique was not simply about style, but also about the manner in which buildings were constructed, particularly the question of adapting style to climate. Although not disapproving of Gothic churches, Medley found shortcomings in the way they were currently built as they were not well accommodated to the climate. In contrast, he praised the architecture of mosques for maintaining a good temperature in hot and cold months. Similarly, he found native houses with their thick walls and few doorways more suited to the climate than Anglo-Indian houses with their large rooms and numerous openings. He had no hesitation in recommending the use of courtyards, typical of houses constructed by natives and in the East, for adoption by Anglo-Indian architecture. Medley made clear that he was not recommending that Europeans live in native houses, but merely that Anglo-Indian architecture had to find a way of building that was appropriate

FIGURE 3.5. M. C. Murzban and John Adams, Sir Cowasji Jehangir Readymoney, Kt., building for the Elphinstone College and State Record Office, Bombay, opened in 1889. The building was originally designed to house the Government Central Press and was built by M. C. Murzban, at that time executive engineer of the Presidency. To the right is the Sassoon Mechanics' Institute. From Murzban, *Leaves from the Life of Khan Bahadur Muncherji Cowasji Murzban*, 64.

for the climate.[25] Unlike discussions on style in architectural journals (see chapter 2), the discussion by engineers put the practical problems of suitability above ideological questions and thus could include ideas from India in their building designs.

Medley's discussion on materials also allows one to get a sense of what these buildings were like on the inside. Although bungalows with their surrounding verandahs in the compound have been discussed in terms of their effectiveness in social distancing, their interiors were often shabby.[26] On the interior of houses in the cantonment, we find "high bare whitewashed walls, a barn-like roof, with perhaps a dirty ceiling cloth shaking in the wind, a dilapidated plaster floor and square holes cut in the wall doing duty as doors and windows."[27] This shabby plainness was only relieved by the fireplace whose ornamentation was described as "a grotesque mass of ornaments" carved by native masons that would "perhaps be more effective if unblackened by the smoke from the ill-constructed chimney."[28] It was not just domestic structures that suffered from inadequate attention to materials but all kinds of buildings. Medley criticized the application of lime whitewash on inferior plaster finishes on building interiors, which then whitened the coat of those who stood against it. We hear of fans—the commonly used Bombay punkah, a wooden stick of wood with a "heavy deep fringe," or the much inferior and often used "white-washed rectangle"—and while the author gave advice on these types, he pointedly remarked, "Let the fringe be of good material and color, *and above all, clean.*"[29] The details give us a sense of the lack of refinement in the experience of many buildings. Far from the lofty discussions of the meaning of style, one catches a glimpse of the lived realities in buildings where whitewash marked clothing, of floors where dust particles rose up, and of fringed fans that were in need of cleaning. In this short piece Medley discussed a wide range of practical topics, including climate, plaster, roof materials, flooring, fans, and fireplaces, criticizing contemporary practices and offering practical advice for improvements.[30] Instead of a suitable Anglo-architectural style, practical suggestions to everyday problems were viewed as central to the improvement of Anglo-Indian architecture.

Medley goes on to note, "Treating of Architecture as distinct from mere building, it is an art, not a science, and therefore does not fall under exact rules of instruction; one consequence, of which is, that while Engineering advances and improves, Architecture stands still and copies."[31] If architecture was considered by engineers as mere copying, it is hardly surprising that Murzban's biography highlights his abilities in the science of building. He may have copied Gothic details in his architectural designs much as an architect did, but as an engineer he showed skill and took pride in solving structural problems, thereby assisting in the advance of engineering.

Two incidents treated in his biography reveal that Murzban saw himself not only on par with but also superior to Europeans as an engineer. In 1874, he went on leave and traveled for over seven months in the Continent and England where he visited many sites. This visit combined pleasure with education. He went specifically to Dundee, for example, to examine a large bridge then under construction that spanned the river Tay. His son notes that in his diary Murzban recorded his apprehensions about the design of the bridge, fearing that it would not be long before it would collapse. However, he did not have the courage to voice his fears before the notable engineers who designed the bridge. Murzban's concerns proved prescient, as the bridge collapsed soon after.[32] Here we see that Murzban was unable to voice his apprehensions, but just by observing the bridge Murzban could detect the flaws in its design, to which the supposedly more superior European designers were blind.

The second incident recorded in Murzban's biography has to do with the General Post Office building located near the Flora Fountain and used since 1914 as an adjunct to the General Telegraph Office. The construction of this building was based on designs sent out from England by an English architect. The building was designed in such a way that the entire weight of the two upper floors was to fall on the substructure of the ground floor, composed of columns and arches. As the building construction commenced based on the English plans, Murzban alerted his superior officer of the inherent weakness of the under-structure. When work on the superstructure of the two upper floors was almost complete and work on roofing had begun, the inadequacy of the stone columns became clear—one had a complete vertical crack. Realizing that a structural collapse would tarnish the reputation of the PWD, Murzban took matters in his own hands and immediately replaced the cracked column with a new one. As he was in the process of supervising the repairs, chief engineer and secretary to government Sir Michael Kennedy and executive engineer Hart appeared on the scene. Noticing the dangerous nature of the construction, they rebuked Murz-ban for embarking on this work without getting permission. This was followed by a stern letter, in reply to which Murzban stated that he was concerned that if the columns failed, it would not only create a scare but it would also impugn the reputation of the PWD. Not long after the fractured column had been replaced, several other columns were found fractured because of the excessive weight of the superstructure. People in Bombay began to talk about how the Post Office building was collapsing. The matter even reached the attention of the governor of Bombay, Sir Seymour Vesey FitzGerald. It was decided that the eight col-umns beneath the two upper floors should be replaced, and Murzban was put in charge. It was a risky enterprise, and several Indian and European engineers, the chief engineer, and the executive engineer stopped by to see how this was being handled. Murzban's successful resolution of this structural crisis resulted in his promotion.[33]

Here we see Murzban portrayed as a heroic and loyal figure who, by his daring and ingenuity, saved this building from sure collapse, an endeavor that was followed closely by both Indian and European engineers in order to learn how this was done. He was also revealed to be loyal to the British government, and selfless and zealous in his desire to maintain the good name of his depart-ment. The two examples of Murzban's engineering expertise are also notable; they do not impugn the reputation of his European superiors in Bombay because the engineers and architect at fault resided in Europe. The veracity of these incidents is not important. What is important is what they seem to indicate. While remaining loyal to the colonial government, it appears that the tutelage of the British was no longer necessary, for Murzban at least, as these incidents reveal him to be at the top of his game not just in Bombay but in the empire. Murzban wanted to be seen primarily as a good engineer, and all the evidence points us in that direction.

THE INTERMEDIARY: A LIFE ON THE MIDDLE VERANDAH

I concentrate on Murzban's official career to examine his meteoric rise and his role in the construction of Victorian Bombay. Murzban's abilities as an engineer, his facility in nurturing mentors, the wide range of official activities he undertook that made him indispensable to the colonial elite, his role as an intermediary between the government and Parsi philanthropists, the prominent association of his family with social reform, and his membership in Masonic lodges all contributed to his success. In other words, if we accept that Murzban was an excellent engineer, what is otherwise striking was his ability to participate in diverse though sometimes overlapping arenas and networks of power. By examining Murzban's varied involvements, I will shed light on how we might understand what meaning many members of Bombay's citizenry would have read into Murzban's public buildings.

The Successful Intermediary

Let us begin by sketching the contours of Murzban's early scholastic and professional life. Born on 7 July 1839, Murzban studied at Elphinstone High School and at Poona College. Following this he studied at the Government School of Engineering in Poona (now known as Pune). He passed the entrance examination to join the PWD in 1856. He worked on the creation of plans for the hydraulic works for Poona; and with the officers of the Military Engineering Corps, he worked on the construction of roads, buildings, and bridges.[34] However, this was just a prelude to the important period of his career that began with his move to Bombay in 1863.

Murzban's career was greatly aided by various European mentors who are gratefully acknowledged in his biography, which also contains photographs of many of these gentlemen. All appreciated Murzban's abilities and attempted to reward him by commendations, pay increases, or offers of a job.[35] While working in Poona, he came in "daily contact" with Sir Bartle Frere, governor of Bombay, "and consequent exchange of conversations, had brought about a sort of mutuality of confidences."[36] The governor himself told Murzban of his plans "to erect a new City of Bombay" and asked Murzban to take the job of assistant to the architect who was to come out from England to direct this transformation.[37]

The Rampart Removal Committee was appointed as a result of the decision to tear down the ramparts of the Fort and to construct a new town on the Esplanade. Murzban was appointed as assistant to James Trubshawe, secretary of this committee in 1863. Over time, the committee was disbanded and a new committee known as the Architectural Improvement Committee of Bombay was created with Colonel (later General) J. A. Fuller as secretary and Murzban as his assistant.[38] In other words, Murzban was acquainted with and worked closely with powerful men who were at the forefront of the creation of a new Bombay.

In his biography, we find photographs of the European mentors who were central to Murzban's professional success: the Rev. James McDougall, E. I. Howard, General J. A. Fuller, and J. H. E. Hart, who was architectural executive engineer and surveyor to the government of Bombay in General Fuller's absence. Although McDougall and Howard were instrumental in guiding Murzban toward a career in engineering and the job in Bombay, Fuller's and Hart's recommendations for promotion and salary increase helped fuel Murzban's rapid rise. Murzban was undoubtedly a bright student and excellent professional. However, one of his strengths was his ability to cultivate influential mentors who were favorably disposed toward his advancement.

It was supposedly Murzban's superior engineering abilities that prompted recommendations for his advancement. In 1869, Colonel Fuller proposed to the government that Vasudev Bapuji Kanitkar, Makund Ramchandra, and Muncherji Cowasji Murzban be appointed as assistant engineers. Murzban's son tellingly comments, "In these days, however clever Indian officials were, in the PWD, it was a matter of extreme difficulty to see them placed in the ranks of even assistant engineers."[39] The other two native engineers, who were in higher grades than Murzban, received their promotion while he did not. Fuller repeatedly approached the government in 1870 and again in 1871 for Murzban's promotion, "stating that Muncherji's abilities were on a par with, and in fact, on some points, superior to those of Messrs. Vasudev Bapuji and Makund Ramchandra."[40] Finally, in 1872 Murzban was appointed as assistant engineer in the graded list of the PWD, which, as noted by one of the journals, was "a rare distinction at the time."[41] More distinctions were to follow. In 1877, at the Delhi Durbar, Murzban received the title of Khan Bahadur for his "loyal conduct and services."[42] In 1876, even though he was still an assistant engineer, he was recruited to act as the presidency executive engineer, "a unique appointment" as stated in his biography, "as he was the second native-Indian civil engineer and the *first* Parsi to be appointed to this post."[43]

Murzban was a Parsi as were a majority of Bombay's leading philanthropists. We know of at least one case where Murzban acted as an intermediary

between Parsi philanthropists and the government. In August 1887 he wrote to the government regarding the foundation of an obstetric hospital in Bombay toward which some anonymous donors wished to offer a sum of sixty thousand rupees. Only after their offer was accepted and they gave an additional sum of six thousand rupees were their names revealed as members of the reputable All-bless family. Murzban designed the Bomanji Edalji Allbless Obstetric Hospital (opened in 1891), which was located in the compound of the Pestanji Hormusji Cama Hospital for Women and Children (opened in 1886), also designed by him (Figure 3.6). The Allbless hospital had two special provisions for Parsis: a separate ward for Parsi females and a mortuary or dead house for bodies of Parsi patients.[44]

The Cama family was long associated with social reform, as was the Murz-ban family, and in fact Murzban's grandfather Fardunji Murzban set the reform agenda for the Cama family.[45] In his nonofficial capacity Murzban worked on the Allbless Baug, a community institution for Parsis founded by the Allbless family in 1868. *Baugs* were "religious-cum-social centers . . . public places where initiations, marriages, lectures or meetings might be held."[46] In the 1880s Murzban

FIGURE 3.6. M. C. Murzban, Bomanji Edalji Allbless Obstetric Hospital, Esplanade, Bombay, opened on 8 April 1891. The hospital was constructed in the same precinct as the Pestanji Hormusji Cama Hospital for Women and Chil-dren. From Murzban, *Leaves from the Life of Khan Bahadur Muncherji Cowasji Murzban*, 66.

had already spearheaded a campaign to found a hospital for the exclusive use of Parsis, which fell through. However, the Allbless family not only contributed toward a residential building (opened in 1891) but also paid for the establishment of a dispensary (opened in 1898) attached to Murzban's scheme for Cheap Rental Residential Quarters for Parsis in 1887 (see Figures 3.12–3.15).[47] Murzban was a trustee on many Parsi charitable funds and subsequently designed some public buildings associated with major trustees.[48] Because of these connections, one cannot help wondering whether these Parsi philanthropists specifically requested that Murzban be allowed to design these buildings. Five of the eight public buildings designed by Murzban in his official capacity were funded by Parsi philanthropists and the sixth was founded by a Parsi and fellow Mason.[49] One may never know whether these philanthropists would have objected to a non-Parsi native engineer; the fact that Murzban was a Parsi and from a prominent family could only be an asset.

Engineers in India had to work on a variety of projects, including architectural projects, sanitation, reclamation, sewage disposal, and street layouts.[50] Murzban's work encompassed this great variety of jobs and more. His pavilion at Apollo Bunder, for instance, was the major point of entry for officials before it was replaced by George Ormiston's pavilion and later by Wittet's permanent gateway (Figure 3.7; also see Figure 2.10). More relevant to Murzban's professional success was his ability to make himself indispensable to the colonial elite of Bombay—to those occupying the upper verandah—by organizing fairs, fêtes, official visits, exhibitions, and many other public functions. These were usually events of a temporary nature but necessary in marking and publicizing the achievements of each governor and other senior officials in office, and also in celebrating imperial authority and empire by hosting official visits. Even though senior government officials would have been familiar with his ongoing projects of a permanent nature, it was through these impermanent projects and events that Murzban would have cultivated power on an ongoing basis. Through enabling these events, Murzban's transient and impermanent projects made his expertise necessary and visible to those in power while at the same time bringing him in close personal contact with the colonial elite.

Lady Harris, the wife of the governor, held several elaborate fancy fêtes at the Government House at Malabar Hill to raise money for various institutions. Murzban played a central role in organizing these events and was gratefully acknowledged by Lady Harris in a letter dated 25 March 1892 in which she thanked Murzban for his services. The letter contained a copy of a photograph of the governor and his wife. In its review of these fêtes, the *Times of India*, dated 3 March 1892, acknowledged that in the absence of Murzban, "no Fancy Fair in Bombay could be complete."[51] Here we see Murzban's contribution

Apollo Bunder, Bombay.

acknowledged not only by the governor's wife but also in an influential daily newspaper. A quote from the *Advocate of India*, dated 2 April 1890, which discusses Murzban's role in enabling the visit of H. R. H. Prince Albert Victor, gives one a sense of Murzban's very observable hand conducting most of Bombay's official public events where both his presence and his orchestration was visible to all:

> Among the officials and private gentlemen of this city who have laboured to give weight and grandeur to the public reception lately accorded to H. R. H. Prince Albert Victor, the name of Khan Bahadur Muncherji Murzban, Executive Engineer at the Presidency, must be mentioned. He is to the fore on all such occasions. No Viceroy can arrive on these shores, or depart from them, without his help; without him, all the fairs, all the foundation-stone ceremonies, all the tamashas, of the past decade, would have been robbed of their most artistic effects. He will go down to posterity—we hope—as the author of the gorgeous pavilion on the Apollo Bunder, under which several Royal personages, Viceroys, and Governors have either said farewell to India or received the first words of welcome.[52]

The observation regarding his help confirms that Murzban's success lay partially in his ability to be indispensable to those in power. Such a course of action

FIGURE 3.7. George Ormiston, Apollo Bunder, postcard, circa 1910s. Ormiston's Burmese-style pavilion with a pagoda roof (seen here) is likely to have replaced the pavilion designed by M. C. Murzban that certainly existed in the 1890s. Courtesy Phillips Antiques, Bombay.

was certainly not exclusive to those who were colonized. However, since other avenues of cultivating power were less readily available to the colonized middle, making oneself visible and indispensable to those in power was an important route for anyone with ambition.

"Brotherly Love" and the Cult of Freemasonry

Under colonial rule, the colonized elite and colonized middle found themselves excluded from centers of sociality and arenas of social mobility such as the exclusive clubs where the colonial elite gathered. However, there was an alternative space—the spaces of the secretive and exclusive Freemasonry brotherhood—where elite male members of European and native societies interacted. Soon after coming to Bombay, Murzban was elected as a member of the Lodge Rising Star in 1863. After taking various "degrees" he was elected "master" in 1868 and 1869. Members of his lodge gave him a silver cup and a past-master's jewel at the conclusion of this position. The Masonic lodge (formerly located in Mazagon) hung a life-sized oil portrait of Murzban in its hall. Later, he was also elected member of the Grand Lodge of the Scottish Freemasonry, Bombay, where he held the offices of substitute grand master and honorary deputy grand master. He was also an honorary member of the Lodge Rising Sun, Bombay.[53]

What was the importance of Freemasonry to the imperial project and what was its relationship to religion? In his summary of the importance of Freemasonry to empire, the historian Vahid Jalil Fozdar writes, "Freemasonry was an ideal imperial 'cult': it did not require that one apostatize one's religion, yet it was a quasi-religion with its own rituals and doctrines to which followers of diverse faiths, it was thought, could subscribe."[54] Freemasonry bound its brothers from different races and religious communities together in the British Empire, both of which were headed by the British monarchy, loyalty to whom was expected of the Freemason. Even though Freemasonry was not a religion, Fozdar argues that it had many characteristics of a "universal church." Furthermore, Freemasonry was replete with rituals, many of which came to serve the imperial state. Fozdar draws attention to the deployment of Masonic rituals at foundation-stone-laying ceremonies where loyalty to the Crown and state, forward looking ideals, and an inclusive religion were encouraged. Masonic rituals played a prominent part as early as the 1840s in the foundation-stone-laying ceremonies for the Jamsetjee Jeejeebhoy Hospital, the first major public institution founded by the joint partnership of the government and native philanthropy.[55] Visiting British royalty were invited to conduct Masonic public rituals. On 11 November 1875, the Prince of Wales, in his role as the grand master

HIS EXCELLENCY SIR H. B. E. FRERE LAYING THE CHIEF CORNER-STONE OF THE VICTORIA AND ALBERT MUSEUM, BOMBAY.

of English Masonry, laid the foundation stone of Prince's Dock "according to Masonic rites and ceremonies."[56] In 1882, the foundation stone of the Pestanji Hormusji Cama Hospital for Women and Children was laid by the Duke of Connaught, commander-in-chief and the governor of Bombay. Although the original plan was to conduct the ceremony according to Masonic rituals, a mishap prevented them from doing so (Figure 3.8).[57]

Murzban played a central role in facilitating the visits of royalty and ceremonies accompanying the laying of foundation stones, of which there would have been many since a large majority of Bombay's public buildings under colonial rule were built before 1918. Apart from simply doing his job well and perhaps desiring to curry favor with the colonial elite, we can see that making excellent arrangements for public rituals was a demonstration of Murzban's commitment to Freemasonry and loyalty to its head, the British monarchy. It must have been especially gratifying to have the monarchy participate in ceremonies for buildings that were designed by him as architect and/or engineer. Here, his participation would not simply be instrumental, but a reflection of his commitment to the ideals of Freemasonry and loyalty to the head of the Craft.

FIGURE 3.8. Drawing depicting Sir Bartle Frere laying the main cornerstone of the Victoria and Albert Museum, Bombay, circa November 1862. Courtesy Bhau Daji Lad Sangrahalaya, Bombay.

The Lodge Rising Star of Western India was founded on 15 December 1843 and was the first Indian lodge under European constitution in all of Asia. James Burnes was the leading spirit behind the foundation of the lodge, and one of his central aims was to enroll natives, particularly those employed by the government. As many British government officials were already Freemasons, the inclusion of natives resulted over time in an additional expansion of Masons in the Bombay government. However, until 1872, when four Hindus were admitted, only one Jain had been admitted to the lodge. In contrast its membership included a number of Muslims and many Parsis. This was a result of the low esteem in which Hinduism was held by many Britons in India. In contrast to Hindus, Parsi and Muslim communities did not have the caste system or believe in idolatry.[58] In Bombay, apart from Murzban, all the early native engineers who are mentioned have Hindu-sounding names—Vasudev Bapuji Kanitkar, Makund Ramchandra—and would not have been eligible for membership in the Masonic lodge until 1872. Why is their exclusion significant? What are the implications of Murzban's membership in the Masonic lodge in terms of his career?

Freemasonry imparted to its members social values that were dear to the bourgeois and the nascent global capitalist economy such as punctuality, a realization of the importance of time and labor, desirable forms of recreation, the value of keeping one's word, and civility. In British India such desirable social values were condensed into that indefinable quality called "character" by which the British colonial authorities judged how much they should allow Indians to take part "as equals" in governing the Indian Empire. The central importance given to character in Freemasonry meant that it permitted the British to have faith in Indian Freemasons by giving them charge of important positions both inside and outside the lodge.[59] As a Freemason, Murzban would have been considered a person of character; and just as he was entrusted with positions of responsibility in the Masonic lodge, he would be considered more trustworthy than his native peers who were not Freemasons in his work at the PWD.

The Masonic lodges were arenas where Freemasons, both European and Indian, interacted as "brothers" and forged friendships. Despite the high ideals underpinning Freemasonry, there were few racially mixed lodges in Bombay, although this did not preclude many occasions for social interaction.[60] In a speech given in August 1867 marking the visit of Richard B. Barton, the provincial grand master (Scottish Constitution), Henry Morland, who was his deputy, and James Gibbs, the district grand master for England to Lodge Rising Star in Bombay, Murzban, who was to become the lodge's master in 1868, emphasized that like plants, "brotherly love" has to be tended through recurrent interlodge visits:

Amongst the many and invaluable privileges of Masonry, that of visiting each other's lodges is calculated to increase our Masonic knowledge, and tends to bring together brethren of different countries, of different creeds, and of different denominations, to combine and practice the grand principles of Masonry, Brotherly Lodge, Relief, and Truth. . . . These exchanges of visits strengthen the ties with which we are bound together, and while we enjoy ourselves at these festive boards, opportunities offer themselves for exchanging our sentiments, which do not fail to prove beneficial to those who avail themselves of them. Brotherly love is not a plant of hasty growth, consequently frequent visits to each other's lodges are necessary to become loving brothers.[61]

I have quoted from Murzban's speech not only for evidentiary purposes but also to hear his voice. Freemasonry provided a unique platform where the colonizer and colonized interacted as equals, as brothers. Murzban's positions of authority in the Masonic lodge would have given him confidence and inculcated a certain ease in his interactions with the colonial elite and in conducting public ceremonials, qualities that were assets in the world outside the Masonic lodge.

It was not only his professional work that brought Murzban close to the colonial elite, but the spaces of the Masonic lodges, spaces from which most of his native colleagues were excluded. It is likely that Murzban successfully mastered the distinctions between the two worlds, acting as an equal to his European brothers in Masonic lodges and with the correct deference to his superiors in the profane world, as would be expected of all Masons.[62]

Freemasonry, with its by and large elite membership, was certainly a route to social and professional mobility, but I do not mean to imply that Murzban's membership in this brotherhood was for purely instrumental reasons. Murzban had a family connection to Freemasonry. His grandfather, Fardunji Murzban, founder of the Gujarati Printing Press and of Gujarati Journalism in India, wrote approvingly of Freemasonry in his newspaper columns in 1823, bringing it for the first time into public discussion for Indians.[63] This historic connection to Freemasonry in Bombay and his own membership would have raised Murzban in the estimation of his brothers. In the second half of the nineteenth century, barring a few exceptions, the Indian lodges were dominated by Parsis but also included the educated elite, knights, baronets from other religious groups, and also figures like the Aga Khan, who was the leader of the Khoja community, while the membership of European lodges might include such distinguished personages as the governor of Bombay. Lodge membership also included prominent Parsis—intellectuals, baronets, political players, and social reformers—which, since Murzban was a Parsi himself, was extremely significant.[64]

In Europe, Freemasonry has been seen as important in establishing Enlightenment ideas, and then later, Freemasonry helped to transport these ideas to India. Not surprisingly many Indian Freemasons took a leadership role in setting out to transform their communities—Hindu, Parsi, Muslim—and purge them of superstition, caste, and other supposedly irrational ideas.[65] It is likely that Murzban then would have been associated with reformers and reform movements in the Parsi community. At the same time, as an architect and engineer in the PWD, these worlds intersected in other ways as well.

Manekjee Cursetjee (1808–87), a Parsi and the founding member of Lodge Rising Star, has been described as "the foremost pioneer of English education for native girls."[66] He was responsible for founding the Alexandra Native Girls' English Institution that commemorated the marriage of Princess Alexandra of Denmark to Edward, Prince of Wales.[67] As Freemasonry inculcated a sense of loyalty to the British monarch as the head of the Craft, the naming was surely an expression of such a sentiment. Hindus and Parsis contributed toward the funding of this school, first opened in 1863, which was not only for Parsi girls. "The instruction imparted at the Alexandra was fully in English; to maintain its beneficial and universal character one steered clear of religion and concentrated on general principles of ethics which are basic to all creeds."[68] In its focus on universal standards of ethics, this seems to be a school very much based on the ideals of Freemasonry. The institute was at first sited in a house on Hornby Row, but came to be housed in a new Gothic building designed for it by Murzban. Opened in 1881 (building work began in 1879), and located at a prominent location on the Esplanade, the institution—since its foundation—became a destination in the tourist itinerary of traveling Europeans. The government and the trustees of the institution each contributed half of the cost of the building. Maclean's *Guide* warmly described the building in the following words: "It is an elegant and substantial structure, with a high tower and a roof terraced on either side, with Gothic arches, balconies with conical stone and iron roofs adorned with floriated finals, &c. The total length is 81 feet, breadth 59 feet, and height 45 feet." (Figure 3.9).[69]

Murzban's engagement with this building was not simply professional. The Murzban family was long associated with social reform. Referring to the period of the 1850s and under the subtitle "The Lifting of the Purdah," Sir Dinshaw E. Wacha's reminiscences celebrate the Murzban family:

> Going back to the fifties, it may be said that fair preliminary progress was made with female education among the Parsis during that period, and in 1858 the first Parsi journal for female instruction was published called the "Streebodh," chiefly owing to the efforts of Mr. Sorabji Shapurji Bengali. It was published by the "Duftur Ashkara Press" founded by the Murzbans,

who are indissolubly associated with every liberal reform among the Parsis and who were ever ready by means of tracts and journals to help the cause of social and religious reform. The Parsis should be proud of their Murzbans and the "Duftur Ashkara Press," which is still with us and prospering.[70]

Murzban's grandfather, Fardunji, gave his three sons a start by opening the Duftur Ashkara Press in 1841, where the well-known weekly journal for social reform, the *Rast Goftar*, would later be published. It is likely that Murzban was personally engaged with the issues of social reform that this institution symbolized. It is relevant that these reforms in female education were being spearheaded by a fellow Parsi and a brother Mason, and that his own family was long involved in the cause of social reform. Murzban was himself involved in fund-raising for this institution. He was in charge of the plans and organization of a Fancy Fair held in 1889 to raise money for the Alexandra Institution.[71] Murzban's engagement with this institution was multifaceted: he designed it, helped raise money for it, and was sympathetic to its aims because he was a

Freemason and because he came from a family of Parsi social reformers. As a native, there would have been many barriers to his advancement. On the other hand, as a native who was both a Parsi and a Freemason and came from a prominent family long associated with social and religious reform, there were many opportunities for his advancement, and certainly few European engineers and architects would have had such a multifaceted engagement with institutions as Murzban did.

If, as Kipling argued, Western styles symbolized "enlightenment and progress" for the Western-educated elite, then Murzban and most likely other social reformers and patrons would have been proud of the hospitals and schools designed by him and sheathed in the Gothic Revival style. But this was not just a facile fascination with surface appearances, a shallow admiration for symbols of the colonizer. Instead, these new institutions visually symbolized a reformed and hence purified community, cleansed of at least some of its superstitions and falsehoods. Parsis, for example, came to believe that they were returning to a purer form of their culture, purged from polluting accretions, such as superstitions absorbed from Hinduism over the years. Rather than simply a colonial imposition, social reform resulted from hard-won battles by reformers within communities, hence allowing the transformations to be viewed with community pride by those who approved of them. The new ways of building—the Gothic Revival architecture designed by new professionals rather than craftsmen—were the containers for new ways of being. Gothic Revival architecture outwardly symbolized the transformed and reformed subjects that used them. The enlightened patrons were symbols of the progress in the enlightenment of the community they hailed from. While the Cama and Allbless hospitals were for all natives, the patronage by Parsis allowed many Parsis to believe that they were leading others to the path of progress.

Let us take the example of the Cama and Allbless hospitals, institutions that came to be part of the same complex, designed in the Gothic Revival style by Murzban (Figure 3.10). In terms of plan, these were rectangular in shape, each with a central projecting porch with a terrace above. In other words, one approached the hospital entrance from the porch and arrived at the entrance hall with a staircase that was flanked by wings of equal length on either side. In the case of the Allbless Hospital, the wings increased in width at both ends. In terms of their plan, there was nothing very new. They were both variations of a common plan type, seen for example in Captain H. St. Clair Wilkins's prize-winning competition entry in 1863 for the European General Hospital (see Figures 4.4, 4.5). The Cama and Allbless hospitals were two stories in height, except for the central tower, which was at least three stories in height. The Cama Hospital had gable roofs with decorative crockets and finials seen in other

FIGURE 3.10. M. C. Murzban, Pestanji Hormusji Cama Hospital for Women and Children, Bombay, 1883–86. Behind the entrance hall with a staircase in the center was a room for the lady superintendent, allowing her to easily supervise both wings of the hospital. The right wing contained the general lying-in ward, followed by a dispensary and classroom for the nurses. The left wing housed a separate ward for Parsi females. Each ward could accommodate ten beds. Verandahs ran along the front and rear of the building; the front verandah was enclosed. Bathrooms and lavatories were located to the rear and were reached via a covered passage. The upper floor had a terrace for convalescents, where they could overlook the landscaped grounds. The right wing contained the medical ward, which included a room for nurses, followed by a children's ward with twelve beds. The left wing had the surgical ward, followed by the operation room. The central portion had an additional floor that contained a suite of residential rooms for the house surgeon. The compound had additional annexes to house other special wards and functions, including a block containing separate kitchens for various castes. From Murzban, *Leaves from the Life of Khan Bahadur Muncherji Cowasji Murzban*, 62.

buildings in Bombay, such as the Sassoon Mechanics' Institute, and buttresses that ended in steep triangular gables (see Figure 3.5). The Cama Hospital allowed for a greater articulation of the roof, with the central tower terminating in a pyramidal roof with dormer windows, while the corners of the buildings were emphasized by lower gable roofs and roofs whose pyramidal form was frustrated by a small terrace surrounded by a metal railing echoed on ridge lines. The facades of both buildings were made up of arcades and occasional, carefully placed balconies supported by brackets.

The design of these handsome hospital buildings, which were, architecturally speaking, derivative rather than innovative, tell us little about the meaning they held. To understand the very real social change underpinning these institutions, we need to turn briefly to the story of the foundation of the Cama Hospital. G. T. Kittredge and Dr. (Mrs.) Hoggans established the Medical Women's Fund, Bombay in the 1880s to collect funds for the medical education of females. The fund found few subscribers until P. H. Cama gave a huge donation of 164,300 rupees. Cama also excoriated Hindu traders for their indifference "and expressed rather ruefully that it would be long before the well-to-do Hindus would, as a body, look upon the female medical movement as one that appealed to their pockets as well as to their sympathies." Following his donation, Cama proposed the foundation of a hospital, paid for by him, whose medical staff would be exclusively female, as long as the government would provide a site and the maintenance of the hospital in perpetuity. The government agreed to his proposal.[72]

The Cama Hospital symbolized revolutionary changes—a hospital for women staffed entirely by women. Although the hospital was certainly the product of the joint enterprise between government and a native philanthropist, the author of the project was Cama, who also helped bring about very real social change by making a case for it and paying for it. It is unlikely that all Parsis were behind Cama's scheme; however, his philanthropy and his words showed the Parsi community to be more progressive than other communities, such as the Hindus. The Allbless Hospital that followed reinforced a general perception of Parsi commitment to social change and progressive ideas.

In terms of architectural style, perhaps Murzban was, as Kipling implied of others of his ilk, one of many who were "mere copyists and tracers." However, Murzban's buildings had the ability to transform the meaning of Gothic Revival architecture. He could be read as either or both a native and Parsi architect of public buildings, funded by natives, that were an expression of social reform, but Murzban by his own example demonstrated that Indians were capable of designing and constructing substantial buildings on their own that looked no different from those designed by British engineers. But was there anything special about Gothic Revival architecture for Indians? Or would any architectural style work as well in its place? Gothic Revival architecture was of course the style used by the government for new public buildings, many of which were the product of the joint enterprise. I argue that there was nothing special about Gothic Revival architecture; any Western style that seemed to speak to the present and the future would symbolize "enlightenment and progress" and work just as well. This does not suggest a shallow engagement with architectural style but merely that profound social changes in Indian society required to be housed in buildings whose architectural style was considered symbolic of modernity and progress and hence, at least in terms of external appearance, dramatically different from those traditionally used by Indians.

At least some of Murzban's superiors considered him to have greater abilities than other native engineers senior to him, and we find him competing and winning the position of executive engineer of the Municipal Corporation of Bombay in 1892 over other rivals including a European, Mr. Tomlinson, deputy engineer of the Bombay Municipal Water Works. This appointment was a very public affair, with all the native papers writing in favor of his appointment while two of the local English papers were decidedly against him. He won this appointment in a decisive vote at a Municipal Corporation meeting where he received forty votes and Tomlinson fifteen. Particularly telling were the social reformer Behramji Merwanji Malabari's (1853–1912) comments on this victory in an editorial in the *Indian Spectator* on 11 December 1892 where he opined:

> The election of Mr. M. C. Murzban, as head of the Engineering Department of the Municipality of Bombay, is something of an event in the history of local Self-Government, and, as such, we see it recognised over the Presidency. But it is not so much on sentimental grounds that we welcome the choice of the Corporation. It can be justified on grounds of real practical importance. . . . Mr. Murzban has this advantage, both over his predecessor and his rival. . . . To his natural advantage, Mr. Murzban adds practical experience, ranging over, perhaps a quarter of a century, and a reputation for capacity and independence such as is enjoyed by few servants of the State, or representatives of the rate-paying public. The Municipal Corporation badly needed a veteran like this, if only to clean an Augean stable.[73]

Murzban's victory—as the first native Indian elected to this position—was seen by some of his supporters, such as Malabari, as a victory for local self-government. Malabari's editorial comments are significant, especially in a colonial context, because in his evaluation Murzban's "natural advantages" (which I take to mean his intellect and professional expertise) and his "practical experience" were greater than those of his European predecessor and rival. In the early stages of Murzban's career in Bombay, we saw him being compared to native engineers; at the end of his career in government, in the 1890s, Murzban's qualities were contrasted to his European peers and found by many to be superior. This shift signified a desire by the native elite to assume the reins of self-government rather than simply act as intermediaries for Europeans. Such moves were often spearheaded by Masons who, having achieved leadership positions in the Masonic bureaucracy, wanted a similar parity in government administration in the "profane" world, and so it is hardly surprising to find many Masons among the early nationalists. Murzban himself on 22 May 1869 became a member of the Bombay Branch of the East India Association, an organization founded in 1866 that, along with the Bombay Association (est. 1852), was meant to give Indians a more substantial role in governing India.[74] Murzban's vast body of work—including his buildings, his expertise in architecture and engineering, and his long years of practical experience—were evidence that Indians were ready for local self-governance.

Murzban's election was backed by heavyweights who included the social reformer Malabari; the "'Uncrowned King of Bombay'" Pherozeshah Mehta (1845–1915), who was also a Mason, a member of the Bombay Corporation for forty-six years, and cofounder and president of the Indian National Congress; and the industrialist Jamsetji N. Tata (1839–1904), who first proposed Murzban's name for this position. While this was certainly an important step toward self-government, it is significant that his supporters consisted of prominent Parsis. As Murzban's biography reminds us, Murzban was the *"first* Parsi (and even the first native-Indian, as a Parsi is now considered to be) to receive this appointment."[75] This is an instructive comment, for it shows that Murzban's son certainly saw Parsis as distinct from native-Indians, as did a growing number of Parsis and possibly Murzban as well.

Like Murzban, all native engineers were embedded in a local context where they were involved in the specific communities they belonged to and, depending on their inclinations, were part of political, social, or religious associations or reform movements. These local engagements altered the way they viewed their work and the meaning of their constructions. The "native" engineer was not simply an intermediary between the British and the workers, but was an individual with dense local connections whose own community as well as the larger native community was experiencing an accelerated rate of change. This resulted in a more multifaceted engagement with the city than that available to European engineers.

THE FATHER OF COLONIZATION

It was particularly in the arena of philanthropy that one begins to see Murzban as an independent actor with a unique vision, an innovator, and a player in shaping the form of the city. While his work for the government resulted in the creation of Bombay's public arena, his private philanthropic work was communal or directed to benefit a specific public, the Parsis. In a sense this reflects a larger trend in Bombay of the creation of a common public arena in the 1860s and the reassertion of caring for one's community by the end of the nineteenth century. Here, too, Murzban took the initiative in raising funds to found a hospital for Parsis as well as in founding housing colonies for poor Parsis. Thus Murzban was an architect of the trend for philanthropists to focus not on the larger public but on a specific public defined by community. I should emphasize that throughout the nineteenth century, philanthropists continued to care for their community. However, in the second half of the nineteenth century, the colonial government was able to persuade many of them to underwrite public institutions for the larger public. Now the institutions introduced by the colonial state—particularly hospitals—were being constructed by communities for the exclusive use of their individual community. In the case of housing, even though Murzban was influenced by housing models in Britain, his housing projects not only reflect very local concerns, but also predate the Bombay government's reluctant entry into the field of housing for the poor.

In his nonofficial capacity, Murzban was the architect of public buildings meant for the exclusive use of Parsis. Three of the four buildings listed in Murzban's biography that were designed by him and built under his superintendence in a nonofficial capacity were associated with Parsis; the fourth was a church. Murzban also built buildings for the Parsi community that were religious or part of religious-cum-social institutions. In addition to his involvement in various Parsi charities and associations, these structures are a reminder of his long engagement with charitable, religious, and social institutions of the Parsi community.[76] Thus Murzban's involvement with the Parsi community was longstanding even though his ability to raise secular structures for the exclusive use of Parsis—including hospitals and later, housing and a settlement—was only possible from the late 1880s.

As a member of the committee, Murzban was involved at the outset with the foundation of a hospital for Parsi women—the Parsi Lying-in Hospital, located in a prime site in the Esplanade (Figure 3.11). Murzban designed and superintended the construction of this building, which was completed in 1895 at a cost of 105,000 rupees and was extended later, bringing the total cost of the building by 1914 to 130,541 rupees. Simply planned, organized around a courtyard, the handsome hospital building had space for fifty patients. According to a report in the *Indian and Eastern Engineer*, this hospital had "removed a long-felt want of the community. Owing to a certain custom among the Parsis, females in a delicate state of health are forced to reside, during the period of illness, on ground floor rooms which are generally ill-lighted, ill-ventilated, and badly drained. This hospital has indirectly broken through that custom, and hundreds of Parsi females are taking the benefit of this Institution."[77] Murzban was the architect of this modern sanitary hospital that was instrumental in changing a Parsi "custom" showing that not only was this community willing

FIGURE 3.11. M. C.
Murzban, Parsi
Lying-in Hospital,
Esplanade, Bombay,
1895. From Murz-
ban, *Leaves from the
Life of Khan Bahadur
Muncherji Cowasji
Murzban,* 112.

and able to modernize but that a Parsi was capable of designing an up-to-date structure. In spearheading these changes Murzban was not only continuing a family tradition of social reform but also putting his Masonic Enlightenment ideals into practice by helping to rid his community of superstition. This public building for the women of a specific community—the Parsis—was built in the Gothic Revival style that was used for colonial public buildings. Even though this was the style that Murzban was accustomed to, it showed that Parsis were willing to embrace hospitals—an institutional type introduced by the British that the public had only hesitatingly accepted. In obtaining a prized site in the Esplanade area for this institution from the government, the Parsis were signaling their power.

Although the Allbless Hospital had a separate ward for Parsi women and the Parsi Lying-in Hospital was exclusively for Parsi women, Murzban was the "originator" of the idea of founding a hospital that would be used only for Parsis. He began to raise funds for this purpose from charitably disposed members of the Parsi community and soon collected 55,000 rupees. However, the project fell through. He returned some of the money to the donors, but with the permission of others used the remainder for the construction of the Cheap Rental Residential Quarters for Parsis in 1887.[78] Though not by him, Murzban's dream of founding a hospital exclusively for Parsis would eventually be realized, and subsequently other communities also founded hospitals for their own communities. Ironically, the Parsi General Hospital was housed in a building designed by him.

Before turning to Murzban's work in the creation of housing colonies for poor Parsis, I would briefly like to turn our attention away from Bombay. The emphasis on discussions of the work of architects and architectural style has led to a neglect of the importance given to housing the poor in Victorian Britain and how this issue might relate to Bombay as a city that might resemble it not simply because of its Victorian architecture but in its response to housing the poor. Writing of Great Britain, the author of an editorial in the *Builder* in 1887 looked back on the architectural achievements of the last fifty years of Victoria's reign and observed, "This has not been a great artistic epoch—not in the same sense and with the same extent of meaning in which we call it a great scientific epoch."[79] However, the editorial made note of two areas of exceptional success, both of which were not conventionally thought to be architectural matters. The first was the great steps made in the science of sanitation. The second was the great improvements made in housing the lower classes and the beginnings of an acknowledgment on the part of landlords and the government that they had some responsibility in adequately housing the poor. The *Builder* went on to add, "We may perhaps be justified in thinking that the many blocks of healthy dwellings which have been built during late years, not indeed beautiful architecturally, but representing the possibility of decent, comfortable, and healthy housing for the poor, are as important architectural works in their way as cathedrals and churches."[80]

In Great Britain, philanthropists persuaded the government that the problem of working-class housing could not be resolved without state intervention; in Bombay the crisis produced by the plague in and after 1896 forced the government to begin to take on the issue of housing.[81] Common to both contexts is the reluctance of the state to enter into the arena of housing. Murzban's philanthropic efforts predate the plague and were inspired by British philanthropic efforts. The 1887 editorial in the *Builder* applauded the efforts made in Britain in advancing the science of sanitation and in building improved, healthy houses for the working classes. In the same year, Murzban prepared a plan for the building of sanitary houses for poor Parsis that would be paid for by subscriptions from the Parsi community. Murzban's farsightedness was recognized in a report in the *Indian and Eastern Engineer* from April 1903:

Among private works carried out by Mr. Murzban, it may be mentioned that, long before the plague broke out, it was apparent to him that the best means of improving the sanitary condition of Bombay, was to provide suitable sanitary dwellings for the poorer classes of the people. To carry out such a gigantic work was beyond his power; but, in 1887, he prepared a scheme for the construction of sanitary dwellings for the Parsi poor by means of subscriptions amongst the members of that community. The buildings, constructed for the accommodation of poor Parsis, have been raised through Mr. Murzban's exertions. They are constructed on the principle of Peabody's Homes in England. They are for the accommodation of artisans, clerks, and other people who have not sufficient means to provide, for themselves and their families, accommodation at moderate rents.[82]

I have not come across any additional information on how Peabody's Homes in England influenced Murzban, even though these dwellings were constructed on the same principle. However, a brief introduction to Peabody will allow us to make some comparisons. In 1862, George Peabody, a prosperous American banker, appointed a group of colleagues in business and friends as trustees on a fund established by him. They were to decide how they could best use his gift totaling £150,000 for helping the poor of London. Approving of the trustees' decision to use this money for housing, Peabody raised his gift amount to £500,000. The trustees had no interest in making a profit but instead wanted the trust to be "self-perpetuating, so that future generations might gain some benefit"; thus the 3 percent annual net return was reinvested for the expansion of the trust. In 1864, the Peabody Trust had built its first housing block, a four-story structure, consisting for the most part of two-room units with common facilities including a shared corridor, washing facilities, and sculleries. By 1882, the Peabody Fund had 3,500 "dwellings" that provided housing to a population of over 14,000, and by 1939, there were more than 8,000 "dwellings." Thomas Adam convincingly shows that Peabody's housing shows an embrace of the preindustrial communal living ideal, hence the sharing of facilities between numbers of families. Furthermore, unlike Sir Sydney Waterlow—who in his housing projects embraced capitalism by linking philanthropy and profit, giving rise to the idea of "philanthropy and five percent"—Peabody did not believe that capitalism could be the solution to social problems. Peabody's buildings were deliberately located all over London in order to avoid creating "working-class ghettos." Peabody's buildings accommodated a specific type of person: artisans, rather than paupers, individuals with a steady source of income but not beyond thirty shillings a week. In other words, Peabody wished "to house neither the poorest nor the richest of the working class but a middle stratum of working-class families."[83]

Unlike Peabody, Murzban did not have the means to build this housing all on his own. Instead he collected numerous subscriptions from the Parsi community, allowing a range of people to become philanthropists: from wealthy and famous baronets and leading families to other individuals of more modest means, some of whom remain unnamed. In 1890, Murzban founded the Garib Zarthoshtina Rehethan Fund, or the Poor Zoroastrians Building Fund. By 1890, through these funds, 272 families were housed in the Murzban Colonies at Tardeo and Jacob Circle and 25 families were housed in the Widows Chawl, Gilder Lane in Tardeo by 1899. Individual buildings were usually endowed in the memory of some individual.[84] This was a model found in some subsequent Parsi colonies such as the Khareghat Colony. In such cases, the housing colony as a whole symbolized the many philanthropic individuals from the Parsi community that came together to found it, while each building, even if similar in architectural style, was distinct from its neighbor as it memorialized a particular individual or was paid for by a particular family or group of people and often recorded on the building itself. The multiple donations distinguished like buildings from each other, unlike Peabody's buildings that signaled their singular source. Thus in its multiple sources, this housing was unlike the Peabody buildings but served a similar class of person: the artisan and clerk. However, in not seeing this as a profit-making enterprise and charging low rents, it shared the fundamental premise with Peabody that capitalism could not cure social problems.

Murzban fathered a tradition that resulted in the formation of housing colonies for Parsis that were paid for by philanthropists, often a single family. Britain's philanthropists showed the government that philanthropy alone was inadequate to house the working classes. However, in Bombay, Parsi philanthropists found that by and large they could meet the needs of housing the poor of their community. According to one estimate, by 1966 half of Bombay's Parsis resided in charitable housing in a city that housed approximately 70 percent of its entire population.[85] The Parsi colonies were scattered throughout the city like Peabody's estates, but they were not recognizable by their architectural style. Often designed by the architect H. A. Darbishire, Peabody's estates were architecturally and, by name, distinct.[86]

Let us examine the Murzban Parsi colony at Gilder Lane, which is just off Lamington Road in Tardeo. This is one of the two Murzban colonies—the other is in Agripada near Jacob Circle—founded by Murzban on land leased from the Bombay Improvement Trust. Branching off from busy Lamington Road, Gilder Lane is a quiet, tree-lined street. According to one of the residents of this lane, Murzban owned all the land here; he reserved one side of the road for the dwellings of more well-to-do Parsis, and the opposite side

FIGURE 3.12. M. C.
Murzban, Murzban
Colony, Gilder Lane
Tardeo, Bombay,
circa 1889–1915,
view showing Gilder
Lane and Murzban
Colony. Photograph
by author, 2006.

formed the colony for poor Parsis (Figures 3.12, 3.13). The Murzban colony included four lanes of housing running perpendicular to Gilder Lane, enclosed behind a low boundary wall with a metal railing. Two-story buildings, which looked like cottages and had gable roofs, airy balconies with wooden louvered grills and wooden balustrades, and windows with wooden shutters, faced each other across a wide lane that could be entered through its own gate. The rears of buildings fronted each other across a service lane, making the colony sanitary, as wastes were not only visible to the authorities but could be effectively removed (Figure 3.14). By 1914, thirty-three blocks of buildings had been constructed.[87] The comparatively shallow depth of each lane, the rhythm of gable roofs, the break-up of the massing by the wooden balusters and grills on the balconies, all helped to avoid a monotonous landscape. The colony also included chawls for widows (at least one was called the Allbless Widows Chawl), the Seth Dhunjeebhoy Edalji Allbless Charitable Dispensary, and the Bai Ruttonbai F. D. Panday Girls' High School, which celebrated its centenary in 1998 (Figure 3.15). The health of the community and the minds of the children were nurtured through these institutions.

The Murzban colony at Gilder Lane did not resemble the vaguely Italianate style of Peabody's buildings, so it is clear that their architecture was not a source of inspiration. Although other examples of charitable housing from

England may have influenced the architecture of this colony, Parsi charitable housing did not produce a predictable architectural landscape. Murzban also designed the Murzban colony at Agripada, but these taller buildings with Gothic windows were unlike the colony at Gilder Lane (Figure 3.16). Both of these colonies and many future Parsi housing colonies were gated communities, and while architecturally diverse, they all had planned layouts with substantial open areas, producing very high-standard living environments for their poor.

At the Murzban colony on Gilder Lane is a bust of Khan Bahadur Muncherji Cowasji Murzban (Figure 3.17). The inscription below the bust lists his professional affiliations and titles (C.I.E., F.R.I.B.A., and J.P. [justice of peace]) and professional achievements in the high positions he achieved as executive engineer presidency of PWD and later of the Bombay Municipality. It goes on to describe him as the founder of the Murzban Parsee colony at Tardeo and Lamington Road. This is of course a reference to the colony he founded in his private capacity as a member of the Parsi community. But here Murzban is described as the "originator of the idea of colonization among Parsees and Indians." This is significant; Murzban, not a member of the colonial regime or the Indian elite, is claimed to be the "originator" of the idea of colonization among his own community, which is self-consciously mentioned and differentiated from other "Indians." Murzban is thus a leading architect of the

FIGURE 3.13. M. C. Murzban, Murzban Colony, Gilder Lane Tardeo, Bombay, circa 1889–1915, view showing one lane in Murzban Colony. Photograph by author, 2006.

FIGURE 3.14. M. C. Murzban, Murzban Colony, Gilder Lane, Tardeo, Bombay, circa 1889–1915, view of service lane. Photograph by author, 2006.

idea of community segregation, both at the level of public institutions (such as hospitals) and the private domestic realm.

What is the significance of the idea of colonization? At around the same time that Murzban founded the poor Parsi homes, he bought land in Andheri in a healthy location about fifteen miles from Bombay. Here he established a new town, which came to be known after its founder as Murzbanabad. Many large bungalows by varied classes from the Parsi community were built here. This town was probably established sometime after the plague first struck Bombay in 1896, as a *jashan* ceremony took place there in 1898. It would have been a refuge to many fleeing the city for safer environs. Murzban is credited with helping to establish the town, procuring Tansa water for the town, and providing it with a dispensary.[88]

In the creation of colonies, Murzban obviously thought he was introducing a new idea to the urban landscape of Bombay. What was new about colonies? In order to understand this, we have to look at the native contributions to Bombay's urban form. Bombay's various communities had created neighborhoods in Bombay, such as Bhatiawad, Memonwada, and Israel moholla, a landscape of community institutions and residential quarters heavily populated by members of a community. There were at least two ways by which Bombay's native citizenry contributed to the creation of urban form: through

the formation of a street or a group of streets that formed a larger community neighborhood and through the creation of compounds, such as Allbless Baug, that grew over time to contain religious structures and institutional structures and sometimes housing. Most compounds had well-defined boundaries, and most but not all the compounds served a specific community. Neighborhoods such as Bhatiawad in the Fort were not found on colonial maps, nor did they have precise boundaries. Despite the name, they were also never the exclusive preserve of the community of Bhatias, even though in other cases, some community streets might be exclusively inhabited by a community. As Bhatias moved out of the neighborhood and members of other communities moved in, all that remained of Bhatiawad were fragments of the past, such as the memory of the name of the neighborhood and community institutions, such as the Shri Govardhannathji ni Haveli. In other words, community neighborhoods lacked permanence. Like community neighborhoods, compounds grew over time in an organic fashion, but housing was not necessarily the primary focus, and community compounds have been more successful in retaining the community character and dominance.[89]

In contrast to the organic, gradual growth of these community landscapes, the Parsi colonies, like Greek colonies, were the product of forethought. They were exclusive planned urban developments, often designed by an architect

FIGURE 3.15. Bai Ruttonbai F. D. Panday Girls' High School, Murzban Colony, Gilder Lane, Tardeo, Bombay, school founded in 1898. The edge of the school building can be seen on the right. Photograph by author, 2006.

FIGURE 3.16. M. C. Murzban, Murzban Colony at Lal Chimney, Agripada, Bombay, founded circa 1909, exterior view of colony. Photograph by author, 2006.

who incorporated community institutions, but the emphasis was on housing for a particular community. Whereas the earlier community landscapes had a spectrum of social classes, these colonies were for specific economic classes and, in the case of Parsis, for the poorer members of the community who paid low rents. These planned colonies could be inhabited relatively quickly and were permanent, as non-Parsis were not entitled to rent property here. Managed by community institutions such as the Parsi Panchayat, these colonies were for the perpetual use of the Parsi community. These planned, often gated Parsi colonies formed fragments of exclusive Parsi habitation throughout Bombay, something the British could never successfully fully achieve for themselves. Murzban had shown that he was not simply an intermediary; he was an originator of colonization and community hospitals.

CONCLUSION

The history of British architecture in India is constructed under the general thematic that European architects, familiar with British architectural developments as illustrated on the pages of the *Builder* and *Building News,* designed and thought while Indian engineers and craftsmen enabled their visions to be constructed. The dominant paradigm in the writing of architectural histories is

the tracing of the arc of connections, references, influences, and quotations—the hard work of thinking that makes of architecture an art, albeit a practical art. Murzban did not simply superintend the construction of buildings in Bombay; he was the architect of several Victorian buildings in Bombay. Perhaps he too hungrily perused and plundered the pages of the *Builder* and *Building News*. With great effort, since there does not appear to be any literature on the subject, one could carve a space for Murzban within this history. One sees glimpses of this: His design for the Miss Avabai Mehervanji Bhownagri Home for Nurses (1891) looks similar to the Sir Dinshaw Manockjee Petit Hospital for Women and Children (1890–92) designed by John Adams but constructed under Murzban's superintendence. Both buildings were located in the J. J. Hospital compound. Who was influenced by whom? A history that closely traces the genealogy of designs has a role to play, but this account of Murzban is not such a history nor would it suffice. Instead, I have shown that it is only by looking at the complex networks of Murzban's engagements that one can begin to understand what his buildings might have meant not only to him but also to the local population. Rather than a search for the meaning of Murzban's buildings in a self-referential history of architecture, it is the multifaceted local contextual engagements that give his buildings their meaning.

FIGURE 3.17. Bust of M. C. Murzban at Gilder Lane, Bombay. The canopy over the bust was unveiled on 18 October 1936. To the left is the Cama Building, constructed circa 1898. The well to the right was constructed circa 1900. Photograph by author, 2006.

Native engineers were certainly marginalized and at a disadvantage. On the other hand, they were deeply involved in the transformation of a landscape that was theirs, a feeling very few Europeans in similar positions, with transferable jobs and with a home in Britain, could have. Murzban appears to have been at the right place at the right time. While this may have been true, he appears to have had the skill, the connections, and the desire to grasp every opportunity that came his way. Other native engineers may have been equally or even more talented than Murzban, but perhaps lacked the political skills that are so necessary to the achievement of success. Murzban thus emerges as an ambitious individual with the technical, political, and social skills to get ahead of other native engineers and later even challenge Europeans.

Murzban represented the group—Bhabha's Mimic Men—educated according to Macaulay's Minute who were to act as intermediaries between the colonial authorities and those they governed. Homi Bhabha has argued that "colonial mimicry is the desire for a reformed, recognizable Other, as *a subject of a difference that is almost the same, but not quite.*"[90] Certainly in his attire (in his photographs he is always seen with his turban) Murzban would have been visibly a hybrid subject: "*almost the same, but not quite.*" Parsis, who increasingly saw themselves as distinct from other Indian natives, still fell short of being Europeans. And yet Murzban's architectural designs do not show an excess, a difference. Whether this came from an acute and accurate perception that architectural excess would have been inexcusable from him or whether his sensibility as an engineer introduced a natural restraint is impossible to say. Bhabha emphasizes the destabilizing qualities of excess, where mimicry might be seen as mockery and hence threatening to the colonizer. However, Murzban's abilities as an architect and engineer to reproduce adequate modern public buildings that gave no hint of the origins of its designer could also have been perceived as a threat. The British in India responded to this threat by insisting that native engineers were mere copyists, a group who could be seen as a "type," who needed no individual account of their careers. Murzban's son's biography of his father is a refusal of anonymity for his father.

Murzban's hybridity allowed him to be comfortable in many different situations and with Europeans, Indians, and his fellow Parsis. His architectural projects were also part of different public arenas: secular public buildings for the general public, secular public buildings for the Parsi public, religious public buildings for Parsis (and in one case for Christians), residential colonies for poor Parsis, and a new town for Parsis. He did not simply carry out orders but was the originator of the idea of a hospital for the exclusive use of Parsis and of colonization.

In his role as an architect and engineer who helped to construct the joint secular public landscape of colonial Bombay, and as a Mason who was brother to men of other creeds and races, it seems contradictory to find Murzban as a leading architect of community segregation. But perhaps to him it was not a contradiction to be a Parsi and at the same time a member of Bombay's public. Nor, as we shall see in the next chapter, was this the contradiction it seems to be, for the joint secular public buildings of Bombay were, from the beginning, also divided. The construction of colonial Bombay resulted in a divided public realm even in the common spaces built for its public. Cohesion—the coming together of communities in a common public arena—and their fragmentation into separate communities were a characteristic feature of colonial Bombay from the second half of the nineteenth century.

4 Dividing Practices in Bombay's Hospitals and Lunatic Asylums

THE *BOMBAY CHABUK,* in an editorial on 26 January 1870, praised the philanthropy of the British government, setting this "virtue" in contrast with the native manner of exhibiting charity:

> A Native rájá or nawáb, if of a charitable disposition, will feed thousands of Bráhmans or *faquirs* with dainties, build fine temples or superb mosques, or will do some other acts of a like nature. But, the British government will do nothing of the kind. In giving charity, it is particularly careful that help is given only to those who are willing to help themselves; and it does not encourage or foster idleness. The writer then alludes to great sums the Government generally spends on relief works, on popular education, on hospitals, &c.[1]

The *Bombay Chabuk*'s editorial expressed British opinion on native charity by distorting the practice. It is true that by feeding holy men natives did not distinguish between worthy and unworthy objects of charity and thus differed from the British government. However, native traditions of patronage were long-standing and complex, they supported the construction of both religious and nonreligious buildings, and they realized projects corresponding to the editorial's criteria of "wise and enlightened."[2] Charity was not new to South Asia. Rather it was the partnership with government as mode, the new secular institutions as objects, and the restriction of charity to those who "help themselves" as a guiding ethic that were new.

Native elites were wealthy and leading members of their respective communities. The anthropologist Mary Douglas observes that to be a member of a community one has to pay one's dues in both time and money. Moreover, realizing that great disparity in wealth is troublesome, communities find ways to redistribute wealth. There is the expectation that the wealthier members of the community will subsidize community events and institutions in the religious arena.[3] From the perspective of the maintenance of community, feeding of Brahmans and building temples was not useless. To not participate in this arena, to withdraw one's time and money, was to be an outcast and be denied of the social, economic, political, and other benefits derived from being a member of the community. In other words, participation in the religious arena was not more other-worldly than helping to pay for secular buildings under colonial rule. The colonial government was in a sense asking the wealthy elite to pay in time and money for institutions meant for a new entity—the Bombay public—and thus a new imagined community. At the same time, the colonial regime treated the wealthy elite as leaders of their own individual community. In order to maintain their membership in their own respective communities and also be meaningful in the new emerging arena (the Bombay public with the colonial regime at its head), the wealthy elite were engaged in a delicate balancing act. One method was to pay for projects meant for the general public while also making special provisions for one's own community.

In Bombay, the colonial government encouraged natives to imitate their way of exhibiting charity by convincing them to pay for projects they considered useful such as wells, charitable dispensaries, hospitals, educational institutions, and so on. In Britain, wealthy individuals often subscribed to or endowed hospitals and lunatic asylums; in Bombay, the state encouraged the native elite to do the same. While natives continued to feed Brahmans and pay *zakat*, build fine temples and mosques, they also cooperated with the British in founding public institutions or works in the public interest, apparently secular in nature and for the use of the general public. The native elite learned that only by combining British ways of exhibiting charity to specific colonial projects would they be rewarded with the honors and titles they sought for their own varied reasons.

This chapter explores the role of philanthropy in the creation of this joint public realm of Bombay in which new public institutions were established, especially in and after the 1860s. This was distinguished from early philanthropy where the efforts of philanthropists were directed mainly toward the building of wells and tanks and less often toward the building of common institutions for the entire public. This new public realm was truly a joint venture between the colonial regime and the natives where the British publicized the type of institution it wanted to create and the locals brought in their own concerns and cultural rules to building such public institutions as new schools, colleges, hospitals, and dispensaries.

The British government's mode of exhibiting charity—toward those who would help themselves—was one of the means meant to force the indigenous population to turn to wage labor for income. The creation of secular public institutions where people of all castes, religions, and races would interact at a more intimate level was a new phenomenon. While people of various castes and religions did interact with each other in common spaces, such as the shared sacred spaces of popular religion, these new shared public institutions and types of interactions were modern and fundamentally different.[4] Activities such as sleeping near each other in hospitals, sitting next to each other or touching each other in railway stations and trains, or dining with each other were difficult to practice for Indians. The goals of the colonial government were contradictory: it promoted the establishment of common public institutions and spaces, yet the Europeans maintained their own separate institutions.

I argue that both European racial prejudices and a nineteenth-century obsession with counting, sorting, and separating met their counterparts in Indian prejudices of ritual pollution and local interests to create a divided public realm. The nature of this public domain was compromised as issues of caste, class, community, race, and religion divided it. In particular, I focus on the role of the Parsi philanthropists in creating special provisions for their own distinct or separate community. The first section of this chapter examines the dividing practices of the colonial regime in Bombay's lunatic asylum at Colaba in the mid-nineteenth century, which had both native and European patients. The second section examines the dividing practices in Bombay's European and native hospitals. The third section examines issues of race and religion at the end of the nineteenth century in the foundation of new lunatic asylums in Nowpada and Yerwada, located in the Bombay Presidency.

Focusing on hospitals and lunatic asylums, I show how both the British authorities and the Indian philanthropists created a divided public realm, a fractured landscape, through their dividing practices. We can understand the philanthropy exercised by Bombay's native elites better by seeing its connections to these dividing practices and not by essentializing generosity as a universal virtue. I examine two types of social dividing practices or modes: stylistic marking and spatial exclusion. Drawing on Michel Foucault's work, the anthropologist Paul Rabinow defines "dividing practices" as "modes of manipulation that combine the mediation of a science (or pseudoscience) and the practice of exclusion— usually in a spatial sense, but always in a social one."[5] Such division was also achieved visually through what Dell Upton calls "artifactual modes" that serve to create new differences.[6] The European sick, for example, were distinguished from the native sick in Bombay; they were housed in different hospitals, located in different spaces in the city, and the name "European Hospital" called attention to the fact that it served a differentiated population. When similar architectural styles were used for European and native hospitals, then other elements, such as location or the name (such as "European" or "native" hospital), were necessary to distinguish between groups. Parsis sought to separate themselves from natives in Bombay's native hospitals, but they only succeeded in visibly distinguishing themselves from the natives if their sick were housed in a separate block. Since Parsi wards were located in the same compound of the native hospital, they could not entirely escape being categorized as native.

The British had no problem accommodating religious communities in separate spaces in secular public institutions or visually dissecting South Asia's architectural heritage along religious lines. However, they were unwilling to allow religious rituals at these sites. Nevertheless, they had no objection to Masonic rituals at foundation-stone-laying ceremonies at these sites that encouraged loyalty to the British monarch and the Empire and helped to provide the foundation for the creation of a shared civil religion. The sociologist Robert N. Bellah has argued for the existence of what he calls a civil religion (in America), one that is distinct and accompanied by its own institutions and rituals, although it may also borrow from dominant religious traditions.[7] Over time there is a set of beliefs, symbols, and rituals in connection to new sacred things that are celebrated or institutionalized for the collective.[8] Even as practices of shared popular religion were being eroded in South Asia, a new civil religion was being forged that encouraged reverence of the British monarchy and empire.

COLONIAL DIVIDING PRACTICES IN THE COLABA LUNATIC ASYLUM

Lunatic asylums and hospitals were introduced to Bombay in the nineteenth century under colonial rule where capitalism had not developed deep roots.[9] This section describes the implementation of dividing practices in the Colaba Lunatic Asylum. These practices reflected the racial and class hierarchies in colonial society and, in the asylum, created an ideal hierarchical order that was not entirely possible in the real world. Archival sources suggest that both the knowledge and the disciplinary power exercised over lunatics were quite rudimentary or crude and not a well-developed science or even pseudoscience.[10]

The lunatic asylum at the far end of Colaba had long been considered inadequate to meet the needs of its patients (Figure 4.1). A plain and functional-looking building, the Colaba Lunatic Asylum was established in 1826 and expanded over time as the number of patients increased (Figure 4.2).[11] The

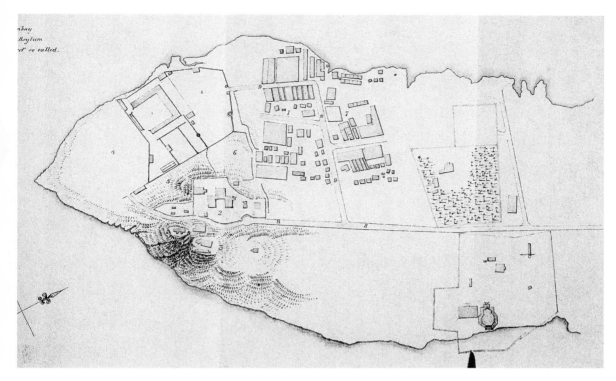

FIGURE 4.1. Island of Colaba, Bombay, 1853, sketch map of the southern end of the island showing location of the lunatic asylum and surrounding buildings. Note the lunatic asylum (1 in plan) and superintendent's bungalow (2). The road to Bombay (8) lies between the bungalow and the lighthouse (3). The road to the asylum (9) cuts through a village (7) to its north, while the English burial ground (4) lies to the asylum's south. Courtesy Maharashtra State Archives, Bombay. Photograph by author, 1998.

expansion of the asylum in 1851 allowed the main building to be devoted to patients and for an elaboration of the system of classification, both within and without the asylum building on the basis of race, gender, class, and type of insanity. In 1852, Dr. William Campbell, the superintendent of the asylum, praised the new building extensions to the asylum as "a vast addition to the means of classification, occupation and amusement, and strengthened and increased in every way, the resources of humane, and efficient treatment" of the patients.[12]

The plan of the building was simple (Figure 4.3). The main building consisted of a two-story U-shaped block where most of the patients were housed. Staircases at the center and between the wings and corners of the front of the asylum allowed access to different wards and sections of the upper floor.[13]

In contrast to hospitals with their large wards, insane asylums were typically spaces that required a greater number of subdivisions for treating patients.[14] After 1851, in the Colaba Lunatic Asylum, the main block contained the staff

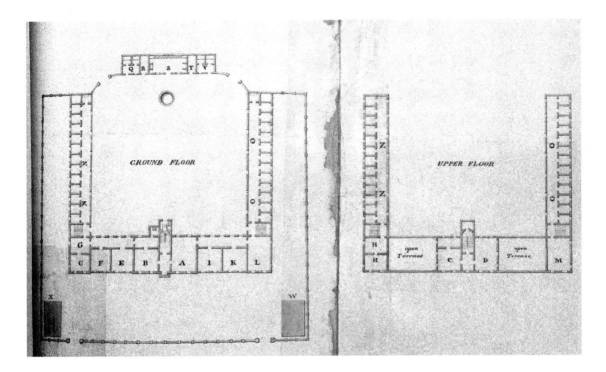

GROUND FLOOR

UPPER FLOOR

areas and common services at the front on the ground floor—the matron's room (B in the plan) and the dispensary (A) flanking the staircase, and the servant's hall (I) and the infirmary (L) to the right. The lower floor was also the realm of the violent, dirty, noisy, and destructive patients. Violent and suicidal European male patients faced the front on the lower floor (KK) while women occupied the eastern front of the building (EFG). The insane officers were the asylum's elite: white, male, and upper-class, occupying the central position on the upper floor facing the front (C and D). Waltraud Ernst notes that being declared insane was better than facing disciplinary punishment in the military and navy and that pleading insanity was often used as a method to terminate a long career by soldiers and even officers, so it is hardly surprising to find special accommodations for insane officers.[15] Insane officers were flanked by wards for clean, harmless females on one side (HHH) and by wards for lower-class European males (MMM) on the other side. Female lunatics may have included European as well as native lunatics because of a lack of space. If the upper floor was the domain of upper-class, clean, and passive lunatics, the lower floor was occupied by violent, dirtier patients.

In contrast to the generous allocation of spaces and bathing facilities for the predominantly European population, the native male patients and some harmless patients had to make do with much less and were quartered in the wings. In general, having achieved separation on the basis of gender, the asylum

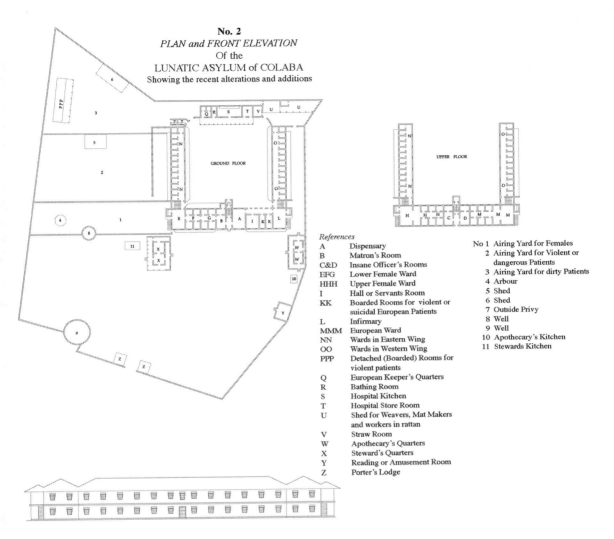

No. 2

PLAN and FRONT ELEVATION
Of the
LUNATIC ASYLUM of COLABA
Showing the recent alterations and additions

GROUND FLOOR

UPPER FLOOR

References

A	Dispensary
B	Matron's Room
C&D	Insane Officer's Rooms
EFG	Lower Female Ward
HHH	Upper Female Ward
I	Hall or Servants Room
KK	Boarded Rooms for violent or suicidal European Patients
L	Infirmary
MMM	European Ward
NN	Wards in Eastern Wing
OO	Wards in Western Wing
PPP	Detached (Boarded) Rooms for violent patients
Q	European Keeper's Quarters
R	Bathing Room
S	Hospital Kitchen
T	Hospital Store Room
U	Shed for Weavers, Mat Makers and workers in rattan
V	Straw Room
W	Apothecary's Quarters
X	Steward's Quarters
Y	Reading or Amusement Room
Z	Porter's Lodge

No 1	Airing Yard for Females
2	Airing Yard for Violent or dangerous Patients
3	Airing Yard for dirty Patients
4	Arbour
5	Shed
6	Shed
7	Outside Privy
8	Well
9	Well
10	Apothecary's Kitchen
11	Stewards Kitchen

was moving toward a complete separation on the basis of race with not only more space but also different kinds of spaces—wards that included cells and apartments—being allocated to Europeans. The plan of the wings consisted of a row of twelve cells that opened into a corridor that ran from one end of the wing to the other. In 1853, the clean, harmless patients and convalescents occupied the upper-floor wings to the rear of the building. This was to change and they would soon be replaced by native patients as this was the largest category of the asylum's inhabitants of about one hundred men. In the meantime, native males were divided into two classes for the purpose of placing them in one of the two wards reserved exclusively for them. The "violent dangerous and unruly" tenanted the lower ward in the eastern wing (NN), while those who exhibited "dirtiness, and indifference to decency and propriety" occupied

FIGURE 4.3. Lunatic asylum at Colaba, Bombay, 1853, plan and front elevation. Original plan courtesy Maharashtra State Archives, Bombay. Redrawn by Robert Batson.

the lower floor of the west wing (OO).[16] Each cell was to be occupied by one person, and thirteen patients were accommodated in the corridor, which would have afforded little privacy.[17] After the criminal lunatics acts of 1849 and 1851, criminal lunatics had to be admitted to asylums even though asylums were overcrowded. The solution to prevent further overcrowding was to provide for criminal lunatics and to avoid the classification of Indian lunatics as "harmless" or "idiotic" to prevent their institutionalization.[18] Thus public safety was prioritized over the needs of noncriminal Indian lunatics who did not receive treatment because they were classified into categories that did not require institutionalization.

Class certainly played a role in the administration of lunatics just as it did in England. Samuel Tuke's Retreat at York, an institution opened by his father William Tuke in 1796, had special provisions for the upper class.[19] In Bombay, the upper classes were presumed to be cleaner and the lower classes dirtier; and since dirt or cleanliness were symptoms, by implication, I would argue, they embodied different kinds of insanity. The articles of clothing and bedding for Europeans were of two categories: one for persons of lower ranks and the other for people of higher class, based on the kind they would normally use when healthy. They were provided in different quantities: articles of clothing required to be washed would be sufficient in number so that upper-class Europeans could change every day and those of the lower class every second day.[20] Clearly, the lower classes were deemed and doomed to be dirtier than the upper classes.

The classification allows us to make some broad generalizations that help us get a sense of where people might be located in the space of the main building of the lunatic asylum. The ground floor housed violent patients while the upper floor housed harmless patients. Female patients and European males were housed on both floors at the front of the building; once the final changes were made, native males were housed in the wings to the rear of the building. Finally, the administration and common services were housed in the front of the building on the ground floor. Thus the three main categories used to divide patients were violent patients, harmless patients, and insane officers. The first two categories of patients included female patients, lower-class European males, and native males, while the third category was made of a singular group, insane officers.

The compound of the asylum was also classified and separated. The women's wards opened out into an airing court (No. 1), and the violent, dangerous patients occupied their own (No. 2), as did the dirty patients of the lower ward of the west wing (No. 3). The square enclosed by the main buildings was reserved for the natives on the upper ward on the eastern side. Plans were made to ensure that there was no interaction between women in the lower female ward and the men outside by the erection of a wooden railing and a screen to the front and rear of the ward.[21] The largest space was reserved for the convalescents and the Europeans: the open space by the seaside and the large open ground to the north, in front of the building.[22] Dr. Campbell often accompanied European lunatics for a walk on the beach, conversing with them, while savoring magnificent views of the harbor, sailing ships, and the hills in the distant horizon.[23] One can see that, apart from the women, the residents of the upper levels of the asylum had access to larger spaces. The Europeans and convalescents, who may have included native patients at this time, were given the largest and perhaps best spaces in the compound of the lunatic asylum. Overall these spaces revealed that lunatics were not subject to "chains and lashes" as had been the case in England until the idea of "moral treatment" developed by William Tuke and his son Samuel became influential.[24] The approach to treating lunatics as practiced by Dr. Campbell, who was asylum superintendent from 1849 to 1864, were generally influenced by the ideas of moral therapy.[25]

Apart from social class, little attention was paid to the separation of lunatics in eighteenth-century England until Samuel Tuke emphasized the importance of classification in the segregation and treatment of patients.[26] Thus one can see how important it must have been to Dr. Campbell to classify patients in Colaba's lunatic asylum. Incomplete though the new system of classification in the asylum was, it reflected the racial and class hierarchies in colonial society and created an ideal hierarchical order that was not entirely possible in the real world. Here patients could be kept "separate and distinct." Dr. Campbell described with some horror the earlier period where lunatics of all types lived, loved, and hated together:

> In former times, the male and female, the dark man and the white, the dirty and the cleanly, the noisy and the quiet, the dangerous and the harmless, those who loved, and those who hated each other, all met together, or if they did not, it was only by bolt and bar and padlock that they could be kept apart. But now each great division of our Patients can be kept separate and distinct, and the largest class of all are distributed as has been shown above, into four different sections.[27]

According to Dr. Campbell the new improvements also allowed an improved system of supervision and hence control of the patients. Although the asylum caregivers spent long hours with the patients during the day, by night, in their previous quarters, they were unable to "exercise that unremitting surveillance" as necessary during the night as the day.[28] A new bungalow was erected for the superintendent on the high ground toward the east, two hundred feet from the garden wall. His original quarters in the asylum building were converted to other uses.[29] According to Dr. Campbell, with the new arrangements the apothecary's bungalow (WW) "commands" the European wards and western wing, the stewards' (XX) the female wards and eastern wing, and was within earshot of the patients' voices (see Figure 4.3). The European keeper (Q) could hear what was going on in the galleries overlooking the inner court, and apparently in his new bungalow the superintendent was even more readily aware than earlier of any disturbance by residents in the eastern wing.[30] Thus, in Colaba, specific sets of patients could be heard or partially observed by particular persons from known vantage positions surrounding the wards. However, only the matron's room (B) was located in the main asylum building adjacent to and opening into the lower female ward (EFG), while it is not clear whether anyone resided in the servant's hall (I). In contrast, in lunatic asylums in England provision had to be made for separate bedrooms for attendants in every ward or close to dormitories.[31] The living quarters of the staff reflected its own hierarchies. In the transformed asylum, the superintendent's bungalow was farther away from the asylum building and was probably the largest of the residential units. The apothecary and steward's bungalows, almost identical in plan, flanked the front facade of the asylum, whereas the European keeper's smaller quarters were located in the rear block of the asylum. The size of accommodation was in direct proportion to their positions in the hierarchy. Only the European matron within the same block as the insane was subject to the surveillance of the male staff, just as the insane were.

At the turn of the century, European matrons were poorly paid and did not have the means to take a drive or to get away for a short period of recreation. Writing in 1904, the surgeon general to the government of Bombay sympathetically reported that "the former matron of Colába died with her nervous system shattered and out of her mind."[32] Among those who moved to the colonies were European women like this matron, who had little choice but to take up ill-paid jobs. This matron led an isolated life away from society, in a lunatic asylum at the southern tip of the island, ending her days in madness. Miles away, in the new remote lunatic asylum at Nowpada in Thana, the European matron there was also in a poor state of health because of the "confinement."[33] One can only hope that madness was not her fate as well.

In 1872, the building of two new blocks effected further separation of females and European male patients respectively; however, by and large the classification of patients remained unchanged till the end of the nineteenth century.[34] Archival documents reveal the classification of non-European male patients at the Colaba Lunatic Asylum on 15 May 1899 under a number of different categories. The same categories were used for female patients. The two categories of insanity, violent (including epileptics) and harmless, were further subdivided into criminals and noncriminals. The corresponding numbers under each category were tabulated by race/community. Class did not appear on this table. Perhaps natives were all deemed to be of the same class. The number of uncategorized European patients was also listed.[35]

There is nothing specifically colonial about classifying patients. However, colonialism was relevant to systems of classification in two ways. First, natives and intermediary groups were lower in the hierarchy as compared to Europeans. This may have affected both the treatment they received and services such as clean clothing. Second, segregation on the basis of a system of classification was considered necessary for effective treatment. However, neither race nor class is a category of insanity, nor is gender, but it makes sense to separate patients on the basis of gender. Categories that are not medical have spatial consequences as patients in each large category (such as gender or race) had to be subdivided. Each refinement of classifications for treatment would require additional space, which probably resulted in inefficiencies.

Budgetary constraints in Bombay were important and asylums fulfilled the functions both of prisons, where patients were kept "in custody" away from society, and of hospitals, as places for bodily treatment but not for the "cure" of patients. Writing about the asylum system in India in 1904, Lieutenant-Colonel J. P. Barry, the superintendent of the Colaba Lunatic Asylum, bemoaned the fact that there was "very little anywhere in the nature of system," and "in one word, there is no specialisation."[36]

> The preamble to the Asylums' General Rules gives the cue to the purpose generally held in view, "the proper care and custody of the inmates." The word "cure" is strangely absent. And so our asylums partake partly of the nature of a prison where the inmates are kept in "custody" to prevent mischief to themselves and others, and partly of a general hospital, where they are treated on ordinary lines, for ordinary physical ailments. The "special" character of asylum, the real treatment of the mind, has been left in the background not through medical neglect but through the impossibility of special work with the means placed at our disposal. In all the essentials of a proper lunacy administration—suitability of site and buildings, space, equipment, gardens, pay—chaos reigns supreme. This branch of public service has been so starved as to make it the veritable Cinderella of the family.[37]

The asylum served as a warehouse for people of various types rejected by society. As Andrew Scull points out, asylums became important during that period of transformation from the mid-eighteenth to mid-nineteenth centuries when all kinds of "deviants," including lunatics, whose care was once a family and communal responsibility, were now viewed as "problem populations" who had to be separated from society in special institutions.[38] The Colaba Lunatic Asylum should be seen as an institution that encouraged Indians to do the same, to identify "problem populations" in their society who needed to be segregated from society, their care no longer a family or communal matter. Despite the construction of lunatic asylums in South Asia during the colonial era and their use by local populations, it is far from clear that the walls of asylums completely divide madness and reason in South Asia.

DIVIDING PRACTICES IN BOMBAY'S HOSPITALS

We will now turn to hospitals in Bombay, institutions whose foundational histories in England were quite different from the colonial context. A brief examination of England's past allows us understand why the colonial regime was eager to enter into partnerships with the native elite for the foundation of hospitals for the native population. In England, monastic hospitals had taken care of the sick and suffering for centuries, a system that abruptly came to an end with the Reformation. Under Henry VIII, church lands were confiscated and churches and buildings associated with the church were destroyed. From 1536 to 1544, the poor, beggars, paupers, and the ill of London received no help and as a consequence wandered on the streets. In order to resolve the situation, a group of London's wealthy citizens under the lord mayor petitioned the king to revive the old hospitals and promised to pay for the running expenses.[39] This can be seen as an example of joint enterprise in Britain where the Crown and bourgeoisie's fruitful cooperation served to resolve a problem of governance. It is not surprising that the Bombay government sought a similar partnership. Although the English bourgeoisie were certainly motivated by charitable motives, their main goals were to ensure the health of the public in the city and to create a structure for funding and managing social problems.[40] In the second half of the nineteenth century, Bombay's hospitals were primarily meant to serve the lower classes, the government was responsible for Europeans, and the native elite in partnership with the government built palatial structures for the care of natives.

In the nineteenth century, native philanthropists in Bombay played important roles in the colonial structure of governance as justices of the peace, members of the legislative assembly, and committee members. As leading members of their community, they often worked in the interests of their community. In many public institutions philanthropists tried to make special provisions for their own communities. In principle, these new nineteenth-century institutions were open to all citizens without prejudice, but in practice this was not so. These special provisions, made by both the colonial government and Indians, were most evident in the city's hospitals and mental institutions. As far as possible, the British tried to maintain separate institutions for the Europeans. However, the Europeans were not a monolithic community as revealed in the categories used to divide patients in the European General Hospital.

In hospitals for the native public, separation among different castes and religions existed, in theory at least, from the beginning of the formation of these public institutions. Caste and religious segregation was related to attitudes toward ritual pollution that encoded strict rules regarding dietary restrictions, dining with other castes/religious groups, or coming in contact with certain polluting groups in society. However, I argue that race became an additional factor within the native populations by the end of the nineteenth century as the case of the Parsis illustrates.

European Dividing Practices in the European General Hospital in the Nineteenth Century

In 1863, the Bombay government invited architects from England and India to participate in a design competition for a European General Hospital. Out of seventeen received entries, five or six were from England. Captain H. St. Clair Wilkins of the Royal Engineers received a first in merit for his design although it was never executed. According to the committee all the designs submitted exceeded the cost stipulated in the brief. Even though it was never constructed, we will examine Wilkins's design because it tells us a lot about European dividing practices and reveals a fractured rather than a unified community.[41]

Wilkins designed a three-story building (ground floor plus two stories). Plans of the building show it to be a long, rectangular building, 480 feet in length (Figure 4.4). The ends of the building are nicely terminated by projections of increased width. The design emphasized the width of the center of the building, which could be entered from either side by covered carriage porches, with the western porch carrying a chapel above it. Steps from the east and west porticoes led through an open arcade to an octagonal hall where two flights of staircases led to the upper stories. The staircases were at the heart of the building and were illuminated from above by four rose windows. To light the space, enhance the vertical ventilation, and provide an impressive and visually unifying feature, a tall octagonal lantern was the towering finale of the entire composition. Unsurprisingly, the style chosen was Gothic from southern Europe, where the climate was closer to Indian conditions than that of England (Figure 4.5). The steep hipped roof was designed to repulse Bombay's heavy rainfall.[42]

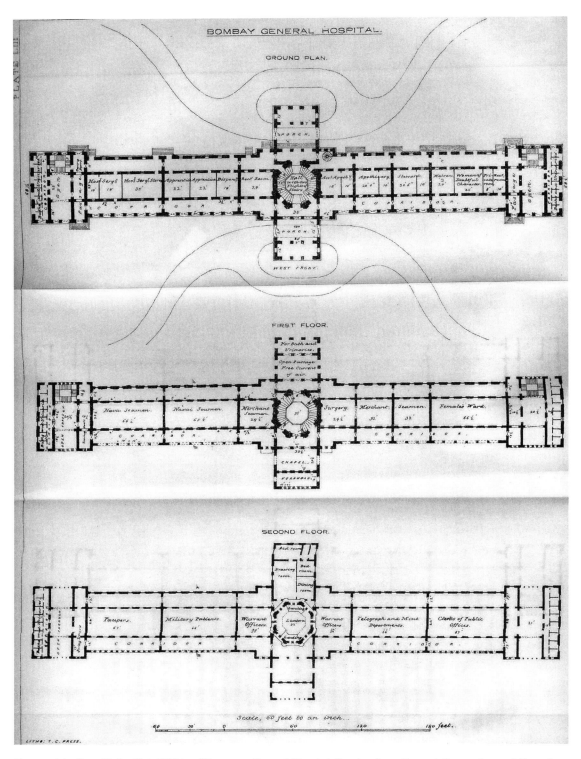

FIGURE 4.4. Capt. H. St. Clair Wilkins, "European General Hospital, Bombay," n.p. Ground, first, and second floor plans of Wilkins's design for the hospital, 1863.

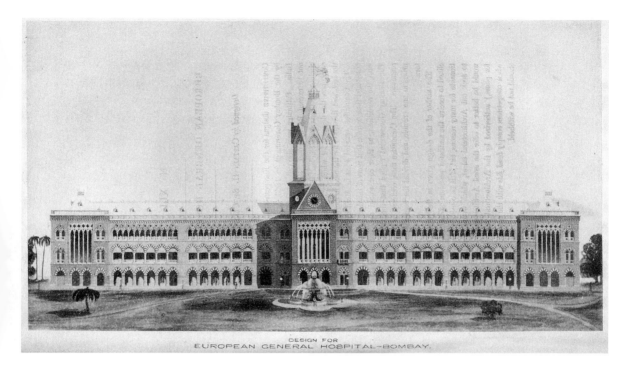

DESIGN FOR
EUROPEAN GENERAL HOSPITAL—BOMBAY.

The building plan was simple and in general identical on each floor. Behind the arcade and flanking the center were the left and right wings of the hospital. Each wing consisted of a single row of rooms flanked by verandahs on either side. Only the western verandah was referred to as a corridor so it might be assumed that the entrance to the rooms was from this verandah. This simple plan ensured cross ventilation of all the rooms. The protuberances at the ends held the services—toilets and additional staircases—and care was taken to ventilate the space between the toilets and the other rooms by an open passage. In terms of its plan, it was a corridor-type hospital distinct from most English hospitals because Bombay's climatic conditions allowed the corridor to be constructed behind an arcade rather than within the walls of the building. Although perhaps reducing privacy, it easily allowed for cross ventilation. The spaces above the porches were put to different uses. On the first floor were a chapel and bathrooms; on the second floor was a suite of rooms: dining rooms, drawing rooms, and bedrooms. It is not clear who used these rooms. Even though in terms of plan type it could be characterized as a corridor-type plan, it was hardly an unusual arrangement. More to the point, a building block surrounded by a verandah was used as a plan type for bungalows as well as public buildings not devoted to medical needs. In fact, Wilkins's design for the Public Works Offices in Bombay, constructed around 1872, was a Gothic Revival structure whose plan consisted of a central staircase tower flanked by a wing on

FIGURE 4.5. Capt. H. St. Clair Wilkins, "European General Hospital, Bombay," view of hospital in Wilkins's design, 1863, opposite 406.

either side—an arrangement similar to his design for the European General Hospital.

The floor plans of the hospital reveal wards and rooms reserved for specific groups. Most of the ground floor was reserved for administration and housing hospital staff but also included two receiving rooms, a larger one next to the entrance on the left wing and a smaller room tucked away at the end of the right wing. Between the matron's room in the right wing and the receiving room were two rooms: a small ward for "Women of doubtful character" and a "Private Room." There was only one room in each category in the hospital and their location seems to indicate that both categories needed to be under the direct supervision of the staff. Women of doubtful character had to be kept away from men, for example, while a paying customer would be housed in a private room. The single private room indicated that hospitals were still largely seen as charitable institutions shunned by the wealthier classes who preferred to be treated at home.[43] The wings of the first floor housed merchant seamen and naval seamen, the surgery, but also a female ward that was next to the wards for merchant seamen. The second-floor wings had wards for paupers, military patients, warrant officers, Steam Telegraph & Mint departments, and clerks of public offices. Most of the wards in the hospital were reserved for merchant and naval seamen and for specific departments of the government including the military, which was separate from civil administration. It is not clear where a patient not included in these categories would turn for help.

It is not surprising that the hospital catered mainly to specific groups. The European General Hospital (later called St. George's Hospital) was founded by the East India Company for the care of servants of the Company and seamen from the ships in the harbor. Certainly by 1913, the growth of the large nonofficial European and Anglo-Indian community had expanded the scope of the hospital so that it admitted members of the nonofficial community after the claims of the former groups were met. It was a hospital primarily intended for the use of those too poor to pay for some or all of their medical expenses.[44] Although divisions on the basis of gender, class, and occupation were seen in England,[45] divisions based on government departments were an entirely colonial invention.

These multiple divisions in spatial arrangements had nothing to do with the medical maladies that assailed these various populations. However, they point to great divisions based not just on gender and class but also on morality and culture. Seamen, military patients, and those who worked in government departments were culturally distinct. Perhaps their segregation had something to do with bookkeeping, but it is equally possible that these divisions reveal fault lines. The categories remind us that neither Europeans nor the British were a homogenous group, and we get a glimpse of the caste-like divisions that existed in British colonial society. Even as these spatial arrangements replicated some of the divisions seen in England—particularly gender and class—most of the other divisions were a reflection of the distinctions made between the members of European society in colonial Bombay.

Indian Dividing Practices in Bombay's Native Hospitals in the Nineteenth Century

Right from the start Indians were divided on the basis of gender and religious community in Bombay's native general hospitals, and yet philanthropists attempted to make special provisions for their own community. In 1904, Sir Jamsetjee Jeejeebhoy (his real name was Cowasji, fourth baronet, 1852–1908) protested against a proposal to move the Parsi Male Ward of the Jamsetjee Jeejeebhoy Hospital, commonly referred to as J. J. Hospital, into the General Hospital of the J. J. Hospital. The J. J. Hospital was the first major public institution founded for the care of the native poor in Bombay, built at the joint expense of the East India Company and Sir Jamsetjee Jeejeebhoy (the first baronet, 1783–1859). Jeejeebhoy contributed Rs. 164,000 toward the building, which was opened in May 1845. Located along the Parel Road, this hospital formed the nucleus of a complex of related institutions that sprung up around it including the Sir Cowasji Jehangir Ophthalmic Hospital (opened in 1865) and the Grant Medical College. In 1892, three medical facilities focusing on women and children were opened: the Bai Motlibai Obstetric Hospital, Sir Dinshaw Manockjee Petit Hospital for Women and Children, and the Dwarkadas Lallubhai Dispensary for Women and Children (Figure 4.6).[46]

In 1904, Sir Jamsetjee Jeejeebhoy requested that the Parsi Ward, if moved to the General Hospital, continue to be a separate building, or if that were not possible, "that the Parsee ward be located in a wing, or floor, or part thereof of the proposed general Hospital buildings *entirely by itself, separated and kept distinct* from any of the other wards of the Hospital" (emphasis added). The second clause asked that accommodation for the same number of patients be provided. The third clause asked that he be allowed "first choice" in case the matter came to the selection of a ward for Parsis "from among the best ones in the new building."[47] The desire for a separate building for the Parsi ward indicates the desire by Parsis for artifactual modes that would distinguish them from the natives.

Government records reveal that there was indeed a special provision for providing separate wards for Parsis. In 1840, the governor believed that the best way of carrying out the philanthropic intentions of the Honorable Court and

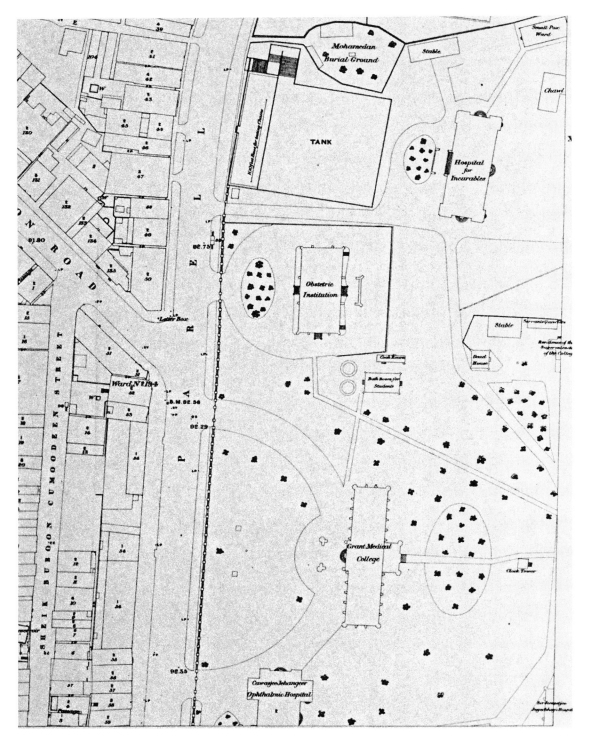

FIGURE 4.6. Colonel George A. Laughton, Tarwaree, sheet no. LXXXIX, Bombay, surveyed in 1868, 1869, and corrected up to 1 June 1870, plan showing part of J. J. Hospital compound in lower right. This detail of the map shows the Obstetric Institution, Grant Medical College, and part of the Cowasji Jehangir Ophthalmic Hospital. North of the Obstetric Institution is a Hospital for Incurables. Courtesy Maharashtra State Archives, Bombay. Photograph by author, 1998.

Jeejeebhoy was for the "establishment of *one* Hospital capable of accommodating 300 patients, as much regard being paid as may be found practicable to the classification and separation of the sick according to caste and sex."[48] Additionally, a range of wards, called the Jamsetjee Jeejeebhoy's Wards or Sir Jamsetjee's Wards, depending on what name was preferred by Sir Jeejeebhoy, were set aside for the accommodation and treatment of sick persons who produced a "ticket of recommendation" from Jeejeebhoy "or his representative."[49] In practice however, there was a provision for Parsis. A newspaper article reporting on the opening of the hospital in 1845 observed:

> The wards are to be arranged according to the divisions of the Poor; thus there will be two large wards for the Hindoos, in which they will be placed according to their castes, two for the Mahomedans, two for the Native Christians, two or more for females, two for contagious disorders, two for surgical cases, and two for Parsees, which last are to be left to the disposal of the Founder.[50]

By 1905 at least, and probably long before, the separation of patients according to religion was not practiced, except for the "Parsi Wards."[51] Different religious groups probably shared the wards for contagious disorders and surgical cases. In 1881, Hindus and Muslims shared the same wards, while "separate" cooks prepared their food.[52] The Parsi ward was constructed in 1851 as an obstetric hospital and was converted into a male Parsi ward in 1892 when the Motlibai Obstetric Hospital was opened in 1892.[53] During fieldwork in Bombay in 1999 and 2007, I found that a separate Parsi ward still exists in J. J. Hospital (Figure 4.7).[54]

The first baronet Sir Jeejeebhoy's argument for separation of castes was primarily motivated by issues of ritual pollution, whereas in 1905, the fourth baronet Sir Jeejeebhoy's desire to *separate* the Parsis was related to notions of racial superiority and the need to mark Parsis as *distinct* from the natives. This will become clearer in the example of the lunatic asylum at Nowpada later in the chapter. In other words, the racial landscape of Bombay with all its contradictions was marked in the city's institutions. Eckehard Kulke points out that as late as the mid-nineteenth century the Parsis still saw themselves as "natives." Around 1850, Sir Jamsetjee Jeejeebhoy referred to himself as a "native of India." By the turn of the century, the majority of the community refused to be called "natives." There were some who even saw themselves as a "purely white race."[55] As Parsis were among the most prominent philanthropists in the city, these changing attitudes were reflected in Bombay's hospitals and lunatic asylums.

The British encouraged Parsis to think of themselves as separate from the "natives." As early as 1838, Mrs. Marianne Postans wrote of the Parsis, Baghdadi Jews, and Armenians as "foreign settlers" in Bombay, explaining that she

FIGURE 4.7. Parsi Ward, J. J. Hospital Compound, constructed after 1845. Photograph by author, 2007.

had chosen to exclude other groups because their numbers were not sufficient to form "distinct classes":

> In speaking of the Parsees, Jews, and Armenians, only, as foreign settlers in Bombay, it will be supposed that this classification includes but a small proportion of emigrating Asiatics, as have selected the Presidency of Western India for the scene of their speculations. Others, however, are not sufficiently numerous to form distinct classes, being scattered among the social community, rather under the character of individual adventurers, than merchant settlers.[56]

To view the Parsis, settled in India from Persia since between the eighth and tenth centuries, as "foreign settlers" is rather ingenuous and is entirely a colonial invention, aided and abetted by the Parsis themselves, but by no means acceptable to all Parsis.[57]

Special provisions for Parsis were made in other Bombay hospitals as well. Another group of medical institutions related to women's health was erected on a prominent location on the Esplanade. In 1882, G. T. Kittredge, the Parsi reformer Sorabji Shapurji Bengali (1831–93), and others started a movement that urged that medical assistance be given to Indian women. The next year Pestanji Hormusji Cama made an offer of Rs. 164,300 for a hospital for women and children to be run under the charge of medical women. A prominent site on the Esplanade fronting the Cruickshank Road was granted for the Pestanji Hormusji Cama Hospital for Women and Children (see Figure 3.10). In 1886, a dispensary known as the Jafar Suleman Dispensary for women and children was constructed on a site adjacent to the Crawford Market through a donation of Rs. 20,000 by Cumoo Jafar Suleman. In 1891, a third building, the Bomanji Edalji Allbless Obstetric Hospital, was erected at a cost of Rs. 59,640 (see Figure 3.6). In practice these three buildings functioned almost as one institution. Associated with the hospital was a training school for nurses and midwives, opened in 1887. On the same triangular piece of land as these hospitals but fronting the Carnac Road lay the Gokuldas Tejpal Native General Hospital, also known as the G. T. Hospital. In 1865, the public demanded a second native hospital. Arthur Crawford, the municipal commissioner, persuaded Gokuldas Tejpal (1822–67), a wealthy Kutchi Bhatia merchant who was on his deathbed, to contribute Rs. 150,000 toward the cost of this building. Designed by Colonel Fuller, it was built between 1870 and 1874.[58]

In 1886, Dr. Edith Pechey, honorary physician to the Cama Hospital, wrote a letter to the government with a proposal that a block of rooms constructed in the hospital compound for the accommodation of servants be converted to a ward for Bania, Bhatia, and other high-caste Hindu women who were unwilling to go to the general ward and also forwarded an estimate for this conversion drawn up by the executive engineer. The government could not accede to Pechey's proposal because it had agreed with the donor to pay for the cost of the staff and maintenance of the hospital, while the donor, Pestanji Hormusji Cama ["Káma" in records] was to pay for the cost of the building. Cama had given an additional donation of Rs. 44,311 for a separate ward for Parsi females, and he was unlikely to do the same for Hindu women. The government observed the needs of these Bania women would be met in the proposed Harkisandas Hospital where the donor, Harkisandas Narotumdas, had stipulated that a ward or part of a ward be set aside for women and children of the Bania caste.[59] An additional consideration for the government was that an inscription would have to record government funding for the conversion of the servants quarter. They believed that Cama might not like this because up to this point he had provided all of the funds for the building of the hospital.[60]

Parsis were not the only ones who attempted to make special provisions for their community. In 1885, Harkisandas Narotumdas, on behalf of his mother, Bai Putlibai, and other members of his family, wrote to the government offering a sum of Rs. 100,000 for the building of a fifty-bed hospital to treat women's diseases and children. In this hospital, clinical instruction could be given to the students of the Grant Medical College. While also giving relief to the poor, it would serve as a memorial to his father, Narotumdas Madhavdas, and his uncle, Vurjeevandas Madhavdas. Harkisandas came from a wealthy and prominent family of the Kapole Bania caste. His ancestors had immigrated to Bombay from Kathiawar in Gujarat over two hundred years ago. His uncle, Vurjeevandas Madhavdas (1817–96) was, according to one opinion, considered the leader of the Hindu community in Bombay.[61]

Narotumdas's offer came with a number of stipulations, some of which will be considered here. He offered Rs. 100,000 for the construction of the main buildings of the hospital and the dispensary while the government had to purchase a site near the J. J. Hospital that Narotumdas had selected and pay for the maintenance and "competent" staffing of the hospital. Presumably, the government was to pay for the additional outbuildings required for this hospital. The hospital was to be named after Narotumdas's father and uncle, and no portion of the hospital or building erected in its compound was to bear any other name than that of the donor family. Finally, a ward or portion of a ward was to be reserved for women and children of the Bania caste.[62] Narotumdas's offer fell far short of the government's expectations. According to the government's estimates a new obstetric hospital would roughly cost Rs. 150,000, and a large separate children's hospital would itself cost several hundred thousand rupees. The government was beginning to feel the impact of the additional expenses entailed by this partnership with native philanthropy where the government had to expend money on buildings or toward the maintenance of buildings or both. The surgeon general suggested that in future the government should announce that an endowment or a contribution toward an endowment should go with a building contribution.[63]

Dr. Moore, the surgeon general, attached six rough sketches of a fifty-bed hospital to a report to the government concerning the required staff and cost of the hospital. These plans were arrived at after consultation with the first physician and obstetric physician of J. J. Hospital and reference to some "continental hospital plans." The six sketches showed a one- or two-story main building with outbuildings (Figures 4.8 to 4.13). The plans for the outbuildings were the same for all six sketch plans with some variations in 5 and 6 (as numbered on the drawings). The overall plan consisted of a large bilaterally symmetrical main building with a prominent entrance at the center. Small outbuildings hugged the edges of the compound, and larger outbuildings were hidden behind the main building (Figure 4.14). Undesirable, polluting, unhygienic activities were pushed farther toward the end of the plan, opposite the entrance, including the servants' latrine and washing platform, the dead house, and the disinfecting room. The layout was not entirely dissimilar to that of a north Indian Hindu temple complex with a prominent central building and smaller shrines around, easily added or subtracted.

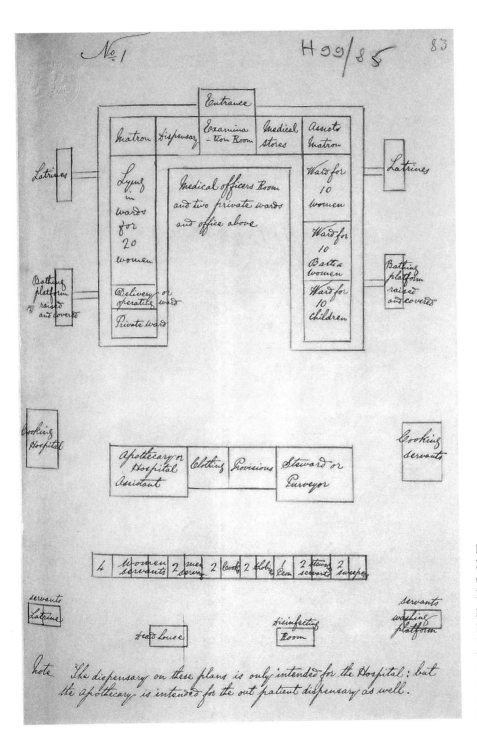

Entrance

Matron	Dispensary	Examina-tion Room	Medical stores	Assist. Matron

Latrines

Lying in wards for 20 women

Medical officers Room and two private wards and office above

Latrines

Ward for 10 women

Ward for 10 Battia women

Ward for 10 Children

Bathing platform raised and covered

Delivery or operative ward

Private ward

Bathing platform raised and covered

Cooking Hospital

Apothecary or Hospital Assistant	Clothing	Provisions	Steward or Purveyor

Cooking servants

4	Women servants	2	men servts	2	cooks	2	Dhobis	1	Peon	2	Steward servants	2	sweeper

servants Latrine

Dead house

Disinfecting Room

servants washing platform

note   The dispensary on these plans is only intended for the Hospital: but the apothecary is intended for the out patient dispensary as well.

FIGURE 4.8. Harkisandas Narotumdas Hospital, Bombay, 1885, sketch plan no. 1 of proposed hospital. Note the ward for Bhatia women in plans 1–6. Courtesy Maharashtra State Archives, Bombay. Photograph by author, 1998.

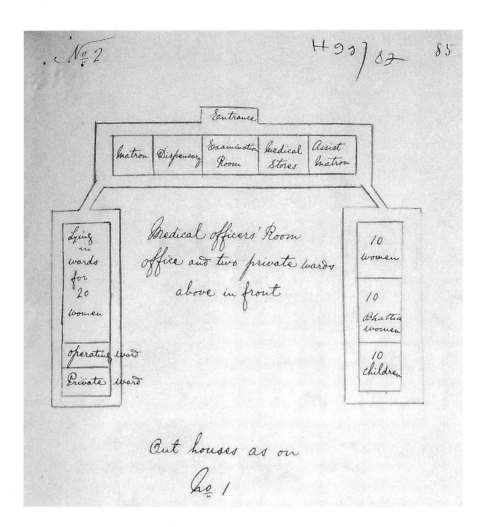

The handwritten sketch plan contains the following labels:

No. 2   H99/82   85

Entrance

| Matron | Dispensary | Examination Room | Medical Stores | Assist Matron |

Medical officers' Room office and two private wards above in front

Lying in wards for 20 women

Operating ward
Private ward

10 women

10 Bhattia women

10 children

Out houses as on
No. 1

FIGURE 4.9. Sketch plan 2 of proposed hospital.

The sketch plans of the main building were all bilaterally symmetrical in terms of the building footprint—variations of a corridor plan that was made up either of a single block of rooms with an administrative core surrounded by verandahs or of a multiple block model that consisted of a central administrative core connected to ward blocks through a corridor. In case of multiple blocks, each block was surrounded by verandahs and connected by corridors. In the central building or block—the administrative core—the entrance or entrance hall was fronted, flanked, or surrounded by the offices of the matron, dispensary, examination room, and medical officer. The patients' wards lay on either side of this central core. This basic pattern was repeated on the upper story, if there was one; latrines and bathing areas, if drawn, appeared as undesirable append-ages attached to and distanced from the building. Architectural historian Ann-marie Adams has noted, "British hospital architects were particularly proud of

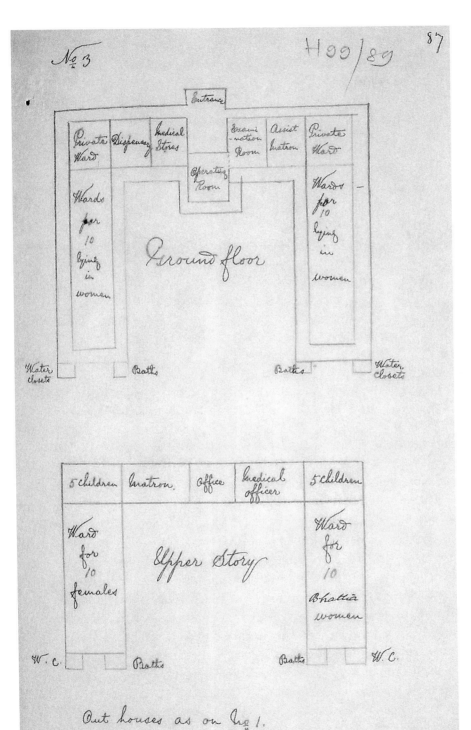

FIGURE 4.10. Sketch plan 3 of proposed hospital.

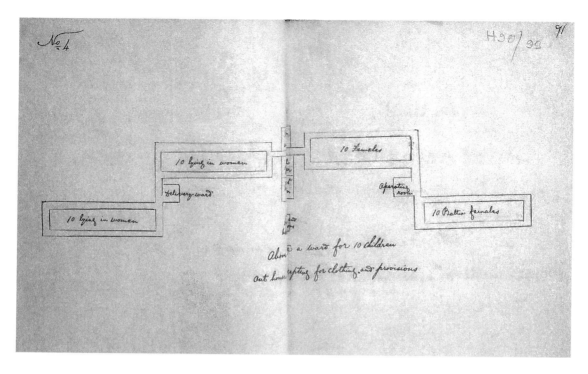

FIGURE 4.11. Sketch plan 4 of proposed hospital.

their design of sanitary facilities, and quick to compare their own standards to those of both Europe and the United States. The main difference was that toilets in British hospitals were frequently accommodated in disconnected and thus heavily ventilated spaces," as we can see in these sketch plans.[64] Sketch plans 1, 3, and 5 were all variations of a single block plan. Plans 1 and 3 were C-shaped buildings with forward facing wings; plan 5 was a rectangular block without wings. Sketch plan 2 was a variation of plan 1 with the wings containing the wards separated and connected to the central block via a corridor. In plan 4 a narrow administrative core was flanked by a linear staggered formation of wards that were connected by corridors. Sketch plan 6 had a prominent rectangular central administrative core perpendicular to and intersecting with a well-defined C-shaped corridor off of which wards and other rooms open. Two wards, parallel to each other but separate, open into the corridor on the left wing and right wing respectively. Even though sketch plan 6 may have been influenced by pavilion hospital designs, the separate ward blocks did not contain services and thus were not pavilion ward blocks, which often terminated with a typical sanitary end tower.[65]

Despite the reference to "continental plans," none of the sketch plans considered erecting the "pavilion plan" hospital, the most influential design type for hospitals from the end of the 1850s to the 1930s.[66] In every sketch plan, a separate ward for ten Battia (Bhatia) women was outlined, and one may assume

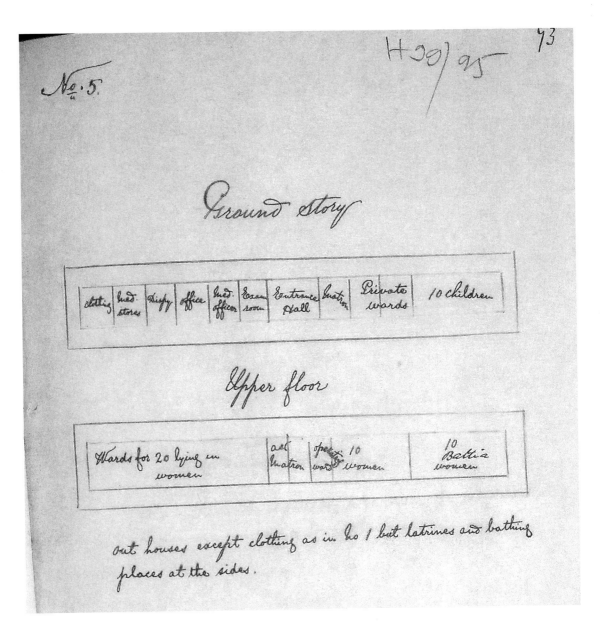

that this was the separate ward for the Hindu women of Bania caste. The sketch plans also showed provision for two private wards for classes who could afford to pay. What the sketch plans left unsaid was that women would be separated by religion.

Estimates showed that unless the sum offered by the donor was increased, the number of beds would have to be reduced to thirty or, including children's cots, to forty. Dr. James Arnott, obstetric physician, J. J. Hospital, drew a rough plan of the hospital that was later redrawn by the executive engineer and used

FIGURE 4.12. Sketch plan 5 of proposed hospital.

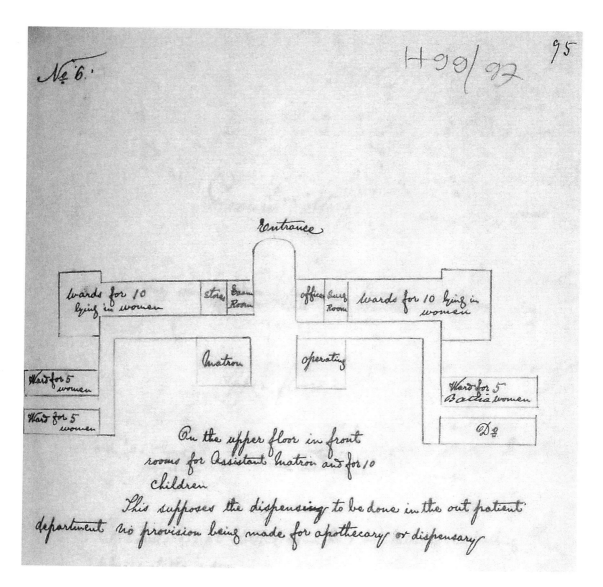

In the drawing (handwritten labels):

Nº 6.

H 99/92   95

Entrance

wards for 10 lying in women | store | Exam Room | office | Surg Room | wards for 10 lying in women

Matron | operating

Ward for 5 women

Ward for 5 women

Ward for 5 Bania women

Dº

On the upper floor in front
rooms for Assistant Matron and for 10
children
This supposes the dispensing to be done in the out patient
department no provision being made for apothecary or dispensary

FIGURE 4.13. Sketch plan 6 of proposed hospital.

to make cost estimates. Arnott reduced the number of beds to approximately forty. These were to be divided into four wards intended for Hindus, Muslims, Parsis, and others. He emphasized that no ward should "on emergency" be reserved for any one caste, except for a small ward of four beds to be reserved for the Bania caste, adding that he would prefer to divide each approximately twelve-bed ward by a five-foot-high screen into two sections. He offered suggestions on the architecture: a handsome, well-proportioned, two-story building of inexpensive design, devoid of decorative architecture such as turrets and carved stone works, would suffice. Large, spacious, and well-ventilated wards, as well as verandahs, with venetian blinds to keep out the sun and rain, were

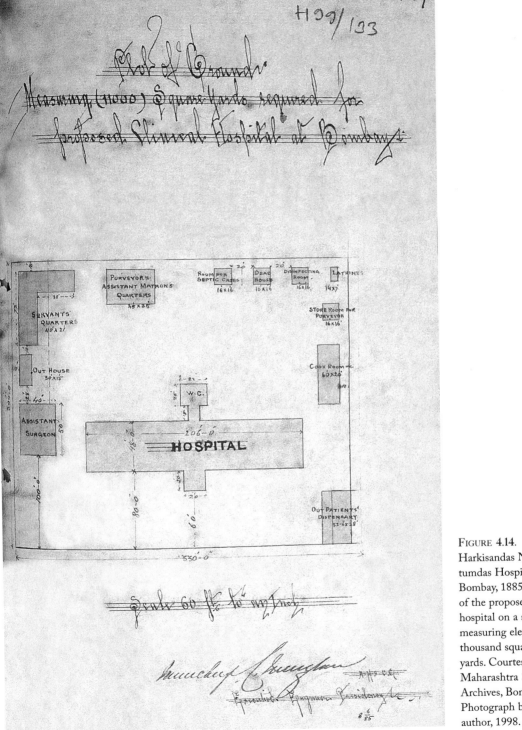

FIGURE 4.14.
Harkisandas Naro-
tumdas Hospital,
Bombay, 1885, layout
of the proposed
hospital on a site
measuring eleven
thousand square
yards. Courtesy
Maharashtra State
Archives, Bombay.
Photograph by
author, 1998.

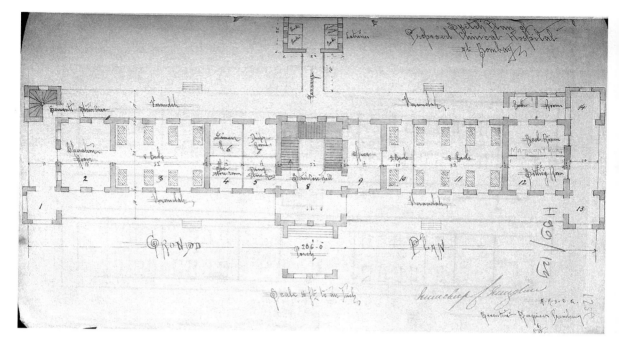

Figure 4.15. Harkisandas Naro-tumdas Hospital, Bombay, 1885, ground floor plan of the proposed hospital drawn up by M. C. Murzban, executive engineer. Courtesy Maharashtra State Archives, Bombay. Photograph by author, 1998.

required. Additionally, the plan should have provision for the extension of an upper ward. The plans drawn up by Khan Bahadur Muncherji C. Murzban, the executive engineer, based on Dr. Arnott's plans, are similar in principle to the early sketches (Figures 4.15, 4.16).[67]

The design selected for development and drawn up by Murzban was a variation of sketch plan 5. Here one sees windows placed between two beds showing that cross ventilation was a consideration. The plan of the upper floor shows a room for a nurse pupil on the left wing overlooking a ward with eight beds and a nurse on duty on the right wing supervising the patients (see Figure 4.16). But the nurse on duty on the right wing could not have supervised all sixteen of the patients from her room because screens between sets of beds would have removed those patients beyond the screen from her line of vision. It appears that there was a single point of entry and exit for patients in the left wing through the nurse pupil's office, but in the right wing there was an alternative route of entry and exit at the far end of the right wing. Thus not only would the nurse on duty in the right wing have been unable to supervise who entered the ward, but it is not clear that access to the toilets would have been straightforward. Despite the decades separating Wilkins's design for the European General Hospital and the Harkisandas Hospital and the major developments in hospital design, there is not much difference between the hospital designs.

A ward type that with additional developments came to be known after the 1860s as the Nightingale Ward had only one point of entry and exit. It was

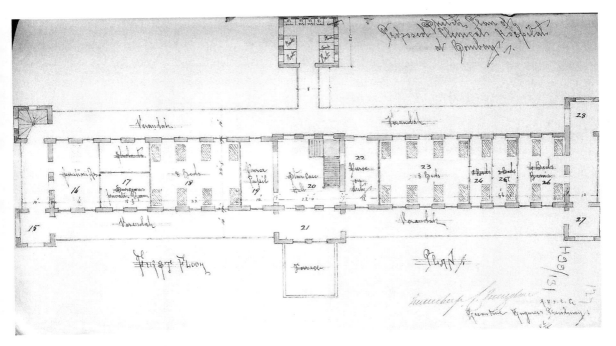

hoped that this would prevent polluted air from traveling to other parts of the hospital. Additionally, it allowed the nurses to keep a close eye on the ward and also to supervise the movements of visitors and patients. The bathrooms and toilets were at the other end of the ward.[68] While the Bombay hospital wards surveyed so far provided for cross ventilation, the various social divisions precluded the easy implementation of something like a Nightingale Ward, although the Harkisandas Hospital plan certainly seems to have been influenced by some of its principles by locating a room for a nurse that overlooked a ward. Government estimates showed that the total cost of this forty-two-bed hospital, including the cost of the site, was Rs. 245,000, and Narotumdas's offer was refused because the government's share would have been approximately Rs. 150,000.[69] This example shows a willingness of other communities, other than the Parsis, to carve out separate spaces for themselves in the city's hospitals.

Subsequently, in 1887, the government received an offer of Rs. 125,000 from Sir Dinshaw Manockjee Petit (1823–1901) for a lying-in hospital. However, the government would have to provide the land for this building within the hospital compound. It was thought that the Mazagaon Parsonage land held by the government on a fifty-year lease would be the most suitable site, but since it was private property it was not available. Soon after this discussion a wealthy Parsi lady, Bai Motlibai (1811–97), widow of Maneckji Navroji Wadia, who was in touch with the governor on this subject, gave the Parsonage site, measuring approximately 20,000 square yards and located behind the J. J. Hospital, to the

FIGURE 4.16. Harkisandas Narotumdas Hospital, Bombay, 1885, first floor plan of the proposed hospital drawn up by M. C. Murzban, executive engineer. Courtesy Maharashtra State Archives, Bombay. Photograph by author, 1998.

government.[70] She also gave an additional sum of Rs. 150,000 for the construction of a charitable hospital to be maintained by the government. She made the condition that the building be designed in such a manner that a wing or section or a proportionate number of beds be set aside exclusively for Parsis.[71] These negotiations resulted in the foundation of the Bai Motlibai Obstetric Hospital and the Sir Dinshaw Manockjee Petit Hospital for Women and Children, which were constructed in 1892.

This examination of Bombay's hospitals has revealed deep social divisions where communities desired to be segregated. While the Europeans were sequestered in their own hospital, the ward divisions revealed fissures beyond those of gender and class. Of the native communities, only the Parsis consistently made special provisions for their community in all of the city's native hospitals by the end of the nineteenth century except for the G. T. Hospital. Parsi philanthropy assured that this segregation would be permanent. Certainly in the case of the J. J. Hospital, the early community segregation based on religion had given way over time except in the case of Parsis. Even in the case of the Harkisandas Hospital, Dr. Arnott made the point that no ward should be reserved for any community except for the Banias and temporary screens rather than walls should be used to segregate patients of different religious communities. However, even if the divisions between most communities would not remain in practice, it is likely that the need for planning for community segregation influenced the design of hospitals, perhaps inhibiting designers from introducing innovations in hospital designs being undertaken in Europe. The colonial regime was only too willing to allow community segregation on a permanent basis if the community was willing to bear the cost. In carving out a separate space for themselves in the city's native hospitals, the Parsis spatially articulated their intermediary status in society, a position they willingly chose to occupy—"foreigners" who were distinct from natives but not quite European.

ACCOMMODATING RACE, COMMUNITIES, AND RELIGIOUS PRACTICES IN THE NEW LUNATIC ASYLUMS OF THE BOMBAY PRESIDENCY

Serious discussions of the building of a new lunatic asylum began only in the 1890s, but earlier decades were marked by discussions on the inadequacy of the lunatic asylum in Bombay and of such asylums in the Bombay Presidency as a whole. As a result, consideration of a new asylum for Bombay was linked to the issue of how to handle lunatics in the Presidency. Here, too, Parsi philanthropists were able to carve out a separate space for their own community. While the British were comfortable with divisions based on community, they could not tolerate religious spaces and practices in the lunatic asylum.

In 1893, a committee selected by the government inspected and reported on the site at Nowpada near Thana for the proposed lunatic asylum.[72] Subsequent medical and sanitary opinion found the proposed site, particularly its climate, unsuitable for the treatment of lunatics and opened the discussion of the suitability of different locations for disparate sets of patients including Europeans. Surgeon-Major Clarkson, acting sanitary commissioner for the government of Bombay and one of the members of the committee appointed in 1893 to examine the Nowpada site, argued that the climate of Thana was unsuitable for the treatment of lunatics, especially Europeans.[73] Surgeon General Turnbull with the government of Bombay concurred with Clarkson's opinion. He found the climate of the Thana Valley unfit for both the physical and mental health of a large proportion of the patients. The monsoon downpour would make it impossible (presumably for the inmates) to undertake any outdoor labor in the garden and fields during that period. A "bracing" rather than a "debilitating and depressing" climate was necessary for the successful treatment of inmates; it was unlikely such a climate could be found in the plains of the Konkan where Thana was located. A more appropriate location in his opinion would be above the western ghats, sufficiently close to a railway line as a large number of European soldiers had to be accommodated in the asylum. He suggested Nasik as an alternate location for the asylum as it was close to Devlali where a large number of soldiers were stationed at the depot. While European cases in the asylum required "special consideration," other groups that had been accommodated in the Colaba asylum—Eurasians, natives of the Deccan, Gujarat, and foreign countries—would also be adversely affected by the "moist steamy heat" of the Konkan plains.[74] In short, the insalubrious climate of the Thana Valley was unsuitable for Europeans as well as all other groups that were not native to the Konkan region.

The government considered the conflicting advice on the suitability of the site and came up with a solution that placed insane patients in asylums located near their home regions by expanding existing facilities or planning new asylums. The government decided against making the asylum at Nowpada a central asylum for the whole Presidency because it was felt that, apart from climatic considerations, lunatics should be confined near their friends, relatives, and former neighborhood. The government approved the site at Nowpada for Konkanis, who would also use the asylum at Ratnagiri. The Nowpada site was also to be for Bombay natives; for non-European foreigners, who would only use the asylum until they could be returned to their home; and for natives from other parts of India until they could be returned to their homes. Officials were to explore whether to expand the Ahmedabad Lunatic Asylum or build a new one to accommodate the Gujarati lunatics. Similarly, officials were to study whether the Deccani lunatics could be accommodated in the Poona asylum and to study Yerwada as a suitable location for a new one. The government also planned to build an asylum at Nasik for civil and military Europeans.[75] Toward the construction of the Nowpada asylum, the government received a donation of Rs. 100,000 from Bai Putlibai, widow of the late Narotumdas Madhavdas, and her sons. By 1895, with interest it had accrued, this amount was now Rs. 118,000.[76] This is the same family whose earlier offer of Rs. 100,000 toward the building of an obstetric hospital fell through.

The government had no problem accepting the separation of religious communities in principle, which was by now a well-established tradition in Bombay's public buildings. In 1894, the government received a letter from Dinsha Bamanji Pestanji Master, Honorary Physician for the Nasarvanji Manekji Petit Charity Fund for destitute, insane Parsis. He was writing on behalf of Bai Dinbai Nasarvanji Petit, widow of the late Nasarvanji Manekji Petit, who wished to offer the government Rs. 15,000 for the construction of two separate wards, one for males and another for female Parsi patients who were admitted to the Nowpada lunatic asylum. Each ward was to be provided with associated rooms for patients who were convalescent and padded rooms for violent patients. No patients hailing from any other "nationality" were to be admitted to these wards unless there was not a single Parsi patient in the hospital. On the other hand, if there were more Parsi patients than could be admitted in these wards, they should be admitted to the wards in other parts of the asylum, where patients of other "nationalities" resided. The government turned down this offer, because according to their estimates these wards would cost Rs. 52,512.[77]

This was merely the beginning of a protracted series of financial and spatial negotiations between Parsi donors and the government, in which the donor clearly stated the need for the separation of Parsis from natives of other nationalities. Master, on behalf of Bai Dinbai, wrote to the government again in 1895 increasing the offer to Rs. 20,000. Master clarified that this amount was sufficient for two wards and separate blocks of building were not required. He reminded the government that the Nasarvanji Manekji Petit Charity Fund defrayed fifteen rupees every month toward the maintenance charges of Parsi patients, thus relieving the government of a considerable financial burden.[78] Furthermore, Master conveyed the specific request of Bai Dinbai that Parsis be segregated from other native patients, not on religious grounds but on the grounds of cleanliness, as the latter were filthy in their habits:

She [Bai Dinbai] hopes that His Excellency the Governor in Council will be pleased to grant the concession of segregating Pársi patients from those of other nationalities. This concession is asked for specially because it is found from experience that Pársi patients, however poor, do not, as a rule, like to resort to a hospital where patients of all nationalities are put together in the same ward, and this reluctance is shown not only on religious grounds, but also on the grounds of cleanliness. The lower classes of natives who, as a rule, resort to hospitals are very filthy in their habits, and the Pársis, as a rule, being of more cleanly habits, do not therefore like to associate with them in the same wards. For these reasons arrangements have been specially made by the Pársi community in all the hospitals of Bombay—except in the Gokaldás Hospital—for segregating Pársi patients in separate wards.[79]

The government showed considerable flexibility in accommodating the needs of Parsis after Bai Dinbai's inadequate offer of Rs. 20,000. Two separate wards were designed for the use of male and female paying Parsi patients; a portion of at least one general ward was partitioned to accommodate pauper Parsi patients.[80]

The characterization of Parsis as a community, by and large, of clean habits seems to indicate the use of new criteria by Parsis for distinguishing themselves from the natives and aligning themselves with Europeans. Racial hierarchies were related to notions of civilization and were in turn related to cleanliness. Cleanliness was also a criterion applied to lunacy, and upper-class patients were deemed cleaner in their habits than those of the lower class. In the city of Bombay, cleanliness was a central concern of colonial administrators, particularly the municipal and sanitary commissioners. Quarters occupied by lower-class natives were much dirtier than those occupied by Europeans and upper-class natives. At the same time, the sums expended by the municipality on the maintenance of the latter areas were many times more than it spent on areas occupied by the lower classes.

In 1898, the government of India noted that it heard that the construction of a separate asylum for the Parsis had been considered and, if this were the case, it was desirable that it be built in Yerwada, near Poona. They also concurred with the medical opinions and with the view of the government of Bombay that the Nowpada asylum was unsuitable for European and Deccani lunatics, and that they should be accommodated in the new asylum proposed to be established in Yerwada, near Poona. If the changes it proposed were carried out, including the amalgamation of some asylums, then the government of India was of the opinion that the asylum at Poona would be the most important in the Bombay Presidency, requiring a full time commissioned medical officer for its superintendence.[81] In other words, the lunatics here would get the best medical attention.

The scheme for a separate asylum for the Parsis was not widely known, but the government gave the Parsis special treatment, accorded to no other native community, allowing them the choice of alternative sites for their wards or asylum. In 1899, the superintendent to the Colaba Lunatic Asylum alluded to a rumor of a plan to leave Parsis as well as Europeans at Colaba. He warned that such a scheme of partiality would harm the reputation of Nowpada and the Parsis: "If Nowpada is not good enough for the Pársis, there will be plenty to cry out that it is not good enough for other people."[82] In November 1898, Bai Avabai Framji Petit, daughter of the late Bai Dinbai Nasarvanji Petit, expressed her objections to the transfer of Parsi lunatics to Poona, stating that it would be inconvenient to relatives of patients residing in Bombay.[83] By August 1899, Bai Avabai had changed her mind, citing an article in the *Times of India,* 27 July 1889, which talked about the extreme unsuitability of the Nowpada site. Now, it was "her particular desire" to see the Parsi wards erected at Yerwada.[84]

From about the 1880s, this desire by some sections of the Parsi elite to separate their community from the natives was reflected in the establishment of entirely separate institutions for the Parsis in Bombay. The Parsi Lying-in Hospital was opened in 1895 on the Esplanade (see Figure 3.11).[85] In 1892, Sir Dinshaw Manockjee Petit set aside a sum of Rs. 5,00,000 for the establishment of a hospital for the Parsi Zoroastrian public. The money was used for other projects to benefit the Parsi community, as there was not enough financial support for this scheme from other members of the community at that time. However, his grandson pursued the scheme and the Parsi General Hospital was opened in 1912.[86] Significantly, this hospital was planned in 1892, before the plague broke out in Bombay. After the plague in 1896, temporary hospitals were established for different communities. However, it was only later in the twentieth century, following the model of the Parsi General Hospital, that other communities also founded separate hospitals for their communities.[87]

RELIGION AND THE PUBLIC REALM

In contrast to the desire for segregation in secular public institutions, people of various castes and religions did interact with each other in common spaces such as the shared sacred spaces of popular religion—the *samadhis* (tombs of Hindu holy men), *kabars* (graves), and *khanaqahs* (major shrines of Muslim *pirs*). The older shared landscape was under threat from a number of quarters. Sections within communities themselves discouraged practices of popular religion. In

Bombay, for example, attention was drawn at a Parsi Panchayat meeting on 4 November 1819 to certain superstitious practices followed by Parsi women that had to be counteracted by issuing certain rules of conduct.[88] The British encouraged Indians to shed caste prejudices; however, their practices of counting and separating in activities such as the census operations fostered and in some cases created hard divisions among various Indian communities. British official categories were disparate, and one had to decide, for example, whether one was a Hindu or a Sikh. Furthermore, through policies such as quotas, they encouraged Indians to maintain these divisions.[89] Such policies discouraged an older shared landscape based on popular religion while at the same time it promoted a new shared secular institutional landscape.

While the British were only too willing to analyze architecture according to religious categories[90] or spatially accommodate different religious communities in separate spaces in hospitals, they were unwilling to accept religious practices in these shared secular public institutions. A bequest left for high-class patients of the lunatic asylum opened the question of the introduction of religious practices into these shared institutions, which the British found unacceptable. This was a general problem for the British across South Asia. Harkisandas Narotumdas, son of the late Bai Putlibai, wrote to the government in 1896 that his mother left Rs. 30,000 in her will to be placed at the disposal of the government and the interest to be used for certain charitable purposes. The main object of the fund was to give financial help to "high-class Hindu inmates" in the Narotumdas Madhavdas Lunatic Asylum at Nowpada, Thana, to be able to conduct their customary religious rites and ceremonies. The balance of the money was to be used according to the discretion of the trustees, to supplement the diet, clothing, and medical needs of high-class Hindus and other pauper patients of the asylum. High-class pauper Hindu patients were to have such articles of clothing, food, and additional medicines as they were accustomed to before they became inmates of the asylum.[91] We may infer that "high-class" refers to "high-caste."

The government asked Narotumdas about the probable income of the endowment, the nature of the ceremonies to which they were to be devoted, and the amount to be spent on nonreligious objects, as well as why he desired government officers to be associated with this trust.[92] Narotumdas replied that the ceremonies referred to were those performed by every orthodox Hindu at home after his morning ablutions. These consisted of worshipping certain idols. In the lunatic asylum, this would not require the building of a temple, but merely the setting apart of a small room where small statues of Withoba, Radha, Krishna, and other deities could be installed and the Hindus could pray. A Brahman would be required to worship the idols every day, and the Brahman cook hired to prepare meals for high-caste Hindus would be able to fulfill this task for an increase in salary. Assuming the income from the endowment to be Rs. 950 to Rs. 1,000 per annum, after certain initial costs, Narotumdas estimated that no more than Rs. 50 per annum would be required for religious purposes. This left the bulk of the income to be applied toward the extra dietary and medical needs of high-caste Hindu patients.[93]

The religious aspect and possible public reaction to the association of government officials with religion led to much discussion. In the words of one official, "Still there is no knowing what the religious world might say to the setting up of idols, however cheap, by Government officers."[94] The possibility of separating out the religious and charitable endowments was debated so that government officers would have no association with the religious endowment. Although it was legal for government officers to be appointed trustees by name, the governor thought, "It would be wiser for government officers to keep clear of these religious trusts."[95]

However, the other issue was the carving out of religious spaces in public buildings, which was unacceptable. In the words of one official:

> We cannot start Hindu temples in public buildings, and whatever Mr. Harkisondas may say "setting apart a small separate room" in the asylum for the erection and consequent worship of idols representing various Hindu deities, where high caste lunatics may say their prayers, is converting that room into a temple. If we admit to this we may be asked to allow other rooms to be used as mosques, fire temples, Jain places of worship and the like.[96]

The government informed Narotumdas that they were unable to accept his offer because they could not make the "necessary arrangements" required for religious observances.[97] Following further negotiations Narotumdas agreed to omit the reference to religious observances and the government accepted his offer of Rs. 30,000 in the new modified form.[98]

One might see the government's rejection of Narotumdas's offer as a triumph of the principles of the Enlightenment, of the separation of church and state and the separation of religion from the public realm—something Indians might be considered reluctant to do due to their spirituality. However, religious spaces and practices were accommodated in many of the hospitals and asylums in both Europe and England in the past.[99] With the Reformation most Roman Catholic churches and monastic buildings were destroyed in England. However, this did not end the place of religion in hospitals and lunatic asylums constructed in England. When St. Thomas's Hospital (founded before 1173) was reconstructed in 1871, the chapel occupied a central location. Chapels were found in many but not all hospitals constructed in English hospitals from 1840 to

1914.[100] However, after 1845, following the instructions of the Commissioners in Lunacy, county pauper lunatic asylums in England were *required* to house a chapel.[101] In India, colonial officials balked at the association of government officials with religion, but religious spaces in England's hospitals and lunatic asylums were hardly an anomaly.

Was religion in medical institutions considered a bad idea in colonial India or was the government just uneasy with the idea of aiding the creation of non-Christian religious spaces in these medical institutions? Wilkins's design for the European General Hospital shows that he placed a chapel in a central location above the west covered carriage porch on the first floor (see Figure 4.4). I take the inclusion of a chapel in his design as an indication that the government would not be opposed to this chapel in principle. The government officials were horrified at the idea of supporting the construction of temples and mosques in the Nowpada asylum but would probably not be opposed to a chapel in a hospital that held Church of England services.

However, religion was not entirely absent in these new secular public institutions. Masonic rituals played a prominent part as early as the 1840s in the foundation-stone-laying ceremonies for the J. J. Hospital. Prominent government officials attended this event including the governor of Bombay, Sir George Arthur, whose son was a Mason though he was not one himself. The historian Vahid Jalil Fozdar reminds us that this reveals "how intertwined the state and Freemasonry had become in Bombay by the late 1840s."[102] As part of the ceremony, a silver plate was buried with the foundation stone. The inscription on the plate read as follows:

> THIS EDIFICE was erected as a testimony of devoted loyalty to THE YOUNG QUEEN OF THE BRITISH ISLES, and of unmingled respect for the just and paternal BRITISH GOVERNMENT IN INDIA; also, in affectionate and patriotic solicitude for the welfare of the poor classes of all races of his countrymen, the British Subjects of Bombay, by SIR JAMSETJEE JEEJEEBHOY, KNIGHT, the first native of India honoured with British Knighthood, who thus hoped to perform a pleasant duty towards his government, his country, and his people and, in solemn remembrance of blessings bestowed, to present this, *his offering of religious gratitude,* to ALMIGHTY GOD, The Father in Heaven of the Christian-the Hindoo-the Mahommedan-and the Parsee, with humble and earnest prayer for His continued care and blessing upon his Children-his Family-his Tribe-and his Country.[103]

This was clearly a religious ceremony where Jeejeebhoy gave the hospital to God as "his offering of religious gratitude." Masonic ideals of an inclusive religion are incorporated by Jeejeebhoy's reference to a universal god of a number of different religious faiths. However, even before god is acknowledged, the building is offered by Jeejeebhoy as a demonstration of secular loyalty.

By the end of the nineteenth century, even as individual buildings from South Asia's architectural heritage were visually dismembered into Hindu and Muslim components and as Bombay's hospitals and lunatic asylums reflected separation on the basis of race, class, or religion, the new public landscape was a shared space. Although religious rituals were disallowed in the new secular public institutions, Masonic rituals were used in the foundation-stone-laying ceremonies of many. Even as practices of shared popular religion were under attack, the Masonic "religion" was a new shared religion—for a selected elite—of all races and religions who forged a brotherhood in the secretive spaces of the Masonic lodge. Even though Bombay's public would never be included in the Masonic brotherhood, the new public spaces of Bombay would reflect the hope that loyalty to the British monarchy and empire could be the new "civil religion" of the public.

CONCLUSION

For the native population of Bombay, the opening of the J. J. Hospital in 1845 was a critical event that forced large numbers of the public from various religious and caste groups to interact with each other in a far more intimate manner. The upper classes—either European or native—were unlikely to resort to the hospital in the second half of the nineteenth century, and if they did, they would require a private room. This chapter shows that both Europeans and native populations found that sharing spaces with people of varied racial, religious, and class backgrounds in common institutions for physical and mental health was difficult.

An examination of Bombay's hospitals and lunatic asylums has revealed a fractured landscape. Patients in the Colaba Lunatic Asylum were classified and divided not only on the basis of gender and mental condition (whether harmless or violent) but also according to race and class. The categories were similar to those in English asylums, but it is the inclusion of natives as a racial category at the bottom of this hierarchy that makes this an imperial space. While Europeans sought to separate themselves from natives, the European General Hospital showed the European community itself to be divided by gender, class, respectability, government departments, military, and seamen. Far from a monolithic community, the fractures showcased spatial divisions that revealed social divisions far greater than those seen in the Colaba Lunatic Asylum. The great number of reserved wards for varied groups was a reflection of colonial dividing practices in Bombay and not those of England, where divisions along the lines of class and gender were seen and where some groups, such as naval seamen, might have their own hospitals. Apart from the separation of wards based on gender and special medical cases, wards for native men in the J.J. Hospital were segregated on the basis of religion. Design of hospitals and lunatic asylums in Bombay revealed a concern with the accommodation of social divisions but not with innovations in hospital design. Far from being specialized, in the second half of the nineteenth century, hospital designs in Bombay were similar to those used for nonmedical public buildings.

The new medical institutions were a product of the joint enterprise, the partnership, between the colonial government and native philanthropists. Native philanthropists who invested in the welfare of their own communities were being asked to help finance institutions run by European experts that served the native public at large. It is hardly surprising that they would have wanted to make special provisions for their own communities. In the second half of the nineteenth century, it was Parsi philanthropists who participated overwhelmingly in the creation of this public realm and who most consistently made special provisions for segregating their community in special wards. The Parsis spatial segregation from natives in the city's native hospitals, and subsequently in the lunatic asylum in Yerwada, contributed to their growing belief that they were racially different from the natives and belonged to the white race even though they were not considered Europeans or housed in the European General Hospital. Their segregation in separate wards in the compounds of native hospitals signified the intermediary racial status the Parsis had achieved, partially through their philanthropy. While the J.J. Hospital maintained separate male wards for different religious groups, this began to break down over time even though food for Muslim and Hindu patients was prepared by separate cooks. Even in the design of the Harkisandas Hospital, apart for the wards reserved for the use of Bania women as stipulated by the donor, Dr. Arnott was against the reservation of wards for any religious group and argued for the use of temporary screens instead. This suggests that in native hospitals, except for the wards paid for by a donor for a specific community—usually, the Parsis— in practice, all other religious communities began to reside in close proximity to each other in hospital wards. The separate community hospitals after the 1896 plague reveal that the tension of sharing space with different groups was hardly resolved.

This tension between fragmentation and cohesion was also apparent in the religious arena. The British encouraged Indians to think of themselves as separate communities, particularly religious communities, and discouraged traditional shared religious practices. While they readily accepted communal segregation, they would not countenance non-Christian religious practices and spaces in lunatic asylums. However, the Masonic rites at foundation-stone-laying ceremonies were those of an elite group—Mason and non-Mason—where new institutions for the common good were dedicated to the god of all religions. While fellow Masons of different races and religions were drawn together in an elite brotherhood, the other elite, many of whom were not Masons, as well as the public-at-large were encouraged to join in the sentiments expressed at these ceremonies where loyalty to the Queen and respect for the British government of India were components of the new "civil religion." This was not a product of forethought or calculation but intrinsic to the ideology of the Masonic elite and performed in public at foundation-stone-laying ceremonies. The public realm produced as a result of the joint venture was, however, a landscape of contradictions where neither the colonial nor the native elite could predict or entirely control the outcomes.

5 An Unforeseen Landscape of Contradictions

ON THE FACE OF IT, one might conclude that the joint enterprise was extremely successful and the colonial government achieved its aims in directing the native elite to collaborate in the creation of public institutions and an urban vision of Bombay that the former desired. However, as demonstrated in chapter 4, local donors did not simply respond to the objectives of the government but brought their own agendas and cultural rules to the mix to create innovative solutions to the building of these new public institutions. Local donors used philanthropy to provide special provisions for their own community and, in the case of the Parsis, to alter their racial status. Chapter 3 showed an individual who used the skills and experience gained from designing public buildings to raise money and design modern hospitals and sanitary housing for his own community. In other words, the joint enterprise also resulted in unexpected outcomes to create a landscape of contradictions.

Moving from a focus in the first four chapters on the implementation of the joint enterprise, this chapter concentrates on its unforeseen consequences to explore the contradictions that troubled this landscape. The intersection of the joint enterprise and the racial policies of the colonial regime created unstable social and spatial hierarchies. Hierarchies of race, community, class, and nationality intersected with space in Bombay to produce unstable identities where an individual could have a privileged status in one space and be denied entry into particular institutions in another space. Thus members of the wealthy Parsi elite who participated in the joint enterprise by constructing palatial institutions for the general public were prohibited from seeking medical aid at the European

General Hospital, a privilege granted to members of their hired help if they were of the right race or nationality.

The construction of the joint public realm was seen by the colonial regime as a division of responsibilities between the government and the local elite. The joint nature of this enterprise was illustrated by names, foundation-stone plaques, sculptural medallions, and busts or statues with which both the governing and native elite sought to advertise contributions. At the same time, especially in the case of medical institutions, we find that these were continually expanded as each community attempted to make special provisions for their own care. In the last chapter we saw that the new public landscape was a fractured landscape. As far as possible, Europeans created institutions that were separate from those for the new entity, the native public. However, an examination of Bombay's hospitals and lunatic asylums in the last chapter revealed that fault lines ran through these institutions as well. Even though these were thought to be public institutions shared by various groups, we saw spaces where populations tried to carve out separate spaces for themselves, creating a landscape of contradictions.

Who owned this public landscape of institutions and public spaces? As a result of joint enterprise, the city of Bombay was transformed in the second half of the nineteenth century, which might signify the colonial regime's success in transforming the city. As local elites contributed vast sums toward the construction of this new joint public realm, they and their descendents attempted to control its current and future use; yet we find that the colonial government, acting on behalf of the public good, worked to limit the claims of elite philanthropists. However, the enormous philanthropic output of the Parsi community made many visitors question whether it was the Parsis, rather than the colonial regime, who constructed Bombay. Furthermore, Parsis attributed their generosity to Zoroastrian religious principles rather than lessons learned from their British masters. In the colonial context it is normal to expect that the ruling race received the best facilities. Undoubtedly the colonial elite did. However, the ruling race consisted of many different groups and classes. How did most Europeans fare in a city built on native philanthropy? How did this compare to the care received by Parsis? If native philanthropists, in partnership with the colonial government, took care of the native population, who was supposed to take care of the Europeans?

In the previous chapter we saw how the joint public realm was compromised as issues of caste, race, and religion led to the division of its hospitals and lunatic asylums. In this chapter we examine colonial Bombay's public institutions at the turn of the twentieth century, where we see class make its appearance as a new category of differentiation between groups. Despite the divisions in the public realm, the shared spaces helped in the construction of an "Indian" identity in contrast to Europeans who had their own institutions. At the turn of the century, attempts influenced by the spirit of "nationalism" tried to bring advanced scientific education and control of public institutions to Indians.

By the early twentieth century, new medical and scientific institutions supported by native philanthropy sought to exclude European expertise. At the turn of the century, the old joint enterprise between the colonial government and native elite was on the wane. An unexpected outcome of the joint enterprise was that native philanthropy would increasingly be applied toward the nurture of native expertise.

UNSTABLE SOCIAL AND SPATIAL HIERARCHIES

Many groups, but particularly intermediary groups such as the Parsis, were subject to unstable social hierarchies. By this I mean that their position in the hierarchy was subject to change over time and dependent on the criteria applied by the colonial elite. In 1902, all the native patients were moved to the Nowpada asylum. At the same time that the Parsis were staying in the Colaba Lunatic Asylum with Europeans and Baghdadi Jews, *only* Eurasians who had adopted European habits were allowed to stay with them.[1] Ann Laura Stoler's work on French Indochina and the Netherlands Indies reveals that even when race was left out of legal categories, cultural distinctions were still made (using such criteria as skills in a specific European language, environment of one's childhood, etc.). Stoler's argument that the origins of cultural racism lie in the colonial era apply to the British Empire as well.[2] In Bombay, as the case of the Eurasians shows, cultural racism flourished; one had to be Western in one's habits, as many in the Parsi community had become. Whereas the Parsis were advancing, the less prosperous Eurasian community in Bombay found itself sliding further down the racial hierarchy.

Hierarchies were not only unstable over time, they were also differentiated across space. "Unstable spatial hierarchies" implies that a particular group may be higher up in the hierarchy in some places and lower in others. Goans, for example, were migrants from the Portuguese dominion of Goa in Western India and were often products of the intermarriage of Portuguese and Indians. As Portuguese citizens, they were foreign nationals and received treatment at the European General Hospital. It is possible that they were also treated here because they were Christians. Assuming that institutions established for the colonial group were the highest in the hierarchy created, then Goans, by gaining admission in that space, might be considered to be higher in the hierarchy than the Parsis. Yet in other spaces in Bombay this was not so. Parsis and Goans shared a close relationship, where the Goans acted as cooks and ayahs for well-to-do Parsis. In 1886, the great Parsi reformer Behramji Malabari (1853–1912) made the point that many educated Parsi girls were becoming strangers to domestic work with the result that in every Parsi quarter in the town there was a colony of Goan ayahs, cooks, and "boys." He estimated that more than 60 percent of the children of prosperous Parsis were nursed and cared for by Goan women.[3] In other arenas in the city, the wealthy and influential Parsi community was certainly considered to be higher up in the hierarchy than Goans. This example merely points to one of the many contradictions in colonial hierarchies.

In colonial India's bustling cities, such as Bombay, Calcutta, and Madras, it was not always easy for the European racial elite to maintain their social and moral prestige. There was no room for spacious civil stations and cantonments. Lower-class Europeans were often found in cities and were an embarrassment to the European elite, while Eurasians had become an uncomfortable reminder of ties between Indians and Europeans. From the 1790s, Eurasians were excluded from appointments in the civil service and commissioned ranks of the army, as the British tried to distance them. British officials often referred to Eurasians as "half-castes," while Eurasian spokesmen preferred the term "Indo-British." In the twentieth century, they were allowed to appropriate the term "Anglo-Indian," which had formerly been used to refer to the British in India.[4] These hierarchies of class and race were reflected in the Colaba Lunatic Asylum, where British officers were separated from lower-class soldiers. By the early twentieth century, the ruling race made it clear that it would not tolerate Eurasians who had "gone native" (see Figure 4.3).

DIVIDING RESPONSIBILITIES AND THE CONTROL OF THE PUBLIC REALM

The joint venture in the creation of medical and educational institutions meant a division of responsibilities between the colonial government and native philanthropists. The government was unwilling to fund institutions for natives unilaterally. The last chapter showed how philanthropists came forward with proposals to fund a section of or an entire medical institution; this chapter extends the discussion on native philanthropy to show how the government both enlisted participation in founding a particular type of institution or constructing additions and articulated expectations of native philanthropists. Under such circumstances it is hardly surprising that native philanthropists tried to make special provisions for their communities, arrange for visual reminders of themselves, and, more important, came to believe that they or their descendents had a right to control the future uses of the institutions they helped found. By naming, placing sculptures of donors, and restricting future developments, philanthropists turned public spaces into memorials for private citizens. While this joint enterprise led many philanthropists to make special provisions for their community, one of the unexpected outcomes of the joint enterprise was that native philanthropists came to expect that they or their descendents had perpetual and private rights over public property.

Dividing Responsibilities

The implicit assumption of the division of responsibilities between the government and the philanthropic native elite was clearly illustrated in 1886 in the government's response to Dr. Edith Pechey's proposal for a new building to be erected in the compound of the Cama Hospital. This building was to accommodate a lecture room and quarters for the resident house surgeon and six resident pupils. To this suggestion the government's firm reply was that it was not up to the government to provide quarters for resident pupils and trusted that a "public-spirited" member of the native public would come forward:

> The Governor in Council would observe that whilst quarters for resident pupils are doubtless desirable it is not, as already stated, for Government to provide them. In Calcutta such quarters have been furnished by private liberality and the Governor in Council trusts that the example set by a native lady in Calcutta will be followed in Bombay where public-spirited and philanthropic munificence is never lacking.[5]

Clearly, native philanthropists were to provide for the accommodation of native pupils, who were not the government's responsibility. In contrast, the government seriously considered the two other requirements—accommodation for the resident surgeon, probably a European, and a lecture room—as necessities for the smooth functioning of the Cama Hospital.

The government made it known that it wanted to build a certain kind of institution and then looked toward some public-spirited person to respond with an offer. To return to what was perhaps the earliest example of the joint partnership, we need go no further than the foundation of the Jamsetjee Jeejeebhoy Hospital (J. J. Hospital) and Grant Medical College (see Figure 4.6). In 1837, Sir Robert Grant, governor of Bombay between 1835 and his death in 1838, made the recommendation that a medical school be established as well as a native hospital, which would form a part of the former institution. "About the same time, or shortly afterwards," Jeejeebhoy, arguably the wealthiest merchant prince at that time, offered to assist in the erection and endowment of a native hospital.[6]

From at least the early 1880s, it was clear that the obstetric hospital attached to the J. J. Hospital, founded in 1851 by Jeejeebhoy, was inadequate. Containing only two wards sufficient for sixteen beds, more accommodation was required for patients and hospital servants. The inadequate accommodation for patients reflected great changes in attitude as well. Whereas earlier native women were reluctant to seek medical aid in hospitals, by 1885 the hospital had to refuse admission to many patients owing to lack of accommodation or the staff's inability to cope with the numbers.[7] Aware of this problem, the government dealt with the subject of a new obstetric hospital in an 1883 Government Resolution to the Surgeon General in which two points were made. First, while a children's hospital would be of great benefit, its "promotion must depend on private liberality." Second, both the governing body of the hospital and Grant Medical College should make "the wants of these institutions publicly known in hopes of evoking charitable aid."[8] In the last chapter we examined Harkisandas Narotumdas's offer to the government in 1885, on behalf of his mother, Bai Putlibai, and other members of his family for the building of a fifty-bed hospital to treat women's diseases and children. This offer is likely to have been a response to this public call.

These cases are illustrative of the methods employed by the government to inform the wealthy native elite that it had certain plans in mind that required their finances to bring to fruition, such as new institutions, buildings for old institutions, and additions to a complex of interrelated institutions. There was no question that wealthy natives had to pay for the institutions that the colonial government wished to set up for the good of native populations. Usually native philanthropists paid for the buildings while the government paid for the maintenance of the institutions, which were to be staffed, at all senior positions, by doctors, surgeons, professors, and other professionals of European descent.

Donors also offered property or money to the government, asking that the property or sum be applied to some specific or general charitable purpose. This is the case of the money donated to the government by mill owner Sir Currimbhoy Ebrahim, Baronet, in 1906, for the establishment of an institution in Bombay to benefit the poor. In 1910, Messrs. Stanley Reed and Fazulbhoy Currimbhoy wrote a letter to the Private Secretary asking that a sum of Rs. 100,354, constituting the balance of the Sir Currimbhoy Ebrahim Entertainment Fund, be applied to the King Edward Memorial Fund for the erection of a hospital on the north of the island. As this hospital was designed to meet the needs of the industrial and poor classes, it would fulfill the terms under which Sir Currimbhoy Ebrahim's money was handed over to the government. It was also pointed out that the baronet approved of the scheme. This offer was accepted.[9]

It should not be assumed that donors merely responded to government intentions or that the public had no role in the foundation of these institutions. A movement begun in 1882 by G. T. Kittredge and S. S. Bengali, urging that medical assistance be given to Indian women, led to the foundation of the Cama Hospital, the Bai Motlibai Obstetric Hospital, and the Sir Dinshaw Manockjee Petit Hospital for Women and Children. Similarly, the Bai Sakarbai Dinshaw Petit Hospital for Animals, opened in 1882, owed its existence in large part to the activities of the Bombay Society for the Prevention of Cruelty to Animals. Sir Dinshaw M. Petit was the major, but not the only, donor, and this hospital was named after his wife (see Figure 2.11).[10]

Special Provisions and Visual Reminders

The donors, whether they were Parsi, Hindu, or Muslim, made special provisions for members of their own community, thereby creating a divided public realm. The colonial government certainly seemed to have no objection to this inequality. The attempt to meet special provisions made by donors or representatives for members of their own community affected the architecture of these complexes. The complexes were never entirely complete because buildings were always being added, as in the case of the J. J. Hospital complex. In 1894, Kazi Shaik Mohamed Murghoy, the kazi of Bombay and also president of the Majlise Taide Amvat Lavarisie Islamie, Bombay, asked the government for a piece of land in the compound of the J. J. Hospital on which to erect a separate mortuary for Muslims. This separate mortuary, he argued, was required for religious reasons and was to be built at the expense of the Muslim community. He also pointed out that the Parsis had a separate accommodation for their dead.[11] In 1896, the government agreed to build one combined mortuary with separate rooms for Christians, Hindus, and Muslims at the government's expense, as the medical authorities opposed building separate mortuaries at various points around the hospital (Figure 5.1).[12]

These institutions—results of the joint partnership between a donor or donors and the colonial government—contained in their architecture the signatures of all the participants. Here, I argue, the native public was left out, ignoring the fact that the government used money extracted from the public through taxes, tithes, and tolls to fund these institutions. The colonial government put its stamp on these buildings through the use of Western architectural styles and the selection of specific sites, such as the Esplanade, where they became part of the new Bombay built by the colonial regime. In the Esplanade in particular, they sat near, beside, or had a view of government buildings or prominent public spaces. Buildings representing new public institutions were often designed

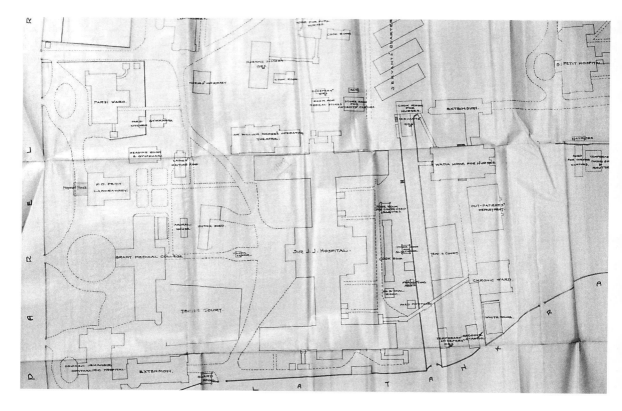

FIGURE 5.1. J. J. Hospital compound, 1907, detail. Note the Parsi ward and Parsi kitchen in the top left corner and the Parsi mortuary, a small structure behind the J. J. Hospital building on the lower right of the plan. Courtesy Maharashtra State Archives, Bombay. Photograph by author, 1998.

by British architects and engineers and followed Western styles of architecture. Plaques, conveniently placed, highlighted the joint nature of these institutions by specifying the sums expended by the government and donors. Through the practices of naming, the donors would alert the public of their philanthropic activities. The donors inserted themselves into the architecture as their masklike faces and coats of arms adorned the facades, blending well with the Victorian architecture, from which strange creatures appeared to leap and spiral towers appeared to disappear into the sky (Figure 5.2). Sometimes their statues appeared or their busts found a place on the grounds of the buildings or in their foyers (see Figure 2.13). At least one statue became the object of veneration and devotion. The statue of Jeejeebhoy, later the first baronet, at the J. J. Hospital has long been garlanded and prayed to by grateful patients. The statue became part of the lore of the building's inhabitants, as student doctors joked about how the statue had heard many a secret that had been whispered in the corridors.

Private Claims over Public Spaces

Donors attempted to keep some kind of control, directly and through their heirs, over the naming, growth, expansion, or future of these institutions, as

Narotumdas tried to do in the case of the obstetric hospital, which was not built (see chapter 4). Another example comes from the offer of a piece of land, known as Dick's Oart, to the government in 1863 from the family of the late Jeejeebhoy. Dick's Oart lay just to the north of the Parsi ward and the compound of the J. J. Hospital. The offer came with certain conditions, the first being that the land being gifted be used only for the extension of the J. J. Hospital or to increase the effectiveness of the Grant Medical College, both institutions being associated with the late first baronet. The second condition was as follows:

> 2nd.—That any buildings which it may be necessary to construct hereafter on this ground, or in the compound of the Hospital, in connection with the purposes before mentioned, shall be built either by Government or by a member of our family, no stranger being allowed this privilege, it being our wish to preserve in all its integrity the right of the Hospital to the designation which it has always hitherto deservedly enjoyed of the Jamsetjee Jejeebhoy Hospital.[13]

Through this stipulation, Jeejeebhoy's family was attempting to keep the J. J. Hospital and its environs as a permanent memorial to him. However, the second stipulation caused considerable concern. John Peet, the principal of Grant Medical College, was against accepting the site offered on these terms. He

FIGURE 5.2. Scott, McClelland & Company, David Sassoon Mechanics' Institute and Library, Bombay, completed in 1870, detail of facade. A sculpture medallion of David Sassoon is set in the tympanum above the arch of the front facade of the entry porch. No members of the Baghdadi Jewish Sassoon family currently reside in Bombay, but the family name is still used in association with the many institutions they founded. Photograph by author, 1998.

showed that while the government contributed Rs. 146,840 toward the cost of construction of the hospital, Jeejeebhoy gave Rs. 58,521 toward the same. Similarly, Jeejeebhoy's endowment of Rs. 100,000 yielded an annual income of Rs. 6,000 per year and was paid toward the maintenance of the hospital, while the government's contribution for the same year was Rs. 52,219. In short, the government made the major contribution toward both the cost of building and maintaining the institution.[14]

Peet pointed out that the government had purchased the ground on which the hospital and Grant College stood. He felt that if a great need was felt to erect new buildings on these grounds, this stipulation meant that no individual, municipality, or member of the public would be allowed to help *even if* the government or members of the Jeejeebhoy family were unable or unwilling to erect such buildings. Given that the major expense of the building and its maintenance was borne by the government, the Jeejeebhoy family were not "entitled to claim as a right that which the munificent and sole founders of some of the large hospitals in England would hardly have been entitled to, and which they certainly have in no instant demanded." The government was being offered a piece of land that was of no use except for location of buildings. In the bargain, the Jeejeebhoy family was placing restrictions on what and who could build on Dick's Oart *and* ground the *government already had* in its possession, namely, the ground on which the hospital and college was built and paid for by the government.[15]

If the government accepted these terms, then even if the hospital were completely rebuilt by the government, descendents of Jeejeebhoy family would continue to exert some influence over the hospital. The government's final decision was a compromise. It accepted the offer of Dick's Oart and in return said that the needs of the Jeejeebhoy family could be met by setting the compound of the Grant Medical College off from that on which the J. J. Hospital stood. The government guaranteed that nothing would be built or added to the grounds within the hospital compound or Dick's Oart except by the government or the Jeejeebhoy family. However, if the family declined to share the expense of additions or extensions, the government could accept aid from the municipal commissioners or other private parties.[16]

Here, the government can be said to have acted largely on behalf of the public interest rather than the private interest of the donors. Although it relinquished some of its control over public property it already owned, namely, the ground on which the hospital stood, to the dictates of a donor family, the latter was ultimately only allowed control over what was built if it agreed to pay for it.

The case of the J. J. Hospital is interesting because institutional buildings, particularly hospitals, have to be renovated or torn down and rebuilt to meet technological changes and new ideas in hospital design. This is not to minimize the contributions of philanthropists such as Jeejeebhoy but to argue that, unless the renovation or rebuilding is paid for by another philanthropist, it is the government, acting on behalf of the public, that bears the major costs for such an institution. Although the government may receive some recognition and the public is forgotten, it is the original philanthropist who is permanently memorialized.

The J. J. Hospital was opened in May 1845 at the joint expense of the East India Company and Sir Jamsetjee Jeejeebhoy (the first baronet, 1783–1859) for the relief of the native poor. Examining the footprint of the original hospital building, one can decipher an H-shaped plan where the middle horizontal bar of the H extended a little beyond the vertical bars on either side. The middle horizontal bar also showed a prominent bulge in the middle for the entrance porches and related spaces (see Figure 5.1). In its plan, the J. J. Hospital resembled the eighteenth-century country residences of British nobility. These country residences usually had symmetrical plans, often drawing on letters of the alphabet such as H, U, or C. After the Reformation, it was the monarch, nobility, or wealthy citizens, rather than the church, who constructed hospitals for the care of the sick and poor. Bourgeois and noble philanthropists constructed hospitals for the care of the poor, and these buildings mimicked familiar forms of palaces and country houses.[17] The plan for the first J. J. Hospital building follows this tradition of copying palaces and country homes in Britain.

An engraving of a painting by W. J. Huggins from 1843, two years before the hospital was opened, reveals the native hospital framed by the foreground consisting of a tropical landscape with palm trees on one side and rocks and vegetation on the other (Figure 5.3). Leading from the foreground to the middle ground is a curved dirt road dotted with various native human and animal figures: a woman carrying an earthen pot on her head, native cattle, figures carrying a litter, and smaller figures near the pool of water to the right and near the building. These are generic figures that provide scale and point to the Indian context. The focus of the middle ground is the gleaming new hospital building. To its right, there seems to be water, and there are hills in the background. This is a picturesque view of the hospital, which speaks to a vision of progress embodied in the new native hospital that is rising amid a still underdeveloped landscape. The hospital was a gothic building with pitched roofs with gabled ends. It had battlemented parapets, in other words, a parapet with higher and lower parts that continued on the gable roofs. The gables were framed by two prominent buttresses that soared above the roofline. The building facades were regularly interrupted by tall, arched windows. The Parsi ward is the only remaining section of the J. J. Hospital whose architecture echoes the original building. Here,

FIGURE 5.3. Mr. W. J. Huggins, Jamsetjee Jejeebhoy Hospital, or the Bombay Native Hospital, Bombay, opened in 1845, engraving of a painting by Huggins published on 1 January 1843. Courtesy The Trustees, Chhatrapati Shivaji Maharaj Vastu Sangrahalaya, Mumbai.

the buttresses are chamfered to reduce the depth as they go up to the next stage and finally terminate in gablets (see Figure 4.7). It is likely that the original building had similar detailing.

Certainly by 1909 there were schemes for the reconstruction of J. J. Hospital (Figure. 5.4). The plan of the 1909 reconstruction shows the footprint of the old hospital in dashed lines indicating that the hospital would have to be completely torn down. The clear outline with dark color infill shows the footprint of the new hospital that was to be built at the same site. While the plan of the old hospital reminded one of an elite residence, the proposed plan had separate ward pavilions and spaces for other functions. The "pavilion plan" hospital was first formulated in the 1850s and was refined by architects and others over the next forty years, remaining an influential model until the 1930s.[18]

Whereas the plan for the first J. J. Hospital building follows the tradition of copying palaces and country homes in Britain, the 1909 plan shows how sanitary concerns and the practice of medicine were now prioritized. I do not know if the hospital was reconstructed according to this plan; however, subsequently

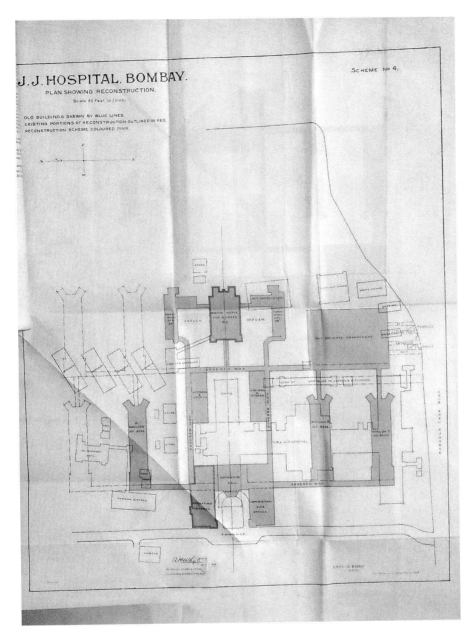

FIGURE 5.4. Scheme 4 for the reconstruction of the J. J. Hospital, 1909. Courtesy Maharashtra State Archives, Bombay. Photograph by author, 1998.

the original building was torn down and replaced by a new building. The government probably paid most of or the entire cost of rebuilding, although the hospital continues to serve as a memorial to the first baronet.

Since the second half of the nineteenth century, philanthropists—private persons and families—exerted undue ownership or control over public institutions and public property, forcing one to assume that the government had no major objection to special privileges being accorded to a particular community.

FIGURE 5.5. George Wittet, Cowasji Jehangir Hall, Bombay, circa 1911–20. Designed in the Renaissance Revival style, the hall is flanked on either side by the Royal Institute of Science. In 1996, the interior of the hall was renovated by Romi Khosla, an architect from Delhi, to house the Bombay branch of the National Gallery of Modern Art. Photograph by author, 1999.

This is seen also in the case of the circular Sir Cowasji Jehangir Public Hall, located at the prominent Wellington Fountain junction, just southwest of the Fort district (Figure 5.5). A plaque informs us that the Sir Cowasji Jehangir Public Hall was made possible by a gift of Rs. 400,000 from Sir Cowasji Jehangir, Baronet, born in 1853. The foundation stone of the building was laid on 5 April 1911 by Lord Sydenham, governor of Bombay. The architect, George Wittet, F.R.I.B.A, designed the building (part of the Royal Institute of Science block of buildings). Wittet designed many other buildings in Bombay, including the Prince of Wales Museum (see Figure 2.9).

Another plaque gives us information about the intended uses of the hall. It gives new meaning to the term "public" hall as it has a special provision for the use of the Parsi community to which Sir Cowasji belonged:

**THE SIR COWASJI JEHANGIR
PUBLIC HALL**

IS AVAILABLE FOR PUBLIC LECTURES, PRIZE GIVINGS AND PUBLIC DAYS OF THE ROYAL INSTITUTE OF SCIENCE, FOR EXAMINATIONS OF THE UNIVERSITY OF BOMBAY, FOR ALL EDUCATIONAL, SCIENTIFIC, LITERARY AND SOCIAL PURPOSES, FOR CONCERTS, PRIZE EXHIBITIONS, LECTURES AND ART AND EDUCATIONAL EXHIBITIONS, FOR PUBLIC MEETINGS SUCH AS

ARE HELD IN THE TOWN HALL AND FOR ALL MEETINGS OF THE PARSIS
CALLED BY THE TRUSTEES OF THE PARSI PANCHAYAT BY PARSI JUSTICES
OF THE PEACE OR ANY OTHER MEETING OF THE PARSIS CALLED BY ANY
RESPONSIBLE BODY ON ANY DAY OF THE WEEK INCLUSIVE OF SUNDAY

One might assume that this hall could not be reserved for meetings of other communities, such as Muslims or Hindus. In this manner, the donor allowed the hall to be used for certain specific activities of the public and for public meetings of a specific public—the Parsi community.

The donors of Bombay's institutions fared better than the builders of Bombay's tanks and wells—many of the institutions they helped establish still exist today. However, just as the decisive sealing of wells displayed the government's ultimate control over this landscape, the government exhibited a similar ruthlessness and ownership in this new era. When necessary, and with the donor's permission, institutions were moved or used for different purposes than originally intended. The donors had little choice but to accede to the government's demands. In 1890, acting contrary to the terms of the agreement they had drawn up with Rustomji Jamshedji Jeejeebhoy, they closed the leper ward attached to the J. J. Hospital. The daughters of the late donor protested to the government against the closure. The government said the applicants "had no right to call government to account" and that in place of the leper ward the government was providing maintenance at the Framji Edalji Allbless Leper Home of more lepers than the ward housed.[19] But as one newspaper pointed out, the troubling part of the government decision was that in the case of a trust, nobody had the right to ask the government for an explanation.[20] It was clear who ultimately controlled this public domain. In colonial Bombay, it was up to the colonial regime to protect the uses and transformation of public buildings for the good of the native public.

PARSIS AND EUROPEANS IN THE CONTRADICTORY LANDSCAPE OF PHILANTHROPY

In his Bombay guidebook, Lieutenant-Colonel H. A. Newell calls Bombay the "adopted country of the Parsis."[21] It is not entirely coincidental that the Parsis played such a prominent role in Bombay, because as a group they made early links with the British, forging what might be called a special relationship.[22] They explicitly attribute their rise from obscurity to the arrival of Europeans and rise of the British, winning many titles for their association with the British and loyalty to the British Crown.[23]

Surat was the most important seaport in Western India since about the beginning of the sixteenth century, forming the nucleus of trade for both the

Mughal Empire as well as European trading companies. Parsis migrated to this port from other regions of Gujarat, making it, by the end of the seventeenth and beginning of the eighteenth centuries, the largest settlement of Parsis. Parsis served as middlemen—agents and brokers—who transacted business with the Indian hinterland on behalf of European merchants. Portuguese, French, Dutch, and English factories used Parsis as their chief brokers. Their in-between role served them well here: they had knowledge of Indian languages and at the same time their lack of caste prejudices allowed them more flexibility in doing business with other foreigners. They moved to Bombay under Portuguese rule and migrated in larger numbers when the British were developing Bombay as a center of trade. The British actively encouraged them to do so, giving them land in 1673 for the establishment of their first *dokhma* (tower of silence).[24]

Did the Parsis Build Bombay?

Parsis date their prosperity to their association with the British and the time that they settled in Bombay.[25] In 1872 about 44,091 Parsis resided in Bombay and represented the largest concentration of the Parsi community in any single place. Fifty-seven percent of the Parsis in India, a population of 48,597, resided in Bombay by 1881. By 1901, they numbered 46,231. At that time, the number of Parsis in India was 93,952, so 49 percent of the Parsi population were in Bombay. In both 1911 and 1921, 51 percent of the Parsi population of India resided in Bombay with populations of 50,931 and 52,234 respectively. The number of Parsis in India in 1911 and 1921 were 100,096 and 101,778 respectively.[26]

The Parsis were a fraction of Bombay's population, yet their dominance in the city and their role in the building of it between 1850 and 1918 was out of proportion to their numbers. In 1901, they formed 6 percent of the city's total population of 776,006. Population figures for 1901 give a sense of the number and proportions of various groups in Bombay City (Table 5.1). By the early twentieth century, Bombay appeared to be a city built and dominated by Parsis rather than colonial rule. The journalist Sidney Low, accompanying the Prince and Princess of Wales on their tour of India in 1906, had this to say about the Parsis and the building of Bombay:

> In the business world of Bombay the Parsis hold a position out of all proportion to their numbers. . . .
>
> They are a mere handful, though it is hard for the European, in his novitiate in India, to believe it. There are only some 45,000 of them, men, women, and children, in Bombay, and well under a hundred thousand in

TABLE 5.1.   Population of different religious groups in Bombay, 1901

Religious group	Population	Percentage of the total population in Bombay City
Hindus	508,608	65.5
Jains	14,248	1.8
Muslims	155,747	20.1
Christians	45,176	5.8
European Christians	12,200	1.5
Eurasian Christians	3,258	0.4
Native Christians	29,645	3.8
Parsi	46,231	6.0
Jews	5,357	0.7
Other	712	0.09
Total	776,006	99.99

Source: Adapted from *Gazetteer of Bombay City and Island,* 1:272–73.

the whole world, including Piccadilly. The fact seems incredible; for at the first aspect Bombay gives the impression of a city of Parsis. They are visible, they and their work, everywhere. The wealth of the place is largely in their hands, so is the manufacturing industry and the real property. Parsi names are painted on the gateposts of many of those desirable suburban residences from which European tenants have been banished. If the eye falls on a handsome public building, it is quite likely to be a Parsi hospital, or a Parsi convalescent home, or the college founded by one wealthy fire-worshipper, or the monument presented to the city by another. Parsis hold most of the shares in the largest of the cotton-mills, whose tall chimneys are blackening the sunlit air all over the northern quarter of the island; the big new hotel, whose imposing sea-front greets the voyager with his first view of Bombay, belongs to a family of Parsi financiers whose names are known in the West as well as the East.[27]

Low, writing in 1905–6, says that "if the eye falls on a handsome public building," it is likely to be a public building built by a Parsi for Parsis or for the public at large. Was Bombay built by the Parsis or the British? Even as the Parsis helped construct the city, they also created an image of themselves as a philanthropic, educated community, Western and progressive in outlook, with high standards of living. In other words, the Parsis contributed toward the building of Bombay and were, in turn, also re-created through this process.

Parsi religious attitudes, which valued the accumulation of wealth and charitable acts, found their fullest expression after the growth of the economy of Bombay in the nineteenth century. According to the Zoroastrian religion, wealth is positive and entails certain social obligations. While enjoying the fruits of wealth, the rich are supposed to help other humans who can then also do "good deeds," which are attributable to the original benefactors as if they were the authors of these second-generation "good deeds."[28] As W. S. Caine observed in his handbook for European travelers, "The 'good deeds' of the Parsis are in evidence all over Bombay, and are by no means confined to their own people."[29]

The Parsis, for instance, in the Parsi-run newspaper *Rast Goftar* in 1862, criticized the Hindus and Muslims for the superstitious nature of their charities, contrasting them to "civilized charities" such as the building of libraries, schools, and dispensaries. In the case of Hindus, these charities included funeral ceremonies, feeding Brahmans, and charitable endowments for distributing food to "idlers and vagabonds" or "vagabond Brahmins." The Muslims spent money on visiting the Ka'ba in Arabia. In contrast, the Parsis had no sacred places of pilgrimage or a powerful priesthood on which to waste their money.[30]

Thus the Parsis, through their religious principles, were supremely well placed in the nineteenth century to exemplify the British government's preferred forms of useful charities. The nineteenth-century historian of the Parsis D. F. Karaka was not shy to point out that Bombay's reputation for generosity and charity derived mainly from the Parsis. While Parsis had always been charitable to all communities, all other charitable Hindu and Muslim philanthropists, with the notable exceptions of the Jain millionaire Premchand Raichand and the Bhatia millionaire Gokuldas Tejpal, had restricted their benefactions to charities for the benefit of their own community.[31] Until the turn of the twentieth century, this statement continued to be true. However, Parsi dominance of philanthropic activities assisted in the creation of a divided public realm. Most of the nineteen wards in medical institutions in the Bombay Presidency that were paid for by Parsis were for the exclusive use of members of the community.[32]

What about the Europeans?

In a colonial situation, it is easy to make the assumption that the ruling race enjoyed the best facilities, accommodations, opportunities, and medical treatment. However, not all the Europeans residing in Bombay were elite or privileged. It was predominantly the poorer sections of the population, including the Europeans, who resorted to the city's public hospitals and dispensaries. In a city where most public institutions were a product of private philanthropy and government spending, one needs to examine how this impacted the Europeans. Were they dependent on private philanthropy as well? How did the racially segregated landscape of Bombay hospitals actually function? Did the Europeans get the best treatment? In what ways were they privileged? In other words, what happened to Europeans in a city where the colonial regime expected the local elite to help in the creation of new public institutions for the use of their own community and other communities?

While philanthropists were erecting grand new hospital buildings for the native public, the Europeans did not get a new hospital until the last decade of the nineteenth century. The Europeans had their own hospital that was known as the European General Hospital in the mid-nineteenth century. A hospital for Europeans existed from about 1677, while it was only in about 1809 that a native general hospital was begun.[33] In about 1824, a new building for the European General Hospital was erected on Hornby Road for the garrison and the European civil population; it was occupied until 1860, when the medical authorities condemned it. James Maclean refers to this as a "wretched structure." The government decided to sell the land and use the money toward the establishment of a new hospital on the Cooperage, a scheme that never materialized for sanitary reasons. In the meantime, the European Artillery barracks in Fort George was used as a temporary hospital from about 1861. Maclean says that it was altered at a cost of £20,000 to an "airy, but not attractive looking hospital." The government, the Port Trust, and the Committee of the European General Hospital decided that proper hospital accommodation was required for Europeans, resulting finally in the establishment of a new hospital, but it was not until 1886 that plans were made for a new hospital, resulting in the laying of the foundation stone of St. George's Hospital in 1889. This building was completed in 1892, for male patients, and the old building was used as the women's ward (Figure 5.6). In 1907, additions were completed which included a new hospital for women, an obstetric ward, a children's ward, and several special wards. Gender, class, and nature of infection were the criteria used to organize the patients. Male and female patients occupied separate buildings. The lower floor of the buildings was reserved for patients who received free treatment, obviously of the lower classes. Located along the edge of the hospital compound were separate buildings for patients suffering from infectious diseases or delirium tremens.[34] In the second half of the nineteenth century, impressive hospital buildings were constructed for the native public while, for most of this period, Europeans had to make do with a renovated barracks building. In contrast to the public hospitals for natives, the site of the new St. George's Hospital, behind the new G.I.P. Railway Victoria Terminus, was of no public significance, and the building was plain.

Whereas entry to the European General Hospital was restricted to certain groups, such as Europeans, Eurasians, Indo-Portuguese, and Baghdadi

FIGURE 5.6. European General Hospital, circa 1895. From Furneaux, *Glimpses of India*, 233.

Jews, the native general hospitals were used by all groups. The following tragic story illustrates the way the principle of separation functioned in practice. On 8 September 1886, an unemployed railway employee of European or Eurasian descent by the name of Charles Henry Couzens took his ailing twenty-seven-year-old wife Margaret Louisa Couzens to the J. J. Hospital, eight days after she had delivered a healthy baby. Charles Couzens had been unemployed for eleven months and lived in Kamathipura, a neighborhood in what was supposed to be the native town. Supported by the Girgaum Mission Charity Fund, he was too poor to send for a doctor to treat his wife at home. His wife was admitted to the J. J. Hospital when she first fell sick and, despite her husband's entreaties, insisted on returning home after a few hours, refusing to remain in a hospital with natives. On the morning of September 11, he took her to the European General Hospital and was advised by Dr. Baker to take her to the Cama Hospital as there was no room for her in that hospital. He took his wife both there and to the Jafar Suleman Dispensary that day and the next day in an attempt to get her admitted into the Cama Hospital. He finally managed to do so on September 13. This delay became the subject of an inquiry after Margaret Couzens died of tetanus later that day.[35] Poor Europeans and Eurasians used institutions founded by native philanthropists, and if they wanted treatment they had no choice but to overcome their racial prejudices. Margaret Couzens could not and refused to remain at the J.J. Hospital. She paid for it with her life.

A newspaper article in 1913 drew attention to the inadequacies of St. George's Hospital, highlighting the particular situation of the European community in Bombay and the special relationship of the hospital to this community. The timing of this article coincided with the arrival of the new governor whose attention they wished to solicit. The article made a number of points about St. George's Hospital. It was a state hospital and not a philanthropic institution, and the staff was mainly honorary. The hospital was maintained by public funds, the medical officers drew salaries according to their rank, and the European public subscribed half the cost of the nursing establishment. At the same time, it was not an entirely free hospital. There were some wards where the government provided free treatment, while in others patients paid a scale of fees outlined by the government. Because there were no nursing homes in Bombay, the hospital answered the needs of large numbers of different classes, including people in Bombay: the *mofussil* who needed to use the hospital despite being able to afford medical treatment in their own homes; young men who had come to India on modest incomes; patients who could not be treated in their homes, including women who lived in private homes but needed to be treated for serious illnesses; and the increasing numbers who lived in flats or the chummery system.[36]

The article painted the medical treatment received at St. George's Hospital in an unflattering light, especially as compared to J.J. Hospital. The three groups of hospitals in Bombay in 1913 were St. George's Hospital, the Gokuldas Tejpal Hospital (G.T. Hospital) and J.J. and its allied hospitals. Each was distinct and separate. The J.J. group was the largest hospital center, having the greatest facilities for research and specialization and was the training center for the Presidency as a whole. The doctors and surgeons were regarded as being at the top of their field. In contrast, in St. George's Hospital, the physician in charge was supposed to be a physician, surgeon, gynecologist, obstetrician, and ophthalmologist in addition to his responsibilities as an administrator. The article complained that the patients at St. George's were cut off from the best medical services at the disposal of the government. Although the government had established a list of consultants who could be called on at any hospital, in practice this rarely happened as most people were unaware that these consultants were available.[37]

It is ironic that colonial policies of separation themselves produced a situation that was disadvantageous to the ruling race. Clearly the native population was receiving better medical treatment in institutions partially funded by their own philanthropy. It was the close proximity of various institutions in the

J. J. Hospital compound that made it such a center of specialization and expertise. The native press had little sympathy with the agitation mounted by the Anglo-Indian community. One paper described St. George's Hospital as "the best equipped, best manned, and best managed in this Presidency" and pointed out that those who preached self-help and ridiculed dependence on the government needed to practice what they preached. In other words, they did not want the provincial taxpayer to pay for unjustified expenditures for the hospital of the Anglo-Indian community.[38] While St. George's may not have been the "best equipped" hospital in the presidency, it should be pointed out that the government gave almost twice the amount of support to patients in St. George's Hospital as it did to those in the native public hospitals. In 1892, for example, the annual cost per patient in St. George's Hospital was approximately Rs. 974, for the J. J. Hospital it was Rs. 414, and for the G. T. Hospital, Rs. 458.[39]

The government sought to resolve the problems of St. George's for the upper classes by taking on the role that it hoped private enterprise would play in the future. Patients who could pay for the special care would now be able to receive it. Recalling the history of its foundation, the government noted that St. George's Hospital (the European General Hospital) was founded by the East India Company for the care of the servants of the company and the seamen from ships in the harbor. The growth of the large, unofficial European and Anglo-Indian community expanded the scope of the hospital so that it admitted members of the nonofficial community after the claims of the former groups were met. It was a hospital primarily intended for the use of those too poor to pay for some or all of their medical expenses. Over time, well-to-do persons had been admitted, their payment being in proportion to the type of accommodation they were provided. However, they were subsidized as this payment did not include professional charges. Responding to the European community's dissatisfaction, the government decided that a portion of the hospital, to be known as the St. George's Nursing Home, would be separately administered. Patients here would be able to select their medical attendants from a range of specialists, and the fees would be negotiated as a matter of private arrangement between patient and physician. Additionally, the patients would have to pay for their accommodation, the actual cost of drugs, and extra nursing.[40]

By the end of the nineteenth century, the partnership between philanthropists and government in the creation of new institutions for the native public was an accepted practice, and by the early twentieth century, the native public agitated against government funding for institutions meant for only Europeans. This became quite clear when the government attempted to establish a separate infectious disease hospital for Europeans. This scheme was under consideration as early as 1906 because it was considered to be against every teaching of modern sanitary science to treat infectious diseases so close to a general hospital as was done at St. George's Hospital.[41] The issue came up for public discussion when the friends of two English custom officers died in the cholera wards of the infectious disease hospital at Arthur Road, which had Europeans as well as Mahars or sweepers. Dr. Turner immediately announced that he was arranging for separate accommodation for Europeans. The *Briton* complained of the lack of facilities for the European and Anglo-Indian communities in Bombay. In an open letter to the governor, Sir George Clarke, the *Briton* complained that he neglected the European and Anglo-Indian communities and urged him to safeguard their interests. The letter pointed to a recent meeting of the Bombay Municipal Corporation (BMC) where a European member drew attention to the complete absence of hospital accommodation for Europeans struck down by infectious diseases. The European member referred to a recent case where a Mr. Ingles and another victim were refused admission at St. George's Hospital, a decision the newspaper defended on the grounds that their admission would have been a risk to other patients. (Mr. Ingles ran from pillar to post before eventually being admitted into the Arthur Road Hospital.)[42] The Indian member of the BMC replied that the Europeans had no right to be in the country at all.[43] Nationalism had inserted itself into this arena.

While there was a range of native reaction, in general it can be said that it was in favor of wards or hospitals for the separate communities but against the use of the taxpayers' money for building an institution exclusively for Europeans. The *Pársi* noted that Indians felt the need for separate accommodation as much as Europeans and that separate wards should be provided to take care of native sensibilities.[44] The *Rast Goftar* advised the BMC to build four different hospitals in separate localities for the four principal communities of the city. The *Bombay Samachar* pointed to the problems raised by the government's letter to the BMC regarding the proposed hospital. The creation of such a hospital, with a racial bias, would go against the Municipal Act. If a community had no liking for a municipal hospital built for the benefit of the public, then it was free to make separate arrangements at its own cost. The small European population in the city would make establishing a separate hospital for five to seven patients an expensive exercise that neither the government nor the municipality could justify. It would also set a bad precedent and invite agitation about allowing only European doctors to be employed there. The newspaper also pointed out that Europeans received large salaries from the government, and while they criticized Indians for not understanding the principle of self-help, they constantly rushed to the government or municipality to aid them in matters to do with education and medicine. The *Parsi* noted the impropriety of the municipality founding a communal hospital and thought that a separate ward, rather than hospital, would do quite adequately in accommodating European patients at the Arthur Road Hospital.[45]

Indians had absorbed the lessons of the British and, with the rise of nationalism since the 1890s, had become bold enough to ensure that the government abided by the rules embodied in the lessons themselves. An earlier example shows the difference. In the 1870s, to commemorate the visit of the Duke of Edinburgh, His Highness Khanderao, Gaekwar of Baroda, gave Rs. 200,000 toward the construction of a new Sailors' Home. The total cost of the home was Rs. 366,629, the balance of which was paid by the government.[46] Built at Apollo Bunder, this magnificent building was located at a prominent junction where the Wellington Fountain was located and six roads met. The Gaekwar's generosity was appreciated by the British, but he met with a barrage of criticism from the majority of the native press who appreciated neither the users nor type of institution his moneys were directed toward, nor his lack of generosity in his own dominions. A writer in the *Arunodaya* of 20 March 1870 angrily observed that the new Sailors' Home "will perpetuate the memory among the people not only of the Duke's arrival, but of the unworthy selfishness of the English government and of its censurable partiality to its own race."[47] The native papers believed that the Gaekwar had been persuaded to give Rs. 200,000 toward the new Sailors' Home.

By the early twentieth century, no native philanthropist in Bombay could be persuaded quite so easily to support a substantial institution solely for the use of Europeans. Moreover, the public had come to believe in a public realm in which public money had to be applied toward institutions for the use of all citizens, whatever its internal divisions. If the Europeans wanted a separate institution, they would have to provide for it themselves.

NEW CATEGORIES, NATIONALISM, AND THE EXCLUSION OF EUROPEANS

Toward the end of the nineteenth century, class became a new category to be accommodated in this public realm. Public hospitals and dispensaries had been created primarily for the care of the poorer classes, and so it may be argued that class had never been absent from this public realm. However, by the turn of the century, class began to be considered in new ways.

The Factor of Class

In 1854, the establishment of the first textile mill in Bombay ushered in the era of industrial capitalism. By the end of the nineteenth century, textile mill workers formed a substantial percentage of the population of Bombay. In

1911, the mill workers formed approximately 10.6 percent of the population. The average daily employment of textile workers in eighty-seven mills in 1911 was 104,500.[48] Public institutions were established for the use of the laboring classes. In the sphere of health, philanthropists and the government began to consider the construction of wards or entire hospitals for the laboring classes. The government also applied to government bodies and industrialists, that is, employers or the owners of the means of production, to pay partially for the treatment of their employees or to act as philanthropists in the creation of institutions for these groups. Employers were asked to act as philanthropists for the care of a particular class that they employed. Hence, this "laboring class" was a particular community for which employers had to care. In the 1920s, a set of interrelated hospitals for the care of the laboring classes was built in the vicinity of the old Government House at Parel, now transformed into an industrial area (see Figure 6.4).

In Bombay, toward the turn of the century, employers were asked to contribute toward the costs of the care of their employees. In the case of the G. T. Hospital, for example, the government and municipality contributed toward its expenses and maintenance.[49] In 1900, the president of the BMC made a proposal to the government that the Bombay Tramway Company and other large employers of labor be induced to contribute toward the upkeep of the hospital. He drew attention to a paragraph from the Report of the Gokuldas Tejpal Native General Hospital, Bombay, for the year 1898, which argued that the company was rich enough to arrange for the treatment of their own employees. The report made the point that the company should not be dependent on a charitable institution meant for the care of the indigent and, if they continued to use the institution, that they be asked to contribute toward its maintenance. The government stated that it would be pleased to hear that employers of labor had been induced to make such a contribution.[50]

Wards in hospitals and entire new hospitals were planned for the industrial working class, and a new set of interrelated hospitals came up in Parel in the industrial area, north of the Fort. In 1909, Mrs. Lily Doughty Wylie wrote to the government to say that she had learned that it was planned to build a hospital from the remainder of the money left from the Sir Currimbhoy Ebrahim Entertainment Fund. If a final decision on this issue had not been made, she wished the governor to consider her proposal that the Rs. 100,000 or so be used toward the building of a ward for mill hands in connection with the Adam Wylie Hospital, which was located in the middle of the mill district. Additionally, she thought that since the various wards and beds in the hospital were memorials to Europeans, Parsis, and Hindus, a ward or wards being a memorial to a Muslim gentleman would be "very suitable."[51] The money from the Sir Currimbhoy Ebrahim Fund was used toward the building of the King Edward Memorial Hospital. The proposal to build a ward for mill hands was a departure from the building of wards for a particular religious group or race.

The Government House at Parel (by now the Haffkine Institute) and its neighborhood were transformed in the 1920s as a result of these new institutions. The King Edward Memorial Hospital, commonly referred to as the K. E. M. Hospital (1926), and the Seth Gordhandas Sunderdas Medical College (1926) were built in what used to be the "park-like grounds" of the Government House.[52] In the vicinity were the Nowrosjee Wadia Maternity Hospital (1926) and the Bai Jerbai Wadia Hospital for Children (1929). Nowrosjee Wadia & Sons, Architects designed the Bai Jerbai Wadia Hospital in the style of the other hospitals and medical colleges, all of which were designed by government architect George Wittet. The K. E. M. Hospital was built as a memorial to Edward VII, King and Emperor, after receiving donations from a variety of sources including the public. The Wadia Hospitals, on the other hand, were built largely through the munificence of the two brothers Sir Nusserwanji Wadia and Sir Cusrow Wadia, mill owners in Bombay. Sir Nusserwanji Wadia and his mother Bai Jerbai contributed large sums toward the building and endowment of the maternity hospital. It was built for the medical relief of women workers—not only for those who worked in the mills under Sir Nusserwanji Wadia's agency but also for the benefit of other women who lived in the Parel district.[53]

The laboring class did not replace communities as objects of philanthropy. The Wadia family, for example, donated large sums for the care of the Parsi community. In particular they contributed generously to the building of several Parsi *baghs,* or charitable housing estates, in the twentieth century. If the mill workers, who were predominantly Maharashtrian, finally became objects of philanthropy, it was as a consequence of their substantial numbers, their growing restiveness since the end of the nineteenth century, and the idea that their physical well-being would be financially beneficial to mill owners and shareholders in the long run. The first major strike in the textile industry occurred in 1919, followed by a second in 1920.[54] However, it was before these strikes, in the first decade of the twentieth century, that the laboring class as a category inserted itself within the existing categories of race, religion, and community. Geography assisted in the separation of these new institutions, which were set amid the *chawls* and factories where millworkers lived and worked (see Figures I.3, 1.13).[55]

The Rise of Nationalism

Historian Stanley Wolpert pointed out that all the leaders of India's first nationalist movement had received some English education. They were generally high-caste, middle-class intellectuals who resided primarily in Calcutta, Madras, Bombay, and Poona. The first annual meeting of the Indian National Congress took place in Bombay in 1885, but nationalism had begun even earlier. Surendranath Banerjea (1848–1926), a Bengali Brahman who was unfairly disqualified from the Indian Civil Service (ICS), founded the Indian Association, Bengal's first nationalist political organization, in 1876. The erudite Chitpavin Brahman, Mahadev Govind Ranade (1842–1901), a graduate from the first class of Bombay University in 1862, whose promotion to Bombay's High Court was delayed for almost a quarter of century because of his Indian birth and public activities, formed the Poona Sarvajanik Sabha in Bombay in 1870. Sarvajanik Sabha can be translated to mean "All People's Association."[56]

The denial of opportunities to qualified Indians in upper levels of governance or in public institutions was linked to the rise of nationalism. In Bombay, since about the 1890s, the unfairness of colonial policies led to the conceptualization or foundation of institutions in which Indians could attain high levels of education and/or reach superior positions in their jobs. While community self-consciousness was a powerful force, the rise of nationalism also linked individuals of different communities together as members of one nation.

The nationalist spirit animated the policies of the Parsi industrialist Jamsetji Nusserwanji Tata (1839–1904), who was instrumental in funding the creation of higher institutions of learning for all Indians. In 1889, Lord Reay, governor of Bombay, pointed out in a speech, as chancellor of the university, the deficiencies in the higher educational system in India, which could not develop further if universities remained merely examining bodies. In 1892, persuaded of the lack of opportunities in higher education in India, Tata decided to organize a strategy to lend money, at a nominal rate of interest, to a few deserving students so that they could pursue higher education in England. Through this scheme he hoped to equip a larger number of Indians with the skills for the Higher Administrative and Technical Services. At first the plan reserved a certain number of seats for Parsis, but this was soon abandoned, and it was decided to choose the most deserving candidates, regardless of religion or province. He also calculated that this idea was a great saving to the country because every Indian who gained admission in the ICS saved the country Rs. 200,000, the cost of a civilian's pay, allowance, and pension, which usually went to Britain.[57]

A more ambitious design, however, was the Indian Institute of Science, which Tata envisioned as an institute for postgraduate teaching and learning. In his choice of a plan and the nature of the institution, Tata exhibited a considerable independence of spirit and was not guided by the needs or dictates of the colonial regime. Tata's scheme for this university and its courses were a result of inquiries into the creation of universities and types of courses in universities in England, France, Germany, and America. In particular, he wished to promote indigenous scientific expertise that could be harnessed to help industry and utilize the natural resources of India. As the largest landowner in Bombay, he decided that the sum of Rs. 3,000,000 could be provided from his landed property. Various locations were considered for the institute and Bombay was a prime candidate. Around 1901, Tata finally accepted the Maharaja of Mysore's offer of three hundred acres of land in Bangalore, Rs. 500,000 toward the building costs, and an annual subsidy.[58]

The government displayed little enthusiasm for the project, probably because it was likely to displace European expertise. In the first days of January 1899, two days after he came to Bombay to take up his appointment as viceroy, Lord Curzon received a deputation from the Provisional Committee on the matter of the Tata research institute. Lord Curzon expressed a number of reservations about the scheme. Would the highly paid professors be able to get an adequate number of students? Were there enough posts for the highly trained scientists?[59] Writing a few months after Tata's death, a number of newspapers in the Bombay Presidency raised the issue of the Tata research institute again. Through Tata's endowment and the annual grants promised by the Mysore Government, there was a deficit of only Rs. 30,000 a year. They pointed out that this was a small sum to a government that was wasting large sums of money on frontier expeditions and military expenditures.[60]

Another successful scheme for natives in the city of Bombay was the medical college in association with the proposed K. E. M. Hospital. In 1913, the great city statesman Sir Pherozeshah Mehta made it clear that he and his friends were in favor not only of a well-equipped hospital but also of a medical college to be associated with it, which would make it a worthy memorial to King Edward. Sir Pherozeshah Mehta and other corporators represented the municipal corporation, which was also donating money toward this project. One paper surmised that the Bombay Presidency King Edward Memorial Association, which was also contributing money toward this plan, did not look on it with much favor because it would become a rival of the current institution, presumably the Grant Medical College, which was the preserve of the Indian Medical Service men.[61]

A year later, it was clear that this idea was considered by some to be an Indian institution, to be run by Indians for the benefit of Indians. In an article, the *Jam-e-Jamshed* pointed out that the K. E. M. Hospital scheme had aroused the interest of the public because of the government's proposal to attach a school of tropical medicine to it. Many members of the corporation wished to report to the government the widespread wish of the Bombay public that the largest possible place in the running of this hospital, in terms of its staff, be given to native talent. It was time for a change in policies of staffing, and this was a good opportunity for the government to remove unnecessary distinctions between Europeans and Indians. The newspaper was unambiguous in its argument that this should be an Indian institution in every way:

> This is to be an essentially Indian institution, an institution not only sub-scribed to, endowed and maintained by the Indians but intended for the benefit of Indians of the poorer classes, and it would be not only appropri-ate but just that its control and administration should be vested in Indians of the requisite talents and abilities.[62]

The inception of medical institutions staffed by Indians had its roots in the late nineteenth century. Qualified Indians were not given positions of responsibil-ity as administrators or teachers in medical colleges or hospitals. Many were frustrated by this situation. Dr. Kaikhosru Nasserwanji Bahadurji (1860–1898) had sought to overcome this prejudice by earning degrees in England. After winning the Gilchrist scholarship in 1882 he went to study in England and received an M.B. (bachelor of medicine) from the University of London. After gaining some research experience he returned to England to earn a B.S. (bach-elor of science) and M.D. (doctor of medicine).[63] According to one account he was the first Indian to receive an M.D. from the University of London, and on his return to India in 1889 he began his medical practice and was soon considered to be one of the leading physicians in the city. Despite Lord Reay, the governor of Bombay's recommendation, he failed to get a position on the staff of the Grant Medical College. Angered by this unfairness, Dr. Bahadurji formulated a project to found a new medical college and hospital staffed by Indians, which would break the monopoly of the Indian Medical Service. He died in 1898, long before his dream came true.[64] Although this might be the more popular account, it appears that Bahadurji was appointed professor of clinical medicine and pharmacology at Grant Medical College and honorary physician, J. J. Hospital, on his return from England. Coming into conflict with his superior Wellington Gray caused him to resign in 1893. Following this, he began a large private practice and became a leader in the movement for profes-sional reform.[65]

In 1910, a group of Bombay's leading physicians formed a committee to raise funds to build a hospital to be staffed entirely by Indians. This scheme evoked a great response, and many people made donations. Thirty thousand rupees was donated by the estate of Dr. Habib Ismail Janmahomed for the construction of a maternity ward or operating theater to be named after him and to be under the supervision of a qualified Indian doctor. The largest donation of almost 1.5 million rupees came from the estate of Seth Gordhandas Sunderdas. As all other funds had been left toward the hospital, this donation was used for the building of the Seth Gordhandas Sunderdas Medical College (1926), or GSMC, which was built next to the K. E. M. Hospital in Parel. The endowment came with several conditions, the most important being that all the professors and teachers employed by the college were to be qualified independent Indian gentlemen who were not in government service.[66]

The successful establishment of the K. E. M. Hospital and the GSMC was significant in several ways. The creation of a space for Indians, to be managed by Indians, was one of the ways toward the creation of what Benedict Anderson calls an "imagined community."[67] That this was almost contemporaneous with the creation of ethnic/religious-based plague hospitals and the B. D. Petit Parsi General Hospital, is to say that people began to imagine themselves as being both Bhatia and Indian, or Parsi and Indian. If the British clubs were "for whites only" then this was an exclusionary space as well, one that said "no whites, please." There was a growing belief that gaining expertise was a matter of training and not innate racial superiority and that Indians had the expertise and skills to conceive, manage, and run an institution on their own. The fruition of this project spoke of native agency and the inability of the colonial regime to prevent the rise of institutions that would compete with their own. The Indians were not trying to relieve the white man's burden but rather hinting that the white man was a burden.

CONCLUSION

By the end of the nineteenth century, wealthy natives, rather than the ruling race, seemed to control the economy and space on the island of Bombay. When James M. Maclean, author of *A Guide to Bombay,* returned to Bombay in 1899, after an absence of almost twenty years, he found it much changed. Maclean resided in Bombay between 1859 and 1880, at a time when the natives "occupied a distinctly inferior position, and did not seem to resent it." Now the wealthy natives lived in the best houses. "The Europeans in Bombay had taken a back seat," and "Englishmen seemed to possess nothing except the fringe of ground adjoining the harbour on which the Yacht Club is built."[68] Unstable social and spatial hierarchies created their own tensions, which came to the fore at the turn of the century. However, in institutions like the lunatic asylum, the colonial authority could maintain the proper hierarchies and change them at will, even though the world outside was rapidly changing.

In the second half of the nineteenth century, the colonial government had set itself a difficult task: to create secular public institutions in a society ridden with divisions. And it had been successful in this effort. However, Bombay's peculiar colonial situation—where the native elite was wealthier than members of the European community—resulted in a number of contradictions. Colonial policies of self-help were adopted by natives but boomeranged on the colonial government when it met with native opposition as it sought to use public money to provide special facilities for Europeans. Segregation had resulted in a peculiar situation where, in hospitals, for example, Europeans did not always get the best treatment. Rather than the colonial elite, the wealthy Parsi community seemed to have the best treatment.

The partnership between the government and native elite, while providing facilities for the public, compromised the public realm. It created inequalities between classes and communities, and by its emphasis on race, the colonial government compromised the quality of care provided in institutions such as lunatic asylums. The colonial government was sometimes the protector of the public realm and at other times gave individual donors too much control over these spaces.

By the early twentieth century, both Indians and Europeans were aware of the very real limits of colonial power. Native philanthropists may have learned the British government's way of exhibiting charity, but they had also begun to assert a greater independence in deciding the projects they wished to fund. These projects sometimes fostered native expertise and excluded Europeans. Colonial racial dividing practices had created resentment among Indians but at the same time tied disparate groups together as "natives." The Indians were to learn that only by looking beyond dividing practices could they begin the task of imagining the nation.

6 Of Gods and Mortal Heroes: Conundrums of the Secular Landscape of Colonial Bombay

IN THE SECOND HALF of the nineteenth century, the city was modernized and a new secular public landscape was created—the joint public realm that was made up of public buildings and open spaces. The Gothic Revival architectural style signified the consensus between native philanthropists and colonial officials on the need for and the aims underlying the new public landscape for all of Bombay's citizens. In contrast, various groups in the city were distinguished by their modes: their distinct clothing, religious buildings, and neighborhoods. Just as the dividing practices in the city's medical institutions separated groups based on various criteria but disallowed religious practices at these sites, modernizing the city meant a clear separation between the religious and secular domains of the city, where local religious structures were not allowed to stand in the way of improvements and were moved, demolished, or rebuilt if the site was required. The religious also had to be contained so that the influence of gods and goddesses was restricted; they had to be restrained within certain boundaries so that the sacred would not get in the way of economic and urban development.

Particularly after the mid-nineteenth century, the colonial regime erected public buildings and urban spaces that were supposedly free of religious symbols. However, statues and images of mortal heroes and royalty substituted for gods in these new arenas that supported the colonial regime's emerging civil religion. In Bombay, many of these new deities were not British. From about the second half of the nineteenth century, busts and statues of Indian philanthropists, and later other prominent Indians, were erected as memorials to their

generosity or leadership, clearly signaling that the British had partners in the building of Bombay (Figure 6.1). These new deities hailed from both Britain and India in a landscape that not only undermined British control and dominance but also complicated the signs of rule with these figures of joint sponsorship. What then is the role of religion in the secular public landscape of the colonial city?

While the British were engaged in the process of converting some Indian religious buildings to secular use, Indians were engaged in an opposite process of inserting the religious into the secular colonial public landscape, and elite Indians were interposing their images amid those of the British. By examining the secularization of Indian religious structures by the British, and the accommodation of the religious by Indians into the secular public landscape, I argue that the meanings of monuments in Bombay became the vehicles of complex associations created by both the colonial regime and the local citizenry. By using the phrase "complex associations," I mean to account for the ways that the secular, the religious, the aesthetic—events, rituals, emotions, to name a few—dynamically shape the meanings of monuments.

The British redirected some associations of monuments by converting certain places of worship to secular use, such as for a governor's residence or as a protected public monument. Public buildings and spaces were meant to accommodate British worthies and underscore the benefits of colonial rule, thereby upholding the myths of the colonizer's civil religion. However, the local population redirected the meanings associated with secular colonial public buildings and public gardens by the introduction of religious buildings and rituals into these sites. Moreover, through acts of philanthropy, the Indian elite ensured that there was space for both British and Indian worthies at these sites.

BRITISH CONTROL OF SPACES OF WORSHIP

A decade after the Portuguese had ceded Bombay to the British in 1661, Gerald Aungier, the British governor of Bombay, inaugurated a policy that granted freedom of worship to caste groups who settled in Bombay.[1] The ability of the British to provide stable conditions for trade and their promise of religious freedom attracted Indian trading communities to migrate to Bombay, a factor that was important in making Bombay the leading international port in western India after the mid-eighteenth century.[2] The Portuguese, in contrast to the British, had destroyed and desecrated temples and converted cave temples into churches.[3]

Despite a general policy of noninterference in religious matters, in certain cases, most notably the western cave sanctuaries, the British did attempt to control religious buildings, ostensibly for preservation. At the same time, British rule brought about changes in the religious landscape of Bombay. In 1760 a Portuguese church and in 1766 the Mumbadevi temple on the Esplanade were given orders to move to new sites. These structures were removed from the Esplanade because the British wanted the sites for building further fortifications and for military maneuvers.[4] Thus, in addition to their control over the cave sanctuaries for preservation, the British moved religious buildings, occupied part of the site, and in one notable case occupied the building itself. In each instance the building or site's use was altered from religious to something approaching the secular.

The Triumph of History over Memory

A novel interpretation of the results of the British policy of religious freedom is illustrated by the story of the foundation of the Mahalakshmi temple (Figure 6.2). The legend is that the image of Mahalakshmi had jumped into the Worli (Varli) creek in the fourteenth century as she was being persecuted by the Muslim rulers. She did not come out of hiding until the Portuguese had given the island of Bombay to the British. In the seventeenth century, the British tried to keep the sea out by building a dam between Mahalakshmi and Worli, but they were continually defeated in their efforts. Then Ramji Shivji, a Prabhu contractor,

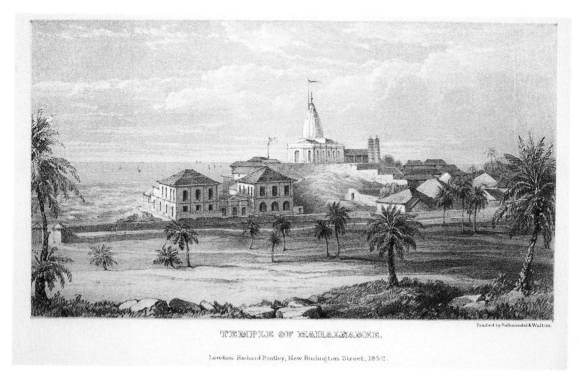

TEMPLE OF MAHALAXMEE.

Printed by Hullmandel & Walton

London: Richard Bentley, New Burlington Street, 1852.

FIGURE 6.2. Mahalakshmi Temple, Bombay, 1852. From Anonymous, *Life in Bombay,* facing 38.

was advised by the goddess in a vision, to work for the government in the construction of the causeway. She promised to ensure the successful construction of the embankment if he would rescue her and her two sister goddesses from the sea and construct a proper shrine for them on land. Ramji did as he was asked; the goddesses were brought back to land after 1680, and they helped the British complete the building of an embankment known as the Hornby Vellard (Figure 6.3). In return, the British presented land to Ramji to construct the temple to the goddesses.[5] These various lifelike actions and miraculous powers of images were not unusual since Hindus customarily believed that the images to which they prayed were endowed with life. Thus images were thought to be alive, owners of property, sometimes rulers, and capable of transforming the course of events through actions.[6] The story of the foundation of the Mahalakshmi temple demonstrates the British acceptance of the Indians' belief that images were efficacious and helped the British build an embankment.

The Government House at Parel was formerly a church and convent belonging to the Jesuits and is probably the only example in Bombay where the British actually occupied a former place of worship (Figure 6.4). When the British acquired Bombay, the Jesuits were a powerful force and controlled the northern parts of the island. Around 1719–20, the monastery was taken from the Jesuits because they were allegedly acting against British interests. It was then converted

VAUCLUSE.

Printed by Hullmandel & Walton.

into the governor's residence.[7] The vaulted chapel was transmuted to house the banqueting hall and ballroom, erasing the former religious associations of this structure.[8] This occupation of a monastery was an assertion of British control over the Jesuits in their role as political players and not an issue of religious persecution of Roman Catholics.

In contrast to this occupation of a former religious structure, a second government house would occupy part of a religious site, forming an alternative center of secular power. At the summit of Malabar Point, another Government House was built after 1812 (Figure 6.5). From this prominence one could get a picturesque view of the Back Bay of Bombay (Figure 6.6). This government house was located next to the ancient Hindu village of Walkeshwar, which consisted of temples and other structures grouped around the sacred tank of Banganga (Figure 6.7; also see Figure 1.5). Near this was an unusually shaped rock on a cliff, called Shri-gundi, or Lucky Stone. This spot and the temple of Walkeshwar were a landmark and an important place of pilgrimage.[9]

The foundation myths of temples such as Walkeshwar encourage us to reimagine parts of Bombay as sacred space, still bearing witness to mythical events that took place eons ago. Walkeshwar, for example, was a place where Lord Rama, the hero of the epic Ramayana, stopped on his way to Lanka. The Portuguese or Muslims destroyed the original Walkeshwar temple, but the

FIGURE 6.3. Breach, Bombay, 1852. From Anonymous, *Life in Bombay*, facing 37.

FIGURE 6.4. Government House, Parel, Bombay, early twentieth century. Originally this was the site of a church and convent belonging to the Jesuits. W. Hornby (1776) was the first governor to establish a residence here, and the building was considerably enlarged and refurbished by a subsequent governor, Mountstuart Elphinstone (1819–27). It was converted into a plague hospital after the bubonic plague first struck Bombay in 1896, then later became the Bombay Bacteriological Laboratory. Courtesy Bhau Daji Lad Sangrahalaya, Bombay.

British donated land for the new temple. It is not clear how the British came to be in possession of the prominent Malabar Point site. The Shenvi community claimed the village of Walkeshwar and argued that the property of the temple included the ground occupied by the Government House compound. Around 1910, a High Court decision disputed the Shenvis' claim of ownership of the village, and the colonial government claimed most of the village and the hill as their property.[10] The British acquired this land because of its scenic location and picturesque views. In the process they complicated Walkeshwar's religious associations by juxtaposing their own names and associations and by building a center of secular power on part of a Hindu pilgrimage site. The British gave Shri-gundi a new name—Malabar Point—and referred to the district of Walkeshwar as Malabar Hill.

The British did not convert local religious buildings into churches, but what they did do was what the French theorist Pierre Nora calls the "conquest and eradication of memory by history."[11] As a site of memory in Nora's sense,

Walkeshwar continued to be a location whose past was tied to mythical events that took place in time immemorial,[12] yet after the arrival of the British one sees a clear rupture with that past. The British recorded past memories of the site, but from that point on memory gave way to a history of the site where only supposedly actual and verifiable events were recorded. In the seventeenth century, the goddesses returned to land to help the British build an embankment. By the nineteenth century, the gods and goddesses were locked in their temples, no longer free to roam the world, help found temples, and influence the lives of mortals.

The Preservation and Secularization of Elephanta

In these examples we see that the British donated a site for a temple, converted a church into a governor's residence, and acquired part of the site of a religious complex for a second governor's residence. In contrast to these religious buildings, the British had a more complicated relationship to the Hindu and Buddhist cave sanctuaries in Bombay's vicinity. Of these, Elephanta was the most prominent.[13]

FIGURE 6.5. Government House, Malabar Point, Bombay, early twentieth century. Governor Mountstuart Elphinstone had a small cottage here but subsequent governors added on to it, especially after the government house in Parel was converted into a plague hospital. Courtesy Bhau Daji Lad Sangrahalaya, Bombay.

MALABAR POINT.

Printed by Hullmandel & Wal

FIGURE 6.6. Malabar
Point, Bombay, 1852.
From Anonymous,
Life in Bombay, fac-
ing 248.

Elephanta's history is intertwined with the history of European encounters that reflected the prevailing intellectual climate in Europe and the growing
colonial power of the British in India. The first European accounts of Elephanta are from the sixteenth century. Visitors to India, like their counterparts
who went to Italy to see the remains of Rome, were struck by the grandeur of
these rock-cut temples and in writings conveyed their sense that these monuments were among the "greatest wonders of the world" and also the oldest.[14]
Elephanta became a secular monument to be analyzed, studied, painted, admired, protected, and worshipped, for its beauty and as a product of human
activity but not as a site of religion, which displayed and made accessible divine
presence.[15]

From the mid-eighteenth century, there were two main trajectories of
European engagement with historical Indian monuments: one group engaged
in a systematic recording of facts of Indian art, and the second reflected on its
"nature and importance."[16] Travelers to Elephanta included artists whose paintings illustrated a romantic view of Indian architecture and scenery and sought
to highlight the sublime and picturesque qualities of Indian antiquities as ruins.
The Elephanta caves were painted by Thomas and William Daniell and appeared
in their volumes of *Oriental Scenery* published between 1795 and 1808.[17] One

might say that these early travelers were overwhelmed by the beauty of caves such as Elephanta and treated them with what Thomas R. Metcalf calls an "uncertain religious awe," related to the secular religion of aesthetics but not religion itself.[18] The eighteenth century also saw the rise of scientific archaeology. After the British had gained control over India in the mid-eighteenth century, it was the English residents who were engaged in measuring and documenting architectural monuments. Many archaeologists were East India Company officials, who persuaded the British government to preserve major antiquities. There were also several important Indian scholars of Indian architecture in the nineteenth century, such as Ram Raz and Rajendralal Mitra. Indian and British orientalists did not always see eye to eye. Mitra, for example, challenged James Fergusson's idea that ancient Hindu and Buddhist architectures were derived from Greece.[19]

In the early nineteenth century, the government erected a protective fence around Elephanta.[20] By the mid-nineteenth century, the government had built a bungalow to house a European sergeant who was to ensure that no further destruction of the temples took place, yet the theft of fingers, toes, and the tip of a nose, allegedly by modern antiquarians, continued. In 1852, one anonymous writer observed:

FIGURE 6.7. Banganga Tank, Walkeshwar, Bombay. Photograph by author, 1999.

Every care has been bestowed by the English Government to guard the relics of Elephanta from further spoliation. A small bungalow was erected some years ago, for the accommodation of an European sergeant appointed to watch over the temples and prevent any additional mutilation of the figures; but the abstraction of fingers and toes still goes on; the tip of a nose occasionally disappears, and various other pilferings of frequent recurrence, remind us pretty significantly, that even Siva himself is less destructive in his propensities than the modern antiquarian.[21]

The British considered the cave sanctuaries to be secular or nonreligious structures and treated them as such. Apart from antiquarians, the caves of western India were popular destinations for English picnickers. At one picnic in the mid-nineteenth century, a table was laid out in the Elephanta cave, where beef was given pride of place on the table. The picnickers were aware that Hindus considered this sacrilegious.[22] In 1875, an impressive banquet was held in the main cave at Elephanta for the Prince of Wales, resulting in "the veritable apotheosis of Elephanta."[23] This event marked the importance of Elephanta to antiquarians, picnickers, and the colonial government itself, which controlled not only India's present but now saw themselves as protectors of its ancient past from its present inhabitants.

While the British observed the occasional Brahman pilgrim at Elephanta, they argued that its desecration by the Portuguese had made it unattractive to Hindus as a regular site of worship.[24] The Portuguese had converted some of these cave temples, such as one at Kanheri, into a church, while Father Antoine, a sixteenth-century Jesuit priest, had rededicated one of the temples of Elephanta to God, after cleansing it of all previous associations.[25] The British were able to take advantage of the gap in religious control created by the Portuguese desecration of the temple, and the disruption of Hindu religious traditions, to gain control over Elephanta. The British justified their occupation of Elephanta by arguing that Hindus no longer considered it to be of religious importance since the Portuguese had desecrated it. This argument would later be concretized in the Ancient Monuments Preservation Bill passed in 1903, which ruled that buildings that were in religious use or the property of a religious group did not come under the jurisdiction of the bill. In the case of such buildings, the government only had the authority to investigate the structures and make recommendations for their conservation and, in case of damage and destruction, to punish the offenders.[26] The ways in which the British came to control many of India's ancient monuments varied. For example, it was only after the British crushed the Indian Rebellion of 1857 (India's First War of Independence) that they came to control Mughal palaces and tombs, which they converted into offices or preserved as old monuments. The latter became tourist attractions.[27] Unlike the Portuguese, the British did not convert these monuments into churches, yet they found other ways of desecrating some of them. According to Bernard Cohn, one might date the beginning of the empire in 1857 to the "desacralization" of the Mughal fortress-palace of Red Fort in Delhi when English officers first imbibed wine and consumed pork there.[28] The very impotence of the Mughal emperor was demonstrated by the consumption of substances forbidden by Islam at this site, rendering it impure.

In 1903, the villagers of Gharapuri, the island on which the Elephanta caves are located, petitioned the government to allow them to enter the caves for religious purposes without the payment of fees. According to government records, fees had been levied on the villagers since 1872, even though the villagers' petition seemed to imply that they were imposed in 1901. The government agreed to issue villagers free passes to enter the caves for religious purposes on three festival days of the year. They were instructed that "no daubing with paint should be permitted."[29] The British were now custodians of this secular architectural site where religious activities were controlled and supervised. Yet the British interest in preserving this site for its beauty, for aesthetic reasons, was also religious in form if not in content, as anthropologist Alfred Gell has argued in his emphasis on the continuity of form in the practice of aesthetic worship.[30]

I began by arguing that for the most part the British did not convert buildings in India from one religious use to another. However, the post-Enlightenment Puritan–Protestant heritage saw the rise of a secular idolatry that honored art. This too, as Gell argues, is a kind of religion or "the substitute for religion."[31] In India, the British took control of many religious "monuments" by converting them from one religious use into temples dedicated to the secular religion of aesthetics. By making the villagers pay to enter Elephanta, the British were not only attempting to control their access to this site and the images within but were also imposing the common practice of paying a fee to enter a museum.

As Elephanta came increasingly under the control of archaeologists, it was transformed from a temple to a museum. Tapati Guha-Thakurta has shown that the two separate trajectories of the museum and archaeology came together in a new arena in the late nineteenth century as conservation became increasingly important to archaeology. The need for conservation was signaled by the formation of a new Department of Curatorship of Ancient Monuments in 1880 under Major H. H. Cole. The desire of museums and the new thrust in archaeology were opposed to each other. While museums obviously desired to increase their collections, Indian archaeologists were now loath to remove anything from a site as it would diminish a historical landmark and the context that contributed to the meaning of the monument, something that could not be replicated or captured in a museum setting. Guha-Thakurta argues that under the Department of the Curatorship of Ancient Monuments, India became conceived of as an "open-air museum."[32] At the same time, she argues that the practices of the museum collection percolated into the way these sites were offered up to the spectator.[33] Elephanta's museumization allowed it to be transformed from a cult space to a space that was subject to secular rituals and the tourist gaze and an object of specialized knowledge.

CIVIL RELIGION AND THE CREATION OF A SECULAR PUBLIC LANDSCAPE

While the British were protecting ancient Indian monuments from what they saw as overly devout Indians, they were also engaged in the construction of grand new urban ensembles and public buildings in Bombay. In the nineteenth century, the colonial regime created a secular public landscape where public rituals, spaces, and buildings were dedicated to contain or remember heroes, government officials, and British royalty. These memorials became the new religious landscape for a publicly secular regime where mortal heroes and royalty replaced gods. However, the associations of this ostensibly secular public landscape were intersected by those of two other sets of players and discourses. The Indian elite also participated in the creation of associations by acts of philanthropy and by helping to fund architectural elements such as gates, clock towers, fountains, and statues dedicated to British government officials and royalty, as well as to themselves or other members of the native elite. The native public also developed associations through everyday practices and acts of reimagination.

The sociologist Robert N. Bellah has argued for the existence of what he calls a civil religion in America, one that is accompanied by its own institutions and rituals and which may borrow from dominant religious traditions but is at the same time distinct from them. Bellah points out that "by civil religion I refer to that religious dimension, found I think in the life of every people, through which it interprets its historical experience in the light of transcendent reality."[34] Bellah is careful to point out that he is not talking about the worship of the American nation but rather that the nation, in this case, is guided by some larger "ethical principles."[35] Such a civil religion is molded over time, thematically transformed by central events such as the Civil War, which introduced "a new theme of death, sacrifice, and rebirth" to civil religion. Over time there are a set of beliefs, symbols, and rituals in connection to new sacred things that are celebrated or institutionalized for the collective.[36] Civil religion is supported by a body of shared myths. Bellah clarifies that "in using the word 'myth,' I do not mean to suggest a story that is not true. Myth does not seek to describe reality; that is the job of science. Myth seeks rather to transfigure reality so that it provides moral and spiritual meaning to individuals or societies. Myths, like scientific theories, may be true or false, but the test of truth or falsehood is different."[37] In India, material culture and landscape—monuments, sites, statues, and memorials—were important to the construction and sustenance of the myths that underlay British colonial rule and its civil religion.

The establishment of British colonial rule in India was accompanied by the slow development of this civil religion for the British colonizers. While in the 1830s and 1840s British rule was theoretically grounded on ideals of Enlightenment, a vision of an expectation of universal progress, by the 1870s most colonial officials of an increasingly authoritarian regime were "convinced of an essential difference between British and Indian that justified indefinite control of political power by a 'superior race.'"[38] The symbols of this civil religion were increasingly marked in the spaces and landscape of British India, in both the institutions and spaces frequented by the British, and increasingly in the public arenas meant for all the citizens.

If, as according to Bellah, the Civil War in America introduced the new theme of sacrifice, the 1857 uprising, which led to the deaths of many British, including women and children, marked the high point of British sacrifice and gave an increased stature to former sacrifices and earlier deaths due to wars or the difficulty of living in India, a land where disease and death always lurked around the corner. By the end of the nineteenth century, British travelers could be reminded of the dastardly behavior of disloyal and ungrateful Indians by going on a pilgrimage of mutiny sites in Lucknow, Kanpur, and the Delhi ridge. Barbara D. Metcalf and Thomas R. Metcalf construct the "mutiny" as bestowing the British with "a cleansing sense of heroism and self-assertion, a confirmation of moral superiority and the right to rule," and one might see the pilgrimage to mutiny sites as rituals of cleansing.[39] But more than this, these civil pilgrimages marked the mutiny as a culmination of earlier sacrifices that formed a strong foundation for civil religion.

Civil Religion's Landscape in Bombay

The sacrifices that upheld civil religion were also reflected in the local landscapes of everyday life. St. Thomas Cathedral, located in the Fort in Bombay and constructed in 1718 as a garrison church and elevated to a cathedral in 1833, was the central place of worship for the Protestant community, a building whose interior was animated by numerous monuments (Figure 6.8; also see Figure 1.8). Not only was this a religious space for Protestant Christians, but it was also one of the spaces that helped to sanctify British rule in India by transmuting the ordinary ambitions underlying conquest into sacred ideals that

FIGURE 6.8. St. Thomas Cathedral, Fort, Bombay, interior view. The structure was built as a garrison church in 1718 and consecrated as a cathedral in 1833. Photograph by author, 2007.

made conquest necessary. The space of the cathedral where the visitor was surrounded by monuments of the dead drove home the message that British rule was built on a history of sacrifice and martyrdom.

Tourists to the city, following guidebooks such as Maclean's *Guide to Bombay* or Murray's *Handbook of the Bombay Presidency,* visited the cathedral and made note of the monuments. Murray's *Handbook,* for example, draws the tourists' attention to several notable monuments, such as the monument to Major Eldred Pottinger, who successfully defended the city of Herat in Afghanistan but died some years later of a fever at the age of thirty-two. It should be mentioned that part of the tourist itinerary would have included a visit to the Afghan Memorial Church of St. John the Evangelist at Colaba, which was built to commemorate the soldiers who died in the campaigns of Sind and Afghanistan in 1835–43. Another monument erected by the East India Company at St. Thomas Cathedral was dedicated to Colonel Campbell, who in 1783 defended Mangalur with a small force against the much larger army of Tipu Sultan. This would have reminded viewers of the subsequent victory over the South Indian king Tipu Sultan in 1799, an important victory for the British East India Company that brought about their final control over southwestern India and subsequently the rest of the subcontinent. On the left-hand side of the chancel lay the tomb of General Carnac, Robert Clive's second in command at the Battle of Plassey of 1757, the famous victory with which the British began their conquest of India. One of the most interesting civil monuments, by John Bacon Jr., was to Jonathan Duncan who was governor of Bombay from 1795 to 1811. The monument shows Duncan supposedly "receiving the blessings of young Hindús" and refers to Duncan's successful efforts in abolishing infanticide in some districts in the vicinity of Banaras and later in Kathiawad through his agent Colonel Walker (Figure 6.9).⁴⁰ On a more personal note is a marble monument to Catherine Kirkpatrick, who died in 1766 at the age of twenty-two, mother of James Achilles Kirkpatrick, resident of Hyderabad. This monument, by the younger Bacon, was paid for by Kirkpatrick's sons.⁴¹

European tourists to the church as well as its regular congregants would have been alive to the various messages encoded in the cathedral's monuments. They revealed the martial bravery exhibited by the British in pacifying the land and the cost of lives exacted by wars as well as by personal misfortune, exemplified by the death of young Catherine Kirkpatrick, a tragedy that left her children without a mother. The monument to Duncan would have comforted viewers and reminded them that these sacrifices were for a higher cause; abolishing infanticide was one of many steps undertaken by the British in the cause of civilizing this land and its people. At the same time, practices such as infanticide were a reminder of India's essential "difference."⁴²

Memorials, naming practices, and the erection of statues, busts, or sculpted medallion faces on buildings played a significant role in practices of colonial place-making linking the city to the history of conquest, settlement, and empire, and to local and larger colonial figures of significance and European residents of the city. In the first half of the nineteenth century, most military memorials erected by the British in Bombay were a reminder of wars and of those who had died fighting; most civil memorials were dedicated to women, children, and officials who died of natural causes. On the other hand, the earliest statues were erected for important officials and heroes. In short, memorials and statues for the British raised in Bombay in the first half of the nineteenth century referred most often to individuals who had played some role—ordinary, official, or military—on the stage of India with no reference to the British monarchy. This was hardly surprising since the conquest of India was accomplished by the East India Company, a commercial entity.

The earliest statues located in exterior public spaces in Bombay were that of Marquis Wellesley, governor-general of India (1798–1805), which was first erected in 1814, and a statue of Marquis Cornwallis, which was commissioned after his death in 1805 and installed in the Bombay Green in 1822.⁴³ Wellesley's statue was first placed on the site later occupied by the Queen's statue but was

FIGURE 6.9. St. Thomas Cathedral, Fort, Bombay, interior view showing a monument by John Bacon Jr. to Jonathan Duncan, governor of Bombay from 1795 to 1811. Photograph by author, 2007.

FIGURE 6.10. Town Hall (1821–33) and Elphinstone Circle Garden (1869–72), Bombay, circa 1880s. This photograph shows the centrally placed fountain in the garden and statues of General Charles, Marquis Cornwallis, and Marquis Wellesley, both by John Bacon Jr. The statue of Marquis Cornwallis was commissioned after his death in 1805 and erected here in 1822; the statue of Marquis Wellesley, governor-general of India (1798–1805), was first erected in 1814 at a site later occupied by the queen's statue. Courtesy Phillips Antiques, Bombay.

subsequently placed in the Bombay Green that later became the Elphinstone Circle Garden, the center of the Fort district, where Cornwallis's statue was located (Figure 6.10; also see Figure 1.8). Both St. Thomas Cathedral and the Town Hall were located adjacent to the garden. Cornwallis was an eighteenth-century British hero who had enabled the conquest of India. Cornwallis had signed a treaty with Tipu Sultan in 1792 and played a prominent role in assuring future British dominance over Mysore. In the decade that followed and particularly after his death in 1805, Cornwallis was hero-worshipped; his portrait was included in the gallery of heroes in the Banqueting Hall in Madras, and monuments were erected in Madras, several parts of Bengal, and in Bombay. The Bombay monument therefore reflected a wider trend of hero worship of Cornwallis in India, but it should be noted that numerous public monuments were erected to other war heroes in various parts of India.[44] Madras's Banqueting Hall, for example, clearly celebrated the military adventures of the

British in India and according to Sten Nilsson "functioned very like a *Heroum*, a neo-classical temple for hero-worship."[45] This trend of hero worship was not unique to India but was also prevalent in England during this period.[46]

Despite the fact that architects working in the Empire often followed the architectural fashions of home, Thomas Metcalf argues that the difference between the practice of architects in Britain and those of the Empire was their explicitly political function of "representing empire itself" in the latter case.[47] A good comparison can be made between Gilbert Scott's designs for the new Foreign Office and the Colonial and India Office buildings in Whitehall, both constructed in the 1860s. While the former had decorated figures on its uppermost story that represented various countries, figures located in the India Office buildings in a similar location did not signify nations but represented "Indian tribes" or "social categories" that the British considered important to the maintenance of their rule over India. The Foreign Office had a plain inner courtyard; in contrast the courtyard of the India Office was animated by busts and statues of well-known civil and military figures associated with the Indian empire.[48]

In Bombay, the political aims of the British Empire's civil religion were effected through naming, architectural style, and particularly through the depiction of British worthies. Governors, colonial officials, or other important members of the European community gave their names to many of Bombay's roads, some institutions, and an occasional fountain, while medallions or more often statues and busts were used to commemorate colonial officials. One of the explicit functions of a public building such as the Town Hall was to house statues (Figure 6.11; also see Figure 6.1). Statues were also found in the semi-public gardens of other buildings, such as those fronting the university and the High Court. Most statues were placed in what could be called the city's public spaces—the Bombay Green or Elphinstone Circle, Apollo Bunder, and Victoria Gardens, with the majority on the Esplanade. Looking at these, viewers would have been reminded of those who toiled in order to bring the benefits of colonial rule to Indians (Figure 6.12).

In 1858, after the First War of Independence, India came under the Crown, and in 1877, Queen Victoria was proclaimed the Empress of India at the Imperial Assemblage in Delhi. Soon after 1858, Bombay was linked to the Crown and later empire of Queen Victoria through naming practices and the erection of statues. The Great Indian Peninsular Railway terminus was named the Victoria Terminus, and the Queen's jubilee year was celebrated in the naming of the Victoria Jubilee Technical Institute. Statues played an important role in these acts of remembrance; the front of the central facade of the Victoria Terminus, for example, contained a life-size statue of the queen-empress forming part of the architecture. Royal visits were memorialized in monuments such as

FIGURE 6.11. Lieutenant-Colonel Thomas Alexander Cowper, Town Hall, Bombay, 1821–33, lobby of the library of the Asiatic Society. To the right is a statue by Sir Francis Chantrey of soldier and historian Major-General Sir John Malcolm (1769–1833), illuminated by a skylight. Apart from statues of British worthies, statues of two Indians are also housed here: Sir Jamsetjee Jeejeebhoy, the famous Parsi philanthropist, and Jagannath Shankarshet, a leading Indian merchant and influential local figure. Photograph by author, 1998.

the statue of the Prince of Wales, who toured India for six months in 1875–76, and the Gateway of India was built in memory of the visit of King-Emperor George V and Queen Mary in 1911 (see Figure 2.10).

The shift of power from the East India Company to the Crown in 1858 was soon followed by changes in Bombay's urban form, particularly after the fort

FIGURE 6.12. Frederick William Stevens, Great Indian Peninsular Railway Victoria Terminus and Administrative Offices, Bombay, 1878–87, detail of medallion portraits of British officials on the facade of administrative offices. Photograph by author, 2005.

walls were torn down in 1862. The walls of the Fort of Bombay were completed in 1715 or 1716 during the governorship of Charles Boone. The Fort formed the nucleus of colonial settlement. In theory, the Fort was divided in two sections, with Indians living in the north and the British occupying the south. At the center of the Fort lay the Bombay Green, a space that was transformed by 1865 into the Elphinstone Circle, Bombay's first urban design scheme. The statues of Cornwallis and Wellesley stood in the central garden. Surrounding the Green/Circle were some of Bombay's major institutions, including St. Thomas Cathedral and the Town Hall. Until 1865, the Green/Circle, St. Thomas Cathedral, and Town Hall contained most of the city's statues and memorials. Outside of the Fort, the Afghan Memorial Church of St. John the Evangelist located in the cantonment in Colaba was a memorial itself. Apart from congregants and European tourists, few members of the public would have visited the churches, while the Town Hall and particularly the Bombay Green were frequented by more members of the public.

The destruction of the fort walls opened up a large new arena for the construction of public buildings, and the open space of the Esplanade provided suitable sites for the erection of statues. The institutions and spaces dominated by the British housed the memorials and statues erected before 1862. Although these were theoretically public spaces, some of them catered almost exclusively to a specific public. After 1862, memorials, medallion sculptures, and statues peopled the very fabric of the large new public buildings as well as the interior and exterior spaces where all members of the public visited, gathered, or passed by. In doing so the colonial regime was simultaneously attempting to invite, incorporate, and accommodate the local population into the ceremonials and beliefs of the British Empire's civil religion in India. This incorporation took place on a scale of India as a whole as well as the local scale, where Bombay's philanthropists influenced the associations of this civil religion.

Philanthropy and the Accommodation of Indian Worthies

After 1862, Indian philanthropists supported the construction of vast public buildings, a fact that was visually represented by depictions of their symbols, by images in the building, or as statues. Sir Bartle Frere, the British governor, may have initiated the construction of these public buildings, but it was the huge profits made by native businessmen in the cotton boom that resulted from the American Civil War that partially financed many of these structures. These buildings and spaces were truly public, the meeting ground of all of Bombay's varied publics. The minor deities memorialized here were both British and Indian and were presided over by Queen, later Empress, Victoria, whose white marble statue was unveiled in 1872 at a prominent location on the Esplanade (Figure 6.13).

The two decades following 1857 marked a change in the status of the monarchy in Britain and in the construction of new forms of authority in India, where Victoria replaced the Mughal Emperor.[49] In the decades following 1858, the British constructed a new hierarchical order under Queen Victoria that incorporated British and Indian subjects, an order that was completed and represented at the 1877 Imperial Assemblage in Delhi. Queen Victoria was at the top of the hierarchy, represented in India by the governor-general and viceroy, and all British and Indians were ranked in status in relation to the viceroy. At the assemblage only the most prominent members of this hierarchy were represented. While native princes and feudal rulers were most prominent, the assemblage also included Indians of other types such as editors, landlords, and journalists. Bernard Cohn points out that in the 1870s the divisions in British theories of Indian sociology were apparent. Some of the British elite believed in a historical India that was a feudal society composed of lords, chiefs, and peasants. Others saw India as a transforming society made up of communities based on religion, caste, region, or educational and occupational categories. For followers of the feudal model, Indians had a "native aristocracy," while for those who believed in the community model, it was thought that these diverse

FIGURE 6.13. Matthew Noble, statue of Queen Victoria, Bombay, unveiled in 1872. The statue was prominently located on the Esplanade near the junction of two main roads, one of which led to the bandstand and the other to the fort. The statue was unveiled on 29 April 1872 as the first public act of Lord Northbrook, Viceroy and Governor-General of India. It cost £18,000 and was the gift of Khanderao Maharaj, Gaekwar of Baroda. The eight-foot statue of the seated queen was placed on a basement that had several steps, and the whole was sheltered by a canopy and Gothic peak. The total height of the structure was forty-two feet. Courtesy Bhau Daji Lad Sangrahalaya, Bombay.

communities could be managed through "representative men," selected by the British, who could speak for their communities.[50] In India's colonial sociology the system of classification had enough flexibility to vary by region. However, at the core, the system was based on two sets of criteria. The first was made up of "natural" criteria such as religion, caste, and race; the second, "social criteria," included achievements—such as education, acts of philanthropy in the construction of works for the public good, and demonstration of loyalty to the British authorities—as well as family history in terms of "descent and genealogy."[51]

Bombay's merchant princes were important components of this newly formulated hierarchy, princes on the basis of social criteria. They were representative men of their respective communities while at the same time earning their aristocratic status or titular awards through acts of philanthropy directed toward projects of public utility or those that displayed their loyalty. While an occasional native prince might demonstrate his philanthropy in Bombay, it was a territory that was dominated by projects reflecting the philanthropy of the city's merchant princes. Individual acts of philanthropy might be directed toward personal glory, but since they acted as representatives of their respective communities, individual philanthropists could also be seen as contributing community philanthropy to the city. At the same time, this reveals some of the possible tensions produced by this system. Communities that were not wealthy could be proud of native philanthropy only if they could think beyond community and see these works as a product of native versus British endeavors.

British civil religion was upheld by the myth of the blessings of British rule that had brought social change, Western education, and works of public utility, and the proof of this was in the material evidence—including educational institutions, institutions of self-government such as the municipality, public buildings, and new modes of transportation that had been established by the British. While the British had a more personal connection to civil religion, it was one they wanted the Indian public to believe in, to participate in, and to feel appropriately respectful of and grateful to the British for the sacrifices they had made in bringing about all the positive outcomes of colonial rule. In Bombay, the satisfaction the British derived in contemplating the positive benefits of British rule was tempered by the reminder that Bombay's achievements were a result of the joint partnership between British and Indians, and the credit would have to be shared with Indians whose philanthropy had made many of these achievements possible. Although the British might pride themselves in directing Indian philanthropy toward projects for the public good, such as hospitals and educational institutions rather than religious institutions and rituals, evidence of Indian philanthropy was everywhere: in the names given to institutions and in statues and busts. Inhabitants of Bombay and visitors to the city could observe the Victorian Gothic Revival architecture of the city while at the same time realizing that much of it had been paid for by Indians. In such a situation, it is likely that the British in Bombay could not have complete confidence in the myths underlying British civil religion in India. Victoria might still reign supreme as the head of this hierarchical order, but even as her statue looked down from above on the Victoria Terminus, Indian and British worthies were depicted in statues in many buildings in the vicinity, hinting that they were at the same level in the hierarchy.

Even though Indian philanthropists were prominent figures as representative men in this new hierarchical order with Victoria at its head, their philanthropy did not only respond to the desires and needs of the colonial regime. Let us take the Parsi community as an example. While there are many famous Indian nationalists who were Parsi, many Parsis had photographs of British royalty on their walls, showing that the community at large saw themselves as subjects of the British monarchy.[52] Hence, the Parsis as a community were largely integrated into the new Victorian order in India. The Parsis certainly flourished under British rule, and many of Bombay's most famous philanthropists hailed from the Parsi community and were suitably rewarded with honors and titles. Yet while simultaneously serving personal ambitions and the purposes of the British regime through acts of philanthropy, wealthy Parsis also served their Zoroastrian faith where the rich are urged to share the fruits of their wealth by helping others, thus allowing them to do more "good deeds" that then go on to bring benefits to the benefactor as if he were the author of these "good deeds."[53] While individual Parsi philanthropists paid for various projects as representative men of their community, their entire community took pride in them and saw these works as typifying the good qualities of their community. Hence, Parsis came to pride themselves on the useful nature of their charities, such as the building of hospitals and libraries, in contrast to the wasteful charities of Hindus and Muslims, who spent money on pilgrimages, funerals, or feeding Brahmans.[54] Thus Parsi philanthropy revealed the superiority of their community versus other Indian communities. Even though the Parsis may have been loyal subjects of the British, they believed they had built Bombay, a widely held sentiment that was even expressed in a comparatively recent play, *Doongaji House,* written by Cyrus Mistry around 1977 and set in Bombay of the late 1960s.[55] This opinion that Parsis built Bombay was echoed by others, such as the journalist Sidney Low, who accompanied the Prince and Princess of Wales on their tour of India in 1906. Low wrote, "If the eye falls on a handsome public building, it is quite likely to be a Parsi hospital, or a Parsi convalescent home, or the college founded by one wealthy fire-worshipper, or the monument presented to the city by another."[56] The British desire to create a single hierarchical order with the Crown and its representatives at its head was undercut by Bombay's philanthropists whose good works sent out the message that Bombay's inhabitants were fortunate to receive the blessings of their philanthropy.

Everyday Life and the Transformation of Meaning

The public landscape was also shaped by a third group: ordinary citizens who influenced it by their reactions to it, by interacting with it in their everyday life, and by appropriating parts of it through acts of reimagination. Native newspapers commented on projects underwritten in part by Bombay's wealthy native elite, and Bombay's citizens could express their disapproval when they felt that native philanthropy was misdirected. In 1864, some members of the Parsi community protested vociferously when Sir Cowasji Jehangir donated a beautiful fountain, at a cost of Rs. 7,000, to St. Thomas Cathedral (see Figure 2.12). Located near the cathedral's western entrance, the fountain has a cross. In his memoirs, D. N. Wacha commented on the reaction of the Zoroastrian community to this gift to a Christian cathedral, remarking:

> For this catholic benevolence, for Sir Cowasji was nothing if not catholic in all his philanthropy, his orthodox community of 1864, was in revolt! It was a profanity of profanities for the scion of the rich Parsi house of the Readymoneys to erect a fountain in a place of worship devoted to Christianity! And some of these Zoroastrian fanatics of the day, a remnant of which class still exists, nicknamed the donor "Cowasji Cross" as the structure is surmounted with a cross.[57]

Parsis who disapproved of Jehangir's generous gift used humor to ridicule the rich gentleman, coining a new name for him that indicated that he had crucified himself with his own cross. While Jehangir's gift was meant to flatter the British and beautify the cathedral, the fountain was used at all times of the day by poor Indians who lived in the vicinity and collected water here for domestic use.[58]

In the restructuring of the city of Bombay to make it more modern, I have argued, the gods and goddesses were locked up, or in other words, the religious was contained.[59] We have seen how the secular colonial landscape created by the British was imbued with the religious even though it was not recognized as such by them. In Bombay, the local population did not recognize the distinction and separation between secular and sacred spaces and transformed secular spaces into religious spaces.

In their everyday life, ordinary Indians interacted with the new and changing public landscape where statues of British worthies were placed. Some

FIGURE 6.14. Monument of Marquis Cornwallis, governor-general of India, Bombay Green, Bombay. The monument shelters the statue of Cornwallis by John Bacon Jr. that was installed in the Bombay Green in 1822. Courtesy Bhau Daji Lad Sangrahalaya, Bombay.

Indians may have thought that early British statues were of gods and treated them as such. Govind Narayan, author of the first complete urban biography of the city that was written in Marathi, points out that when Wellesley's statue was erected, "many of the Maratha simpletons of Mumbai" thought "the Company Sarkar had very kindly imported an English god for their worship."[60] The statue of Marquis Cornwallis was placed in what Narayan described as "a small temple-like structure" in the Bombay Green.[61] This was seen as a shrine and referred to as Chota Dewal, or "small temple" (Figure 6.14; also see Figure 6.10). The natives worshipped the statue, much to the consternation of the British. James Douglas described the statue to Cornwallis in 1900:

> There is a very fine monument, in the Elphinstone Circle, to Cornwallis. Go when you will, you will see flowers placed on the open book, or garlands on the figures. This is not a new custom. In 1825, it was thought by the natives to be a place of religious worship, and they called it *Chota Dewal*. Government tried to stop this, and issued some vernacular notices that it was a mistake. But it was of no use, for when these feelings take possession of the natives they are not easily eradicated.[62]

What was also probably frightening to the British in this early veneration of British statues placed in the public arena was that the religious could not be entirely contained or controlled and could appear anytime and anywhere in this new secular public landscape.

Statues of a nonreligious nature were new phenomena in the urban environment in India. Emperor Ashoka's pillars carved with his edicts and erected in various parts of his empire in the third century BCE were an exception to this general rule, and yet those were not human forms.[63] Under these circumstances it is hardly surprising that these figures were interpreted as gods. But was this necessarily the case? The British interpretation that Indians worshipped statues may have to do with their construction of Indians as religious and their religious practices as being emotional. A good example of the latter would be the Shia Muslim festival of Muhurram, which fascinated the British and was often described by them and involved processions and self-flagellation by some of the participants. However, there were a wide range of ceremonies relating to statues. In the contemporary era, for example, on the occasion of the Hindu festival of Dussehra, one finds garlands adorning the bust of Sir Cowasji Jehangir, the founder of Bombay's Jehangir Art Gallery. The garlands are placed by the workers at the gallery. These workers are well aware that the Parsi gentleman was not divine, and the act of garlanding might be seen as a sign of respect for a deceased elder who participates, in spirit, in the festivities through his statue. One might assume that the participants believe that the respect shown to the statue will have a good effect or, if nothing else, do no harm. Gillian Tindall makes note of similar recent ritual activities taking place at Sir Jamsetjee Jeejeebhoy's (1783–1859) statue at the J. J. Hospital.[64] The deceased Parsi baronet was no Hindu, and one might see the ritual garlands and offerings to his statue as signs of gratitude and respect for his philanthropy and the hospital that he helped to found.

The case of the Cornwallis statue is particularly interesting because it affords a glimpse at an early encounter of Indians with statues of Europeans in a public space in Bombay. Perhaps the Indians paid no attention to the notices issued by the government in the vernacular because they did not understand what the British wanted or did not think that British attitudes were correct, or because they were not worshipping Cornwallis, or if they were they had a right to. In his biography of Bombay, Govind Narayan says of Cornwallis, "This Sahib was very compassionate and a true well-wisher of India." He also criticizes the laborers and poor natives for worshipping the statue, noting in exasperation, "Our people are hopeless! Truly naïve! If they see any shape in stone, they bring a coconut and fold their hands in respect. They do not bother to think."[65] However, we cannot know for sure whether Indians were worshipping or simply paying respect to the statue of Cornwallis. It is entirely possible that they did both, or worshipped the statue at first and later simply paid respect to it. *Chota Dewal*, after all, can be translated to mean "small temple."

Even if Indians were worshipping Cornwallis in some form, would that Cornwallis have the same biography as the figure hero-worshipped by the British? Drawing on the work of Vincente Rafael, I suggest that it is entirely possible that Indians "fished out" fragments of Cornwallis's history, which was subsequently augmented and transformed in the imaginations of the Indians to fit their own categories.[66] The British set up the statue of Cornwallis as an act of hero worship and also as a sign of victory and an assertion of control over the subcontinent. Indians deflected the aims of the colonial regime by adopting the statue and reinventing its meaning through their imaginations in a way that remains lost to us. By garlanding the statue they made it alien to the British, not only because it had been appropriated by popular religious practices but also because it may have reminded the British that their emotions toward Cornwallis were a kind of worship as well.

There are other examples, from India and elsewhere, where statues or other symbols were worshipped by the local population.[67] An interesting case is that of the Didarganj *yakshi* that was found in the Ganges River in Patna in 1917 by Maulavi Qazi Sayyid Muhammad Azimul. The tall, full-breasted, wide-hipped figure may have been sculpted in the third century BCE during the Mauryan period. In northern India during that period, male and female *yakshis* were associated with fertility, wealth, and abundance. Later, the figure was worshipped in the belief that she was a Hindu deity. Not long after that, a British official by the name of E. H. C. Walsh, a member of the provincial Board of Revenue, was informed about the statue. He and D. B. Spooner, the curator of the Patna Museum, took the statue away to the museum, using their knowledge of Hinduism to prove to the Hindus that this was no Hindu goddess. While the villagers probably saw the figure as some version of the Mother Goddess, Walsh and Spooner saw it as an art object, an example of Indian statuary to be displayed, studied, and placed within the chronology of Indian sculpture. Drawing on distinctions made by Walter Benjamin, Richard Davis argues that while the Indians valued the sculpture for its "cult value," the British admired it for its "exhibition value."[68] Implicit in the ability of the British to possess the sculpture was their right to control images that could be considered to be in the realm of art, while Indians had a right to images that had a history of ongoing cult practices.

In Bombay, there was a similar encounter of different kinds of associations in the statue of Cornwallis. The British certainly thought of statues in public spaces as works of art that were to be admired from a distance for their "exhibition value," while certain important statues, such as the Queen's statue, became part of secular state ritual. That the hero worship of Cornwallis or the exaltation of Queen Victoria into almost a Mother Goddess did not seem like religious practice was because the secular rituals of civil religion screened this resemblance from view. However, sculptures of personages are like portraits and are objects that retain cult value in what Walter Benjamin calls the "cult of remembrance."[69] For Indians, there was no such ambiguity about how to view these sculptures, and they saw the statue of Cornwallis as something that could be incorporated into their system of knowledge and cult practices. The British could neither completely control the public space where Cornwallis's statue was located nor deny the superior right of Indian cult practices over the statue in this space. Here, not only did they accede to the religious rights of Indians but it is likely that they feared the consequences of actively preventing Indians from engaging in cult activities at this site. Perhaps what was more frightening was the possibility that any sculpture in a public space could become the object of ongoing ritual practices, thus transforming it into a cult object under the control of Indians. While the British succeeded in transforming many icons into art objects, Indians occasionally succeeded in changing the meanings attached to British statues. As a corollary to this, I add that as it was likely that a large majority of Indians saw the British statues as alive in some way, an attack or defacement of a statue of a British worthy was likely to have meant a great deal more than simple defilement.

Attitudes toward British statues, including that of Cornwallis, were hardly stable. While many Indians may have continued to venerate the statue of Cornwallis, by 1870 it required the protection of a railing. Statues erected to commemorate other British worthies, such as the former governor Sir Richard Temple, had to seriously consider the issue of vandalism. In 1886, when the government was looking for a suitable site for Temple's statue, the Secretariat grounds, facing the Oval, were suggested because it would "probably be there secure from mutilation."[70] In October 1896, the Queen's statue was severely damaged when a bucket of tar and *chunam* (a type of plaster) was poured over the statue. Victoria also received a garland of shoes. The massive marble statue of a seated queen, eight feet tall, shaded by a canopy with a Gothic peak, the whole structure forty-two feet high, must have been overpowering but proved surprisingly vulnerable to attack (see Figure 6.13). The stain and the garland of shoes was a desacralization of the symbol of the Queen and a message that all Indians did not accept her as their monarch. It symbolized the growing public anger at the policies pursued by the government following the 1896 plague. In 1897, Damodher Chapekar, who murdered Mr. Rand, the Chairman of the Poona Plague Committee, admitted to this act of vandalism.[71] Tourists who used Maclean's *Guide to Bombay* read of this incident and perhaps understood that the European deities of Bombay's civil religion were under siege. The larger message was that the British had failed to incorporate Indians into their civil religion. If Bombay's Hindu goddesses were no longer free to roam over Bombay's landscape, statues of former British heroes, governors, and of the Queen herself had to cower behind railings.

THE INSERTION OF THE RELIGIOUS INTO BOMBAY'S SECULAR PUBLIC LANDSCAPE

All the shapers of Bombay's landscape—the colonial regime, the Indian philanthropists, and the native public—participated in the creation and transformation of the Victoria and Albert Museum and the Victoria Gardens in the 1860s, a site where the religious and secular were intertwined. The Victoria Gardens were attached to the Victoria and Albert Museum (1862–72), an Italian Renaissance–style building, which was founded in 1858 to commemorate the change in authority over the government of India from the East India Company to the Crown (Figure 6.15). Central to the foundation of the museum was the "Great Exhibition of the Industry of All Nations," held in London in the Crystal Palace in 1851, where artifacts from India were first displayed. Following this, in the 1850s museum committees were founded in Madras and Bombay to collect and bring together typical samples of art manufacturers of the Presidency. For art schools founded in India in the 1860s and 1870s, the museums were expected to function closely with the schools "as a storehouse of tradition and as a forum of visual instruction" by including the finest examples of Oriental art.[72] The Victoria Museum and Gardens were a result of the joint efforts of the government and the local population. The government donated the site, the native elite contributed toward its foundation, and the museum was built by public subscriptions. Located on a prominent site on Parel Road, the Victoria Museum and Gardens was one of the earliest major public institutions and spaces to be founded in Bombay. The gardens were a popular public space, and even in the early twentieth century, thousands of Indians, men and women, visited the gardens in the evenings.[73]

The museum and gardens contained evidence of individual contributions made by Bombay's wealthy native elite to this complex. Jagannath Shankarshet and Premabhai Hemabhai, for example, paid for most of the cost of the ornamental gateway and railing fronting Parel Road. Rustomji Jeejeebhoy defrayed most of the cost of the triple-arched screen over the garden turnstiles (Figure 6.16).[74]

Sometimes these contributions by wealthy philanthropists acted, in part or entirely, as memorials to themselves. This is particularly clear in the case of

Museum in the Victoria Gardens, Bombay

David Sassoon's two major gifts to the museum. The first was a marble statue by Noble of Albert, the Prince Consort, who had died recently, and for which Sassoon paid £3,100. This served as a memorial to Sassoon's loyalty to the Crown and to his own generosity. He also ensured that the monument contained a Hebrew inscription, a reminder that the donor was a Jew.[75] This large statue was prominently displayed in the large main hall directly fronting the entrance to the museum (Figure 6.17). The second was the illuminated David Sassoon clock tower and fountain, sixty-seven feet in height and designed in a Palladian style (Figure 6.18). Sassoon contributed Rs. 30,000 toward the tower that cost Rs. 51,653 and that ultimately acted as a memorial to him. The clock tower also contained a bust of him that was raised by fellow-citizens in appreciation of his good works and that was, according to Sassoon family biographer Cecil Roth, "in defiance of the second Commandment."[76] While the museum was set back a bit from Parel Road, the clock tower fronted the road. It would have been one of the first structures a passerby or visitor saw. There appears to have been a second statue of David Sassoon, which was placed inside the museum, where his son attempted to install a permanent niche to hold it in a location of his choice. In 1872, Sir Albert Sassoon privately addressed the governor requesting his permission to present a pedestal to the museum to act as a stand for a bust of his father, the late David Sassoon. The bust, at that time,

FIGURE 6.15. Designed by Mr. Tracy, drainage engineer to the municipality, and altered by Messrs. Scott, McClelland & Company, Victoria and Albert Museum (now Bhau Daji Lad Museum/Sangrahalaya), Bombay, 1862–72, postcard circa 1910s. Note the Corinthian columns and rustic basements. Courtesy Phillips Antiques, Bombay.

FIGURE 6.16. Victoria Gardens (now known as Jijamata Udyan), Bombay, opened to the public in 1862, view of triple-arched screen. Photograph by author, 1998.

stood on the ground of the landing, halfway up the staircase leading to the museum's gallery.[77]

The Victoria and Albert Museum and Victoria Gardens also contained busts of British worthies. The museum housed busts of Lord Canning and the Honorable Mountstuart Elphinstone. The gardens contained a building "originally erected to enshrine"[78] a bust by the sculptor Noble of Lady Frere, wife of Sir Bartle Frere, the governor of Bombay who initiated the transformation of Bombay in the 1860s. Lady Frere had opened the gardens to the public in 1862. It appears that Sir Jamsetjee Jeejeebhoy had purchased the bust, or more likely the building for the bust, for Rs. 9,950.[79] This purchase by Jeejeebhoy was surely a demonstration of his loyalty to the British regime. Not far from the main entrance to the museum stood the remnants of the huge elephant that once resided on the western shore of Elephanta Island (also called Gharapuri), and after which the island was named. Relocated and decontextualized in its new domain in the museum grounds, it had been transformed into an art object that was now under the control of the British.

The Victoria and Albert Museum and Victoria Gardens were sites that commemorated and celebrated the change in regime from company control to Crown. It was also a site meant to deify royalty—not only did the museum contain a massive statue of Albert, but Queen Victoria's statue was also originally

FIGURE 6.17. Mr. Tracy and altered by Messrs. Scott, McClelland & Company, Victoria and Albert Museum, 1862–72, interior view showing statue of Prince Albert, consort of Queen Victoria. The eight-foot statue stands on a high pedestal and shows the prince wearing robes of state. He is flanked by two attractive female figures representing science and art. The statue was made by Matthew Noble and cost £3,100. David Sassoon paid the cost of the statue and gifted it to the city. Courtesy Bhau Daji Lad Sangrahalaya, Bombay.

meant to be housed here as a companion to her husband's statue.[80] British worthies stand here on the model of attending deities, but the anxiety of the Indian native elite in this tense period after the Mutiny is evident, and their demonstrations of loyalty to the Crown and its representatives is clear in their individual gifts to this institution. David Sassoon's gifts signaled the friendship of his family and religion to British royalty while his clock tower acted as a space to enshrine his bust. Even though the bust of David Sassoon remained unscathed, sometime around the beginning of the twentieth century Lady Frere's enshrined bust was defaced by some unknown perpetrators for reasons that are not clear, a desecration like that inflicted on images at Elephanta. Lady Frere's bust was sent to England for repair, but since it could not be repaired, Lady Frere's son sent a replica of the bust, which was housed out of harm's way in the Victoria and Albert Museum.[81] This act thus served to empty the shrine of its

FIGURE 6.18. Sassoon's Clock Tower, Victoria Gardens, Bombay, circa 1870s. At the ground level, the tower accommodates a bust of David Sassoon. Courtesy Bhau Daji Lad Sangrahalaya, Bombay.

statue. While the construction of the museum and gardens undertaken with the help of the native elite helped to construct, cement, and demonstrate the new hierarchical order that was fully in place by the 1877 Imperial Assemblage, the defacement of Lady Frere's bust was part of a number of acts that helped to unravel this hierarchical structure, revealing discontent with the government and an incipient nationalist movement.

It is notable that as one of their first public institutions in the construction of a new public landscape, the colonial regime chose to construct a museum, an institution that has long been compared to "a ritual site."[82] Visiting the Victoria and Albert Museum, viewing the objects on display, was certainly an out-of-the-ordinary experience for most of Bombay's citizens. While the museum housed separate sections that displayed materials on agriculture, mythology, pottery, silverware, armory, industry, and even two rooms with holdings of materials on old Bombay, the museum also acted as a shrine for the statue of Prince Albert. The plan of the museum was simple. It was a rectangular, two-story building, with the entry on one short side and the staircase to the upper floor on the opposite side. The two narrower ends of the rectangle were subdivided for the most part into administrative offices, special rooms, and spaces for circulation. Bracketed between these two ends was the main hall of the museum, containing a double-height atrium-like central space that enframed the marble statue of Albert (Figures 6.19 and 6.20; also see Figure 6.17). Although it is true that visitors might move through the museum in various ways, the space of the museum and its exhibits guided movement in particular ways. The entrance to the hall of the exhibits, directly in line with the statue, framed the statue of Albert that appeared to glow with reflected light. As visitors moved around the exhibits on the ground floor and upper floor, they circumambulated the statue. If they looked down into the central space from the upper level, the statue of Albert dominated their visual field.

For the colonial establishment, going to the museum was supposed to be a transformative experience. However, to many Indians, the museum was like the Wonder House of Lahore in Rudyard Kipling's *Kim*. In Bombay, as in Calcutta and Madras, the museums were extremely popular with the public, especially on holidays. However, museum officials were dissatisfied with the way in which museums were viewed by the public, which had more to do with spectacle and wonder and less to do with a well-informed engagement with the exhibits. For the British museum officials, the attitude of the Indian public, who thought of "museums as *tamasha* (show)," must have been particularly troubling because for them museums were, as Carol Duncan has argued, a ritual space where serious and engaged contemplation of exhibits was the proper and fitting deportment.[83]

While secular figures of British monarchy were deified at the Victoria and Albert Museum and Victoria Gardens, the religious was intertwined with the secular in other ways at the Victoria Gardens. In 1874, E. W. Ravenscroft, acting municipal commissioner, reported an encroachment to the government that had taken place in the Victoria Gardens, which he wished to clarify before signing the indenture relating to the gardens. In the indenture laid out between the government and the corporation, it was stated that if the corporation "shall permit the said gardens and premises of any part thereof, to be diverted to any other use, or shall alienate, or shall attempt to alienate the same or any part thereof, to any person or persons, then, or in either of the said cases it would be lawful for the Secretary of State [i.e., the government] to re-enter and re-possess the garden." Ravenscroft reported that a section of the garden had been encroached on "under the very eyes of the Municipal officers" and with the permission of Arthur Crawford, the former municipal commissioner. He added, "It is difficult to speak too strongly of the negligence which permitted the religious edifice of any denomination to spring up in a garden belonging to the public."[84]

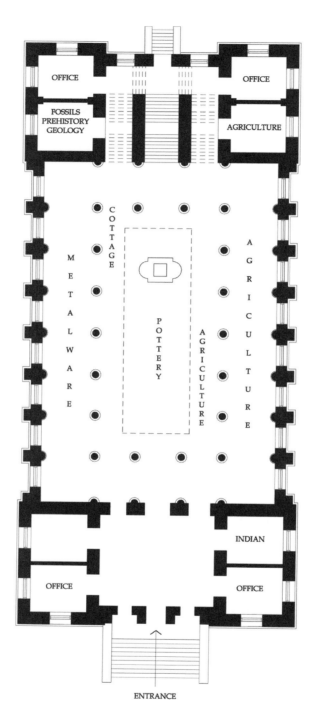

FIGURE 6.19. Mr. Tracy and altered by Messrs. Scott, McClelland & Company, Victoria and Albert Museum at Victoria Gardens, Bombay, ground floor plan, 1862–72. Original plan courtesy Bhau Daji Lad Sangrahalaya, Bombay. Redrawn by Robert Batson.

OFFICE

OFFICE

FOSSILS PREHISTORY GEOLOGY

AGRICULTURE

METALWARE

COTTAGE

POTTERY

AGRICULTURE

AGRICULTURE

INDIAN

OFFICE

OFFICE

ENTRANCE

PLAN OF GROUND FLOOR

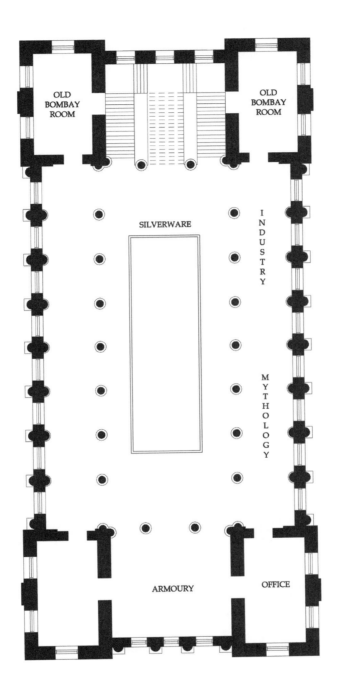

Within the floor plan:

OLD BOMBAY ROOM

OLD BOMBAY ROOM

SILVERWARE

INDUSTRY

MYTHOLOGY

ARMOURY

OFFICE

PLAN OF FIRST FLOOR

FIGURE 6.20. Mr. Tracy and altered by Messrs. Scott, Mc-Clelland & Company, Victoria and Albert Museum at Victoria Gardens, Bombay, first floor plan, 1862–72. Original plan courtesy Bhau Daji Lad Sangrahalaya, Bombay. Redrawn by Robert Batson.

According to Ravenscroft, between 1814 and 1824, a tomb or *dargah* of a Muslim was placed under a large tree on the east of what was then the Victoria Gardens. The encroachments occurred in 1871, when the official in charge of the garden was away for the monsoon months. He returned to find that a fakir or Muslim holy man was constructing a mosque near the tomb. Subsequently, a house and tank were added. In 1873, W. G. Pedder, municipal commissioner, asked the solicitors to the corporation for advice on how to proceed against this fakir who had encroached on about half an acre of the land of the garden and built a house, mosque, tank, and so on. A notice was served to the fakir, with no result.

The British were forced to tolerate this encroachment and decided to enclose it by a wall with a single passage.[85] This ensured that the general population who visited the garden would not be inconvenienced by the large numbers of Muslim devotees who regularly frequented the mosque.[86] The *dargah* and the encroachment on public space was a claim made in the name of an older monument and the practices of popular religion that supported it, which the British seemed compelled to accept (Figure 6.21).

It is important to remember that the Victoria Gardens and the Victoria and Albert Museum were founded to commemorate Queen Victoria. However, on one day of the year the grounds surrounding the museum were used to commemorate Prophet Muhummad. On the last Wednesday of the month of Safar, most Muslims celebrated a day where they went on a picnic, known as Akhiri Char Shamba or Chela Budh. The locations for these picnics included the open areas on Malabar Hill, Mahalakshmi, Mahim or Bandra, and the shrine of Mama Hajiyani.[87] Hundreds, however, took the tram to the Victoria Gardens, and S. M. Edwardes captured their occupation of these grounds in this description:

> To the Victoria Gardens the tram cars bring hundreds of holiday-makers, most of whom remain in the outer or free zone of the gardens and help to illumine its grass plots and shady paths with the green, blue, pink and yellow glories of their silk attire. Here a group of men and women are enjoying a cold luncheon; there a small party of Memons are discussing affairs over their "bidis," while on all sides are children playing with the paper toys, rattles and tin wheels which the hawkers offer at such seasons of merry-making. Coal-black Africans, ruddy Pathans and yellow Bukharans squat on the open turf to the west of the Victoria and Albert Museum.[88]

One cannot help but be struck by the cosmopolitanism of Muslims—differentiated by community, color, culture, and region of origin and yet comfortable

and practiced at sharing space with Muslims from all over the globe at the annual Haj pilgrimage and at sites such as this. Here, at the Victoria and Albert Museum and Victoria Gardens, Muslims commemorated the Prophet's visit to the outskirts of Mecca, as he convalesced after a serious illness, in gardens that were intended to commemorate their Empress.

FIGURE 6.21. Muslim shrine, Jijamata Udyan (Victoria Gardens), Bombay. Photograph by author, 1998.

Michel de Certeau discusses the practice that is known in France as *la perruque,* or "the wig." Wigging can take many forms, from engaging in one's own work during company time or taking unused scraps and converting them into objects of one's own use. What are stolen are not goods but time that the worker uses to be free and creative to indulge in activities that do not bring him or her profit.[89] On Chela Budh in Bombay, Muslims too were engaged in a kind of wigging, where available spaces were used and temporarily stolen so that by the act of reimagination Victoria's domain temporarily became Prophet Muhummad's.

Partha Chatterjee has argued that the spiritual is an "'inner' domain bearing the 'essential' marks of cultural identity," where nationalism first declares its sovereignty and does not allow the colonial power to interfere in this arena.[90] According to Chatterjee, religion, for example, may be a site of resistance, but only in spaces such as the family, which is part of the inner domain. However, we see that religion continued to be a site of resistance in the public or outer domain. Here, Indians expressed their lack of belief in the myths underlying British civil religion by the defacement of statues or, as we see in the case of the Muslims, in a kind of wigging that in the Victoria Gardens.

CONCLUSION

Modernizing colonial Bombay meant a clear separation between the religious and secular domains of the city, where local religious structures were demolished and rebuilt if they stood in the way of improvements such as new roads and railway stations. The religious also had to be controlled, which meant locking up the gods.

However, the new public landscape was only secular on the surface. It was also the arena for the visual representation of the colonial regime's civil religion whose spaces and statues provided new ritual sites and deities, where the cult of remembrance flourished. Indian philanthropists who helped found many of these new institutions and raise subscriptions for statues were quick to raise their own statues and reign as deities. If the Indians thought statues of early British worthies to be gods, the colonial regime converted Indian cave temples into on-site museums. Both museums and monuments became sites of secular worship where artworks and archaeological and agricultural products, among other things, were disassociated from their normal visual contexts and installed in a new setting.

In colonial Bombay, Indians transformed secular public spaces into sacred spaces while the British were engaged in the opposite process of accommodating the secular in Indian sacred spaces. I do not mean to imply that Indians were fundamentally "religious" and the British "secular" but rather that in this cultural encounter each group understood and occupied the secular and religious architectural spaces of the other from the point of view of their own cultural preconceptions and practices. Once a year Muslims occupied Victoria Gardens and remembered the Prophet's convalescence near Mecca while Europeans visiting Elephanta in the sixteenth century thought they inhabited one of the oldest monuments of the world—showing us that to occupy a space was also to reimagine it.

Acknowledgments

I AM GLAD THAT I LISTENED to Dell Upton, my doctoral advisor, when he suggested that I lay my dissertation aside for a year and then ask someone who had written a book to read it. After that year, I turned to my friend Lisa Pollard. She agreed without hesitation and then offered a startling insight: it could result in two books. I thank Lisa not only for reading my dissertation but for this advice, which is directly responsible for the shape of this book, now quite far from where it began.

If it were not for Charles Hallisey, my mentor at the University of Wisconsin–Madison, a wonderful friend and true guide, this book would never have been realized. For several years, he has patiently listened to my ideas, pushed me to think harder and deeper, suggested alternative and imaginative ways to look at a subject, and generously shared his time and insights. He read and commented on my dissertation and on almost everything I have written since then, including the first draft of this book. Much of what is good in this book is a reflection of his faith in me. I was fortunate to meet and befriend Jill H. Casid almost as soon as I arrived in Madison. She generously volunteered to take on the unenviable and formidable task of editing my manuscript—a surgical operation I was incapable of doing myself. Jill's skillful editing was grounded in her own clarity of thought, and she made this an infinitely better book. Aware as I am of my original draft, I appreciate the artistry in Jill's endeavor: a delicate balancing of necessary edits and intuitive knowledge of what to keep and what could not be taken away, an understanding that only a friend who knows one well can have. Thinking of Charlie and Jill, I am reminded of the angels in Wim Wenders's *Wings of Desire*, a favorite film for both of them. I am grateful more than words can say.

I thank Dell Upton, Kathleen James-Chakraborty, Thomas R. Metcalf, and Barbara Daly Metcalf, the members of my dissertation committee at the University of California, Berkeley: their efforts with my dissertation became part of this book. There is no doubt that Dell has been a major intellectual force in my life, and I continue to learn from him. I enjoy working through ideas with Dell over long hours of conversation, and I have benefited from his ability to listen, his broad imagination, and his intellectual curiosity. I always come away from these talks with greater clarity and a gentle nudge in the direction of new ways of conceptualizing my ideas. I thank Kathleen for extensive comments on my work and for continued support of my endeavors. I have enjoyed being challenged by Tom over the years, and I hope that I have had the last word in at least some of our discussions. Barbara has been an encouraging and sure guide during my dissertation, and her insights influenced the shape of this book. I also acknowledge the lasting impact of earlier teachers: I thank Neelkanth Chhaya, who supervised my thesis at the School of Architecture, Ahmedabad, India, and made me realize all those years ago my love of research; and at the University of California, Berkeley, I am grateful to Nezar AlSayyad, Paul Groth, Randolph T. Hester Jr., Allan B. Jacobs, Michael Johns, Michael Southworth, Jim Stockinger, and Richard Walker.

Many of my friends in the Bay Area, some of whom were fellow travelers in doctoral programs and many of whom have now moved to other places, sustained me through the years with friendship and intellectual sustenance. I thank Anil Ananthaswamy, Shilajeet (Banny) Banerjee, Ashok Bardhan, Sharad Chari, Swati Chattopadhyay, Nasreen Chopra, Vandana Date, Kavita Datla, William J. Glover, Alka Hingorani, Mrs. Usha Jain (Usha Mausi), Boreth Ly, Monika Mehta, Emily Meredith, Alan Mikhail, Stella E. Nair, Lisa Pollard, Haripriya Rangan, Simona Sawhney, Arijit Sen, Sriram Srinivasan, and Ved Vatuk (Vedji).

It would not have been possible to satisfactorily complete my research in Bombay (now Mumbai) without the help of Ashok Sohrab Captain. In extremely primitive conditions, Ashok helped me to photograph architectural drawings and maps at the Maharashtra State Archives, and he walked the streets of Bombay with me, exploring places and photographing buildings. I thank him and Leila Captain for giving me a home in Pune and for making so much of this work possible. Rusheed Wadia took me on long walks and generously shared his knowledge of Fort and Parel. Kaushik Bhaumik, Edward L. Simpson, and Clare Talwalker, fellow researchers at the archives, were the best companions and the most generous colleagues one could ask for.

Research at the Maharashtra State Archives in Bombay was efficient, and indeed pleasurable, because of the kind assistance of the staff. Among those who aided me in Bombay, I thank the librarians and staff at the Asiatic Society of Bombay, the Bombay University Library, the People's Free Reading Room and Library, and the K. R. Cama Oriental Institute. I thank Nivedita Mehta of Alpaiwalla Museum; the staff and Suman Tate, librarian, of the Bhau Daji Lad Sangrahalaya for their cooperation; and Farooq Issa and Muneera Daya of Phillips Antiques. Thanks also to Standard Supply Company, which processed all my slides, and Mitter Bedi Studio for printing photographs. In Pune, I thank D. G. Copiers for its high standards of excellence, while Pritam Nahar at Reality Information Systems has for years overseen the digitization of my slides and prints that I now use for presentations and publications. I also thank the staff of the Nehru Memorial Museum and Library and of the New Delhi Oriental and India Office Collections of the British Library in London. I thank Robert Batson for his beautiful drawings.

Many people and friends from Bombay, Pune, and Alibaug shared their memories and knowledge of Bombay with me. I thank my beloved friend Homi Bhathena, who tragically passed away in 2008; Neena Bhathena, Himanshu Burte, Leila Captain, Fali Heerjee, Jay (Bundels) and Kayanoosh Kadapatti, Aparna Kapadia, Richa Kavade, Malini Krishnankutty, Rohit Kulkarni, Geeta Kumana, Amanda (Mandi) Padamsee, Rajani and Shirish Patel, Alpa Sheth, and Veena and Jatinder Singh. I am grateful to Felicia Dias for sharing her home with me in Bombay. Rita and Ravi Khote always reminded me that I had a home in Alibaug. The Nalwa family—Manpreet (Preeti), Tejinder, Tarini, and Tarika—made research at the British Library possible by giving me a home in London. Aboobaker and Munira Lorgat and Veenita J. Singh enabled my research in many practical ways.

I thank Anthony D. King for reading the entire draft of the manuscript and for giving concrete and detailed suggestions that made this a better book. I am overwhelmed by Garth Andrew Myers's attentive, nuanced, and generous reading of the draft of my manuscript, which allowed me to see when the main themes and arguments of individual chapters and the book as a whole worked—and where I needed to further clarify and refine my ideas. Andreas Ferreira Clüver commented on drafts of chapters and was a pillar of support during many difficult years. Stella E. Nair was reliably available, often on short call, to comment and critique my work. Apart from always offering constructive criticism of my work, Swati Chattopadhyay, William J. Glover, and Farina Mir have been the most generous and supportive of friends. Sujeet D. Mehta, Gudrun Bühnemann, and Ellen Sapega read sections of my work, and Gudrun and Ellen have been wonderful mentors at Madison. I thank Ian Morley and Bernard Porter, colleagues from the world of Victorian studies, for their encouragement of my work.

I am grateful to my colleagues at the University of Wisconsin–Madison for offering a productive intellectual environment for the shaping of this book. I appreciate the generous support of the Graduate School of the University of Wisconsin–Madison for funding for summer research, which allowed me to travel to London and Bombay for further research and paid for the digitization of images. My work also received material support from the Center for South Asia at the University of Wisconsin–Madison. The production of this book has been supported by subvention awards from the Graduate School and Provost's Office and the Center for South Asia at the University of Wisconsin–Madison. Initial research in India was aided by the University of California, Berkeley.

Pieter Martin at the University of Minnesota Press was a most excellent editor, ably shepherding the manuscript through various stages of the process, while Kristian Tvedten carefully prepared it for publication. I thank Dawn Stahl and Nancy Sauro for their thorough copyediting and everyone at the University of Minnesota Press who has been involved in the design and production of this book.

My parents, Major General Uttam Chand Chopra and Mrs. Kushal Chopra, and my sister and brother-in-law, Neera and Naresh Kapahi, have supported my efforts over the years. My parents have given me the emotional strength to see everything in this book through from beginning to end.

Finally, I thank the people of Bombay for guiding me through its streets, its buildings, and its history. Through their love of the city and the power of their memories they helped me inhabit it as well. This is a gift that I cannot begin to reciprocate, but I hope this book will be a small reminder of their love of Bombay and an invitation to others to come to love it, too.

Notes

INTRODUCTION

1. Darukhanawala, *Parsi Lustre on Indian Soil,* 83.

2. It is unclear whether this school was open to non-Parsi schoolgirls.

3. Palsetia, *The Parsis of India,* 134, 147.

4. *Gazetteer of Bombay City and Island,* 3:63, 111, 375, 189; 2:171.

5. See Anderson, *Imagined Communities.*

6. See Habermas, *The Structural Transformation of the Public Sphere;* Cohn, "The Census, Social Structure and Objectification in South Asia"; Cooper and Stoler, "Between Metropole and Colony"; for liberal exclusionary practices, see Mehta, "Liberal Strategies of Exclusion" and Oberoi, *The Construction of Religious Boundaries.*

7. Metcalf, *Ideologies of the Raj,* x.

8. *Gazetteer of Bombay City and Island,* 2:171.

9. Baucom, *Out of Place,* 83–85; Maclean, *A Guide to Bombay* (1906), 237–41; Mitter, *Art and Nationalism in Colonial India,* 39, 42, 60–61.

10. Robert Bellah points out that "by civil religion I refer to that religious dimension, found I think in the life of every people, through which it interprets its historical experience in the light of transcendent reality." See Bellah, *The Broken Covenant,* 3.

11. Williams, *Keywords,* 54–55.

12. Oxford English Dictionary Online. http://dictionary.oed.com/

13. *Zakat* is the obligatory or expected payment by every able Muslim adult of a determinate portion of specified categories of their lawful property for the benefit of the poor.

14. For Shahjahanabad, see Blake, "Cityscape of an Imperial Capital." For the relationship between the South Indian temple and the economy, see Stein, "The Economic Function of a Medieval South Indian Temple."

15. Stein, "Introduction," 7 (emphasis in original).

16. Liechty, *Suitably Modern*, 118–19.

17. For English philanthropy, see Owen, *English Philanthropy*.

18. See Habermas, *The Structural Transformation of the Public Sphere*. For development of civil society, colonial governance, and urban citizenship in colonial Bombay, see Kidambi, *The Making of an Indian Metropolis*; Hazareesingh, *The Colonial City and the Challenge of Modernity*.

19. For this interpretation of the role of the census, see Cohn, "The Census, Social Structure and Objectification in South Asia."

20. Writing of colonial New Delhi, Anthony D. King observed that: "The Delhi which had been created was one built for two different worlds, the 'European' and the 'native,' for the ruler and the ones who were ruled. This notion of dualism is the starting point for any explanation of the size and structure of the city." See King, *Colonial Urban Development*, 263.

21. Chattopadhyay, "Blurring Boundaries."

22. Peter Berger quoted in Madan, "Secularism in Its Place," 748.

23. For civil religion, see Bellah, *The Broken Covenant*; for the erosion of practices of shared popular religion, see Oberoi, *Construction of Religious Boundaries*.

24. My argument stands in contrast to many works on colonial urbanism that emphasize the role of the colonial elite in the shaping of urban form. See, for example, King, *Colonial Urban Development*; Rabinow, *French Modern*; Wright, *The Politics of Design in French Colonial Urbanism*; and Norma Evenson, *The Indian Metropolis*. Works that address the contribution of local peoples include Yeoh, *Contesting Space*; Kusno, *Behind the Postcolonial*; and Hosagrahar, *Indigenous Modernities*.

25. Bourdieu, *Distinction*.

26. See Bourdieu, *Distinction*; Upton, "Form and User."

1. A JOINT ENTERPRISE

1. Jagannath Shankarshet, Framji Cowasji, Jamsetjee Jeejeebhoy, Cursetji Cowasji, and Naro Ragoonath Vuckeel to W. C. Bruce, Collector of Bombay, 5 March 1839, Maharashtra State Archives, 1839, Revenue Department, vol. 60/1023, comp. no. 280 (emphasis added). A *lac* (or *lakh*) equals one hundred thousand.

2. King, *Urbanism, Colonialism, and the World Economy*, 39.

3. The Bombay Chamber of Commerce, for example, played a role in fostering the improvement of communications by land and sea, ensuring the provision of port and harbor facilities. In the 1850s, the police force was reorganized, the construction of railways began, and the first train in India ran in April 1853, the twenty-two-mile Bombay-Thana line. Other innovations included the electric telegraph and modern postal service. The Bombay Chamber of Commerce was involved in various ways in all of these schemes. See Sulivan, *One Hundred Years of Bombay*, 56, 222. For more details on the role played by the chamber of commerce in influencing the government to develop the port and railways, refer to chapters 10–13, 21–24; Jacobs, *Edge of Empire*, 36.

4. Prakash and Haynes, "Introduction," 1–22, quote at 3; Scott cited in ibid., 2; ibid., 3.

5. On the island of Bombay, the judge pointed out, *foras* lands usually referred to the new salt batty land reclaimed from the sea; waste grounds lying beyond the Fort, Native Town, and other older settlements; cultivated land on the island; or the quit-rent paid for new salt batty ground and outlying ground. See Westropp, *Bombay High Court Reports*, iv, 40, note in Malabari, *Bombay in the Making*, 386.

6. Malabari, *Bombay in the Making*, 388.

7. Advocate-General Thriepland of Bombay, in *Government Selections*, iii, N.S. para. 17, quoted in Malabari, *Bombay in the Making*, 385–86. For various interpretations for the etymology of *foras*, see ibid., 385–88.

8. See Seed, *Ceremonies of Possession in Europe's Conquest of the New World*, 18–19, 24–25.

9. See *Gazetteer of Bombay City and Island*, 2:367–74 for a fuller account of *foras* lands.

10. Letter from William Acland, East India Company's Solicitor, to H. E. Gold-smid, Secretary to Government, No. 653 of 1847, Territorial Department and No. 1597 of 1848. Transfer from Revenue to General Department, 9 December 1847, Maharash-tra State Archives, General Department, 1848, vol. 54, comp. no. 379, 14–17.

11. Ibid.

12. Letter from Jagannath Shankarshet, Bomanjee Hormusjee, and Dadabhoy Pestonjee, to William Acland, East India Company's Solicitor, 2 December 1847, Maharashtra State Archives, General Department, 1848, vol. 54, comp. no. 379, 18–20.

13. Letter from H. E. Goldsmid, Secretary to Government, to William Acland, East India Company's Solicitor, no. 1595 of 1848, Territorial Department, Revenue, 20 March 1848, Maharashtra State Archives, General Department, 1848, vol. 54, comp. no. 379, 20–22.

14. The conditions were: (i) that landholders give the required land up to the government and be compensated at rates determined by a committee of principal land-holders; and (ii) that a fund be raised from all *foras* landholders, in proportion to the quantity of the land. See *Gazetteer of Bombay City and Island*, 2:372–74.

15. The Foras Act VI was passed on 6 June 1851, which confirmed the holders to the titles of their lands subject to the rents payable to the government. The Foras Commission finished its work by September 1853. See ibid., 372–74.

16. This account of water problems in Bombay is taken from Wacha, *Shells from the Sands of Bombay*, 440–53. For more on the development of the infrastructure of water supply, see Dossal, "The Politics of Municipal Water Supply in Mid-Nineteenth Century Bombay," in *Imperial Designs and Indian Realities*, 95–124.

17. Wacha, *Shells from the Sands of Bombay*, 459–61.

18. *Gazetteer of Bombay City and Island*, 2, 183.

19. Wacha, *Shells from the Sands of Bombay*, 458–59.

20. Sheppard, *Bombay Place-Names and Street-Names*, 53.

21. *Oart* means "a coconut garden" and is a corruption of the Portuguese word *orta*

or *horta;* see ibid., 12. Mugbhat Street extended from Girgaum Road to Khandewadi Lane; see ibid., 104.

22. According to *Gazetteer of Bombay City and Island,* 3:33n.2, Michael's *History of the Municipal Corporation,* 68–69, claims that Framji Cowasji obtained the Powai estate as freehold from the government on condition of always keeping the Two Tanks supplied with a reasonable quantity of water.

23. Wacha, *Shells from the Sands of Bombay,* 454–59; *Gazetteer of Bombay City and Island,* 3:32, puts the date of construction before 1823. Other famous tanks included Gowalia Tank, Mastan Tank, Nawab's Tank, and Sankli Tank.

24. Sheppard, *Bombay Place-Names and Street-Names,* 59; *Gazetteer of Bombay City and Island,* 3:32, gives 1831 as the date of the construction of the Dhobi Talao. The locality is still known as Dhobi Talao.

25. Government Resolution by Under Secretary to Government, Public Works Department, no. 498, C.W. 1185 of 1882, 30 June 1882, Maharashtra State Archives, General Department, 1882, vol. 124, comp. no. 591, 25–26.

26. Wacha, *Shells from the Sands of Bombay,* 453–54; my field research notes, 1998–99.

27. Bomanjee Jamsetjee Moollah to A. Malet, Chief Secretary to Government, no. 2258 of 1850, 12 September 1849; Collector's Report by P. Malet, no. 390 of 1849, 23 November 1849; Secretary to Government, Territorial Department, Revenue to P. Malet, Collector of Land Revenue, no. 1195 of 1850, 16 February 1850, Maharashtra State Archives, General Department, 1850, vol. 47, comp. no. 382, 7–11, 17. It is surprising to find that the government thought this locality to be overcrowded at this time.

28. Messrs. Dinshaw and Nusserwanjee Manockjee Petit to Government, 14 November 1863, in Government Resolution no. 487, "Extract from the Proceedings of the Government of Bombay in the General Department," 11 March 1864, Maharashtra State Archives, General Department, 1862–64, vol. 33, comp. no. 103 of 1864, 521–22. The section of stately buildings lining the grand boulevard stretching between Elphinstone College and Treacher & Company's buildings that was created after the fort walls were torn down in the 1860s was to be called "Frere-town," after Sir Bartle Frere, the influential governor of Bombay who conceived and began this scheme. See Wacha, *A Financial Chapter in the History of Bombay City,* 77.

29. Government Resolution No. 487, "Extract from the Proceedings of the Government of Bombay in the General Department," 11 March 1864, Maharashtra State Archives, General Department, 1862–64, vol. 33, comp. no. 103 of 1864, 517–22.

30. The entire account is in this file. Original petition from Sayad Amadudin Sanaf Sayad Shah Jehan Rafai and Muslim inhabitants of Bombay, 18 September 1880, and orders contained in Government Memorandum no. 3487, 17 November 1880, is in response to this and is referred to in Government Resolution no. 4250, General Department, 16 December 1881. Text of a second memorial from Muslim inhabitants of Bombay, 1881, soliciting reconsideration of the orders in the first government's 1880 memorandum is in the file. All these documents are to be found in Maharashtra State Archives, General Department, 1881, vol. 101, comp. no. 723, 1–9, 281–83, 291.

31. "Annual Report of the Executive Health Officer for 1914," in *Administration Report of the Municipal Commissioner for the City of Bombay* (1914–15), 2:105–11.

32. Manmohandas Ramji and others to Lord Willingdon, Governor in Council, 1 September 1914, enclosing the humble petition from the citizens of Bombay assembled in public meeting in the Town Hall on the 4 August 1914, Maharashtra State Archives, General Department, 1915, comp. no. 191, pt. 1, 11–12.

33. *Administration Report of the Municipal Commissioner for the City of Bombay* (1917–18), 56, 177.

34. The print of the Framji Cowasji Tank is part of the collection of the Alpaiwala Museum in Bombay.

35. According to Max Weber, an "ideal type" is the characterization of a subjective meaning orientation that is constructed by scientists, "a hypothetical actor" who is used to illustrate a given kind of conduct. In *The Protestant Ethic and the Spirit of Capitalism*, Benjamin Franklin is used as an example of an "ideal type," who shows the spirit of capitalism. The "ideal type" is not empirical because perhaps one will not find a single Protestant of the ideal type constructed. See Weber, *The Protestant Ethic and the Spirit of Capitalism*, 47–78; Weber, *Basic Concepts in Sociology*, 32–38.

36. Houston, *Representative Men of the Bombay Presidency*, 67–68.

37. For a list of his public charities, refer to Appendix 3 in Mody, *Jamsetjee Jejeebhoy*, 172–75.

38. Jamsetjee Jeejeebhoy, to Sir George Arthur, Governor and President in Council, 14 February 1844, in *Correspondence Relative to the "Sir Jamsetjee Jejeebhoy Dhurrumsalla*,*"* 1–3. This can be found in Maharashtra State Archives, General Department, 1872, vol. 11, comp. no. 549. "Jejeebhoy" is a variant spelling of "Jeejeebhoy"; "dhurrumsalla" is a variant spelling of "dharamshala."

39. Jamsetjee Jeejeebhoy to J. G. Lumsden, Acting Secretary to Government, 12 September 1847, *Correspondence Relative to the "Sir Jamsetjee Jejeebhoy Dhurrumsalla*,*"* 28–31.

40. J. G. Lumsden, Secretary to Government, to Sir Jamsetjee Jeejeebhoy, no. 3185 of 1847, General Department, 20 November 1847, *Correspondence Relative to the "Sir Jamsetjee Jejeebhoy Dhurrumsalla*,*"* 31–32.

41. Wacha, *A Financial Chapter in the History of Bombay City*, 142–69.

42. Temple, *Men and Events of My Time in India*, 270.

43. Edwardes, *The Bombay City Police*, 44.

44. Edwardes says the lots were sold to English firms. However, the list of names in the conveyance document is of Indian and English firms. The investors mentioned in the conveyance document were Messrs. Dawood (David) Sassoon & Company, the Chartered Mercantile Bank of India London and China, the Chartered Bank of India Australia and China, Mr. Merwanjee Nasserwanjee Bhownugria, Nasserwanjee Ruttonjee Tatah (Tata), Mrs. Ardaseer Hormusjee, Mr. Hormusjee Bomanjee, Messrs. Ritchie Stewart & Company, the Bank of Bombay, Messrs. Remington & Company, and Messrs. Finlay Scott & Company. This can be found in a letter from the Office of Municipal Commissioner with accompanying documents to A. D. Robertson, Secretary

to Government, 11 April 1863, Maharashtra State Archives, General Department, 1862–64, vol. 5, comp. no. 112, 193r, 193v, 199r, 199v.

45. Edwardes, *Bombay City Police,* 39–44. Edwardes puts the date at 1863, but he is wrong, as the following letter shows.

46. See Figure 9, plan of Fort (West) by George A. Laughton, 1872, on page 41 in Edney, "Defining a Unique City," 28–45.

47. Letter from Clerk, Municipal Commissioners' Office, to A. D. Robertson, Secretary to Government, General Department, no. 3777 of 1861, 10 December 1861, Maharashtra State Archives, General Department, 1862–64, vol. 5, comp. no. 112, 3–11. Note that Edwardes makes no reference to the proposal to name the circle "The Victoria Circle."

48. Ibid.; quotes, 9.

49. Memorandum by Colonel H. B. Turner, Acting Secretary to Government, Public Works Department, 28 November 1861, Maharashtra State Archives, General Department, 1862–64, vol. 5, comp. no. 112, 15–18; quote, 16.

50. Government Resolution, 29 November 1861, Maharashtra State Archives, General Department, 1862–64, vol. 5, comp. no. 112, 18; my field research notes, 1998–99.

51. Wacha, *Shells from the Sands of Bombay,* 149–53.

52. Giedion, *Space, Time, and Architecture,* 147–50.

53. Letter from A. D. Robertson, Officiating Chief Secretary to the Government of Bombay, to E. C. Bayley, Secretary to the Government of India, No. 59 of 1864 General Department, 13 January 1864, Maharashtra State Archives, General Department, 1862–64, vol. 5, comp. no. 112, 323.

54. *Report on the Development Plan for Greater Bombay 1964,* xxiv.

55. Temple, *Men and Events,* 276.

56. *Report on the Development Plan for Greater Bombay 1964,* xxiv.

57. Maclean, *A Guide to Bombay* (1906), 207.

58. E. Arnold, *India Revisited,* 55. This quote is from chapter 5, entitled "New Bombay."

59. Temple, *Men and Events,* 276–77; Maclean, *A Guide to Bombay* (1906), 206–58.

60. Davies, *Splendours of the Raj,* 156–57. For a discussion of colonial architecture in Bombay, see chapter 7, "Bombay: Urbs Prima in Indis," 147–82.

61. Hesilrige, *Debrett's Peerage, Baronetage, Knightage, and Companionage,* 208–9, 238–39, 387–88, 471, 564–65, 631; also see Bagchi, "European and Indian Entrepreneurship in India," 223–56. Bagchi does not mention Petit.

62. Gordon, *Businessmen and Politics,* 119–20.

63. *Report on the Development Plan for Greater Bombay 1964,* xxvi

64. Ibid., xxvi–xxvii.

65. See the annual administration reports of the Bombay Improvement Trust for references to the number of settlements made through the courts for each scheme.

66. Burnett-Hurst, *Labour and Housing in Bombay,* 31–32.

67. Ibid., 26.

68. Letter from R. E. Enthoven, Acting Secretary to Government, to the Chairman, City of Bombay Improvement Trust, no. 7382 of 1907, General Department, 9 December 1907, in appendix B of *Annual Administration Report of the City of Bombay Improvement Trust* (1907–8), xxi–xxiv.

69. *Report on the Development Plan for Greater Bombay 1964*, xxvii. It appears that the date is not correct, as at least one body, the Bombay Native Piece Goods Merchants' Association, responded before this date.

70. See letter from the Chairman, Bombay Native Piece Goods Merchants' Association, to the Secretary to the Government of Bombay, General Department, regarding expansion of the City of Bombay, no. 126 of 1907–8, 17 March 1908, Maharashtra State Archives, General Department, 1909, vol. 218, pt. 1, 191–96, for an unsolicited opinion on the issues raised by the government.

71. *Report on the Development Plan for Greater Bombay 1964*, xxviii.

72. Letter from R. E. Enthoven, Acting Secretary to Government, to the Chairman, BIT, no. 7382 of 1907, General Department, 9 December 1907, in appendix B of *Annual Administration Report of the City of Bombay Improvement Trust* (1907–8), xxi–xxiv.

73. "Summary of the replies received to the Government letter" in "Development of Bombay City and the Improvement of Communications in the Island," in Maharashtra State Archives, General Department, 1909, no. 218, pt. 2, 589–608.

2. ANGLO-INDIAN ARCHITECTURE AND THE MEANING OF ITS STYLES

1. Crinson, *Empire Building*, 9.

2. See Begg, "Architecture in India," 342–44; Davies, *Splendours of the Raj*, 192–93.

3. See Metcalf, *An Imperial Vision*.

4. See Frere, "Modern Architecture in Western India," 422.

5. Phrase taken from Smith, "Architectural Art in India," 281.

6. Upton, "Form and User," 158.

7. Ibid., 158–59.

8. Stamp, "Victorian Bombay," 22–24. The Pubic Works Department constructed most of the public architecture in India.

9. See Stamp, "British Architecture in India," 359.

10. For more on the friction between the military engineers and the civil engineers in the Public Works Department, see Anonymous, "Pay in the Public Works Department," 679–80; Anonymous, "On the Public Works Department of India," 1009–10; and Anonymous, "The High Court, Calcutta. Public Works of India," 857.

11. Begg, "The Architect in India," 311. An analysis of the design practices of the Public Works Department can be found in Scriver, "Empire-Building and Thinking in the Public Works Department of British India," 69–92.

12. Smith, "On Buildings for European Occupation in Tropical Climates," 350.

13. Ibid., 350.

14. See Kipling, "Indian Architecture of Today," 1.

15. Ibid., 1–2.

16. Under the Viceroyalty of Lord Curzon, a new position was established in 1902, namely, the post of consulting-architect to the Government of India, and James Ransome (1865–1944), a trained architect, was the first to occupy this position. Begg would move on to work for the Government of India in 1907 and was the second person to hold this position from 1908–21. See Stamp, "British Architecture in India," 359.

17. See Begg, "The Work of George Wittet," 546.

18. See Wilkinson, "The New Professionalism in the Renaissance," 124–60; Wilton-Ely, "The Rise of the Professional Architect in England," 180–208.

19. See Wilton-Ely, "The Rise of the Professional Architect in England," 196–97.

20. Upton, *Architecture in the United States*, 251.

21. See Wilton-Ely, "The Rise of the Professional Architect in England," 180–208.

22. Tarapor, "Growse in Bulandshahr," 48.

23. Schapiro, "Style," 278.

24. Frere, "Modern Architecture in Western India," 422.

25. Ibid.

26. Ibid.

27. Davies, *Splendours of the Raj*, 175.

28. Ibid., 166.

29. Ibid., 167.

30. Napier, "Architecture in India," 681.

31. Ibid.

32. Ibid.

33. Kipling, "Indian Architecture of Today," 2.

34. Napier, "Architecture in India," 682.

35. Ibid.

36. Ibid.

37. Ibid.

38. Ibid.

39. Ibid.

40. Ibid., 723.

41. Ibid.

42. Ibid.

43. Davies, *Splendours of the Raj*, 196.

44. Ibid., 196–97.

45. Smith, "Architectural Art in India," 280.

46. Ibid.

47. Ibid., 281.

48. Ibid.

49. See Anonymous, "Anglo-Indian Architecture," 313.

50. Ibid.

51. Ibid., 314.

52. Rather than "'Italian Gothic,'" it was thought that some in London might describe it as "Manchester Gothic," hinting that its style owed more to Manchester than Italy. See ibid., 314–15.

53. Ibid., 313–15.

54. Bourdieu, *Distinction,* 6.

55. Anonymous, "Anglo-Indian Architecture," 313–14.

56. Baucom, *Out of Place,* 85.

57. Letter from R. F. Chisholm, consulting architect to his Highness the Gaikwar of Baroda, to the *Builder;* and the journal's response, dated 4 June 1888, in *Builder* 55 (14 July 1888): 31.

58. Ibid.

59. Ibid.

60. Anonymous, "Anglo-Indian Architecture," 314.

61. Ibid.

62. Bourdieu, *Distinction,* 2.

63. Begg, "Architecture in India," 342–44.

64. Ibid., 343.

65. Ibid., 344.

66. Ibid., 345.

67. Ibid., 344.

68. Ibid., 343.

69. Ibid., 345–46.

70. Ibid., 345.

71. See Cohn, "Cloth, Clothes, and Colonialism in India," 343.

72. Bourdieu, *Distinction,* 488.

73. Ibid.

74. See Metcalf, *An Imperial Vision,* 94–96.

75. Ibid., 96–98.

76. Calcutta went back to its Classical architectural traditions under Lord Curzon, who was viceroy from 1898 to 1905. See Stamp, "British Architecture in India," 369–70.

77. James Ransome, quoted in discussion following lecture by Begg, "The Work of George Wittet," 548.

78. See Metcalf, *An Imperial Vision,* 106.

79. See ibid., 105–40.

80. See Begg, "Architecture in India," 333–49.

81. See Metcalf, *An Imperial Vision,* 96.

82. Begg, "The Work of George Wittet," 546 (emphasis in original).

83. Ibid.

84. Begg quoting Wittet and Begg quote, ibid., 539 (emphasis in original).

85. Ibid., 539–40.

86. See Anonymous, "The Civic Decorations of Bombay," 137–38.

87. Begg, "The Work of George Wittet," 540. In his many buildings, Wittet developed his own neoclassical style, one that owed much to the Renaissance.

88. These included the Town Hall (built in 1821–33), designed by Lieutenant-Colonel Thomas Alexander Cowper, and the Mint (built in 1824–29). While the former is a Greek Revival structure with Doric columns, the latter is supported by an Ionic portico erected by Major John Hawkins of the Bombay Engineers. See Stamp, "Victorian Bombay," 22.

89. Ibid., 23.

90. Ibid.

91. Davies, *Splendours of the Raj*, 152; See Stamp, "British Architecture in India," 361. For the significance of the Afghan Church to discussions of the appropriate style for churches in colonies, see Crinson, *Empire Building*, 117–18.

92. Stamp, "British Architecture in India," 363.

93. Tarapor, "John Lockwood Kipling and British Art in India," 152.

94. Colonel H. St. Clair Wilkins to J. L. Kipling, 16 May 1873, Kipling Papers; quoted in ibid., 64.

95. Mitter, *Art and Nationalism in Colonial India, 1850–1922*, 60–61.

96. Wacha, *Shells from the Sands of Bombay*, 315–16.

97. Upton, "Form and User," 162.

98. Bourdieu, *Distinction*, 2.

99. Upton, "Form and User," 160.

100. See Stamp, "Victorian Bombay," 23.

101. Khote, *I, Durga Khote*, 23.

102. For a discussion of the reluctance of the British to use native styles for churches in the empire, see Metcalf, *An Imperial Vision*, 98–104.

103. Upton, "Form and User," 161.

104. Davies, *Splendours of the Raj*, 160.

105. Maclean, *A Guide to Bombay* (1906), 218–20.

106. Davies, *Splendours of the Raj*, 162.

107. Wacha, *Shells from the Sands of Bombay*, 143.

108. Maclean, *A Guide to Bombay* (1906), 219.

109. See Cohn, "Cloth, Clothes, and Colonialism in India," 331–42.

110. Upton, "Form and User," 164.

111. Particularly important as models for the Gothic Revival were the competitions held for the Government Offices in Westminster in 1857 and for the new Law Courts in the Strand in 1866. Also influential were Sir Gilbert Scott's buildings, many of which were based on thirteenth-century Gothic, axially planned, and symmetrically arranged around a central tower. Wilkins and Fuller, both Royal Engineers, appear to have been influenced by the works of Scott, Street, Seddon, Burges, and others. Colonel H. St. Clair Wilkins (1828–96) was the designer of the Bombay Secretariat (1867–74) and the Public Works Secretariat/Offices (1869–72), while Lieutenant-Colonel James Augustus Fuller (1828–1902) was the architect for the Bombay Law Courts (1871–78),

also referred to as the High Court, a structure that brought together elements from English Gothic and Venice. In the same line facing the Oval and between the Secretariat and the High Court is the university, whose buildings were designed by the well-known British architect, Sir Gilbert Scott, constructed from drawings sent out by him. It consists of the University Library with the tall Rajabai Tower, which is apparently Scott's interpretation of Giotto's design for the campanile in Florence. Next to the library is the Sir Cowasji Jehangir Hall. See Stamp, "Victorian Bombay," 23, 25; Stamp, "British Architecture in India," 363–64.

112. This was an accepted practice, but the way copying occurred under the Gothic Revival was open to attack by the 1880s when the Gothic Revival was no longer in favor in Great Britain. It was believed that in the present era the best architecture did not merely copy, even while using models, but altered them, thereby aiming at a certain uniqueness. See Anonymous, "Architecture in the Reign of Queen Victoria," 927–28.

113. Even recent scholars who recognize the excellence of Bombay's Victorian architecture often praise it or read it in terms of British models. See, for example, Stamp, "British Architecture in India," 365.

114. See ibid., 367.

115. See Chattopadhyay, "Blurring Boundaries," in *Representing Calcutta*, 76–135.

116. See Smith, "On Buildings for European Occupation in Tropical Climates," 208.

117. See Anonymous, "Anlgo-Indian Architecture," 314.

118. Mitter, *Art and Nationalism in Colonial India*, 54. An appreciation for Indian art would have to wait until the emergence of the Bengal school, the earliest nationalist art movement in India.

3. THE BIOGRAPHY OF AN UNKNOWN NATIVE ENGINEER

1. See, for example, Stamp, "Victorian Bombay," 24.

2. Bhabha, "Of Mimicry and Man," 125.

3. See Murzban, *Leaves from the Life of Khan Bahadur Muncherji Cowasji Murzban*, 90.

4. See Maclean, *A Guide to Bombay* (1906), 214–54.

5. Quoted by Murzban, *Leaves from the Life*, 72.

6. Ibid., 56–58.

7. See Glover, "Objects, Models, and Exemplary Works," 545.

8. Murzban, *Leaves from the Life*, 29.

9. For brief references to Murzban's work, see, for example, London, *Bombay Gothic*.

10. Stamp, "Victorian Bombay," 24.

11. Glover, "Ethnology, Engineering, and Modern Architecture in India," 1–21. I am grateful to William Glover for giving me a copy of his talk.

12. Myers, *Verandahs of Power*, xiii.

13. Ibid., xiii.

14. See Weber, *The Protestant Ethic and the Spirit of Capitalism*, 47–78; Weber, *Basic Concepts in Sociology*, 32–38.

15. In 1871, the Royal Indian Engineering College at Cooper's Hill, England, was established to train engineers and others who could work as telegraphists and forestry officials for jobs in the public services in India, Burma, and other parts of the British Empire. India already had engineering colleges; the Roorkee College of Engineering, the oldest in the empire, was founded in 1847. The training at the Roorkee College was considered to be superior to that of the college at Cooper's Hill, which was one of the reasons the latter closed in 1907. See Glover, "Ethnology, Engineering, and Modern Architecture in India," 20 n. 15.

16. Begg, "The Work of George Wittet," 547–48.

17. See Stamp, "British Architecture in India," 359; Anonymous, "Khan Bahadur Muncherjee Murzban," 121–168.

18. Kipling, "Indian Architecture of Today," 2.

19. Ibid., 2.

20. Ibid.

21. See Murzban, *Leaves from the Life*, 51–52.

22. Quoted in ibid., 70–71.

23. Upton, "Form and User," 160.

24. Medley, "Anglo-Indian Architecture," 201.

25. Ibid., 201–6.

26. See Metcalf, *Ideologies of the Raj*, 177–81; Glover, "A Feeling of Absence from Old England," 61–82.

27. Medley, "Anglo-Indian Architecture," 201–2.

28. Ibid., 202.

29. Ibid., 206 (emphasis added).

30. Ibid., 201–6.

31. Ibid., 202–3.

32. Murzban, *Leaves from the Life*, 52.

33. Ibid., 47–49. Murzban's son does not give a date for the building nor the name of the English architect. The General Post Office, opened on 1 December 1872, was based on designs by J. Trubshawe and W. Paris, architects to the government. See Furneaux, *Glimpses of India*, 214. Murzban was appointed as assistant to Trubshawe in 1863.

34. Menant, *The Parsis*, 331–32.

35. See Murzban, *Leaves from the Life*, 31–32.

36. Ibid., 40.

37. Ibid.

38. Ibid., 39–42.

39. Ibid., 47.

40. Ibid.

41. Ibid.

42. Ibid., 54.

43. Ibid., emphasis in original.

44. Ibid., 67–68.

45. Ibid., 25; Wacha, *Shells from the Sands of Bombay*, 691–92.

46. Hinnells, "The Flowering of Zoroastrian Benevolence,"268. I am grateful to Barbara D. Metcalf for giving me a copy of this article. In the case of Allbless Baug, the layout consisted of a courtyard flanked by spaces for a temple, prayer, and washing room, and so on. See ibid., 268–69. It was under Murzban's supervision that the main hall for the Allbless Baug was designed and constructed. See Murzban, *Leaves from the Life*, 86.

47. See Murzban, *Leaves from the Life*, 118–25.

48. Ibid., 87–89, 115.

49. Ibid., 83–85, 87.

50. Ibid., 115.

51. *Times of India*, 3 March 1892, quoted in ibid., 74.

52. *Advocate of India*, 2 April 1890, quoted in ibid., 73.

53. See Murzban, *Leaves from the Life*, 43.

54. Fozdar, "Constructing the 'Brother,'" p. 1 of abstract.

55. Ibid., p. 1 of abstract, 262–63, 293–98.

56. Wadia, *History of Lodge Rising Star*, 194.

57. Ibid., 231.

58. See Edwardes, *Kharshedji Rustamji Cama*, 50–53; and Fozdar, "Constructing the 'Brother,'" 91, 297.

59. See Fozdar, "Constructing the 'Brother,'" 31–32.

60. Ibid., 455.

61. Murzban, speech in Lodge Rising Star, August 20, 1867, in *Masonic Record of Western India* 4, no. 6 (September 1867): 230–31; quoted in ibid., 10.

62. See Fozdar, "Constructing the 'Brother,'" 15.

63. See ibid., 57–58; Murzban, *Leaves from the Life*, 18.

64. See Fozdar, "Constructing the 'Brother,'" 65, 72.

65. Ibid., 17–30.

66. Darukhanawala, *Parsi Lustre on Indian Soil*, 333.

67. Ibid., 333–34; Wacha, *Shells from the Sands of Bombay*, 695.

68. Menant, *The Parsis*, vol. III, 183. For an account of the foundation of this school, see pp. 181–85.

69. Maclean, *A Guide to Bombay* (1906), 233–34.

70. Wacha, *Shells from the Sands of Bombay*, 691–92.

71. Murzban, *Leaves from the Life*, 25–26, 72. Also see p. 25 for more on Fardunji Murzban's advocacy of female education.

72. Kumar, *Medicine and the Raj*, 59.

73. Malabari, editorial in the *Indian Spectator*, 11 December 1892, quoted by Murzban, *Leaves from the Life*, 78. Malabari was editor of the *Indian Spectator* from 1880 to 1900. See Darukhanawala, *Parsi Lustre*, 332.

74. See Murzban, *Leaves from the Life*, 45; Fozdar, "Constructing the 'Brother,'" 429–31.

75. Murzban, *Leaves from the Life*, 78. See ibid., 75, and Darukhanawala, *Parsi Lustre*, 132–33.

76. See Murzban, *Leaves from the Life*, 85–86, 87–88.

77. Report from *Indian and Eastern Engineer*, n.d., quoted in ibid., 112–13.

78. Ibid., 113–14.

79. Anonymous, "Architecture in the Reign of Queen Victoria," 927.

80. Ibid., 927–28.

81. For England, see Owen, *English Philanthropy 1660–1960*, 372–73.

82. Report in *The Indian and Eastern Engineer*, April 1903, quoted in Murzban, *Leaves from the Life*, 107–8.

83. Adam, "Transatlantic Trading," 330–35.

84. Hinnells, "The Flowering of Zoroastrian Benevolence," 277, 314. For a list of donors, see Murzban, *Leaves from the Life*, 118–27.

85. Hinnells, "The Flowering of Zoroastrian Benevolence," 278. Charitable housing for poor Parsis was also found in other cities apart from Bombay.

86. Barker, "Charitable Architecture," 64; Curl, *Victorian Architecture*, 163.

87. My field research notes, 2006. Mrs. Mistry, a resident of Gilder Lane who lived in a building opposite the colony, said that M. C. Murzban owned the land. However, I cannot confirm this. Also see Murzban, *Leaves from the Life*, 108.

88. Murzban, *Leaves from the Life*, 111–12. *Jashans* "are religious banquets." See Menant, *The Parsis*, vol. II, 381.

89. See Chopra, "La Ville Imaginee," 125–56. For English version, see Chopra, "Imagining the City," 70–87; Chopra, "Refiguring the Colonial City," 109–25.

90. Bhabha, "Of Mimicry and Man," 126 (emphasis in original).

4. DIVIDING PRACTICES IN BOMBAY'S HOSPITALS AND LUNATIC ASYLUMS

1. *Bombay Chabuk*, 26 January 1870, in the *Report on Native Newspapers in the Bombay Presidency* for the week ending in 29 January 1870, 6.

2. Refer to the Introduction for examples from South Asia's precolonial past.

3. Douglas, *Thought Styles*, 106–25.

4. For references to shared religious foci in popular religion, see Oberoi, "An Enchanted Universe: Sikh Participation in Popular Religion," chapter 3 in *The Construction of Religious Boundaries*, 139–203. While Oberoi is writing about Punjab, this phenomenon occurs in other parts of India.

5. Rabinow, "Introduction" to *The Foucault Reader*, 3–29.

6. Upton, "Form and User: Style, Mode, Fashion, and the Artifact," in *Living in a Material World*, 161.

7. Bellah, *The Broken Covenant*, 3.

8. Ibid., 178–79.

9. For the Victorian lunatic asylum in Britain, see Scull, "A Convenient Place to

Get Rid of Inconvenient People," in *Buildings and Society*, 37–60. For Scull's argument about the transformation of English society under capitalism see pp. 38–42.

10. Also see Ernst, *Mad Tales from the Raj*, 130–63.

11. Report on the Lunatic Asylum Colaba for the year ending 31 March 1852, by Dr. Campbell, Superintendent, Lunatic Asylum, Maharashtra State Archives, General Department, 1853, vol. 48, comp. no. 231, 51–136 (multiple pagination systems have been used in this document). The description of the lunatic asylum is based on this document and the drawings it contains. For the foundation of the Bombay lunatic asylum, also see Ernst, *Mad Tales from the Raj*, 21–22.

12. Report on the Lunatic Asylum Colaba for the year ending 31 March 1852, by Dr. Campbell, Superintendent, Lunatic Asylum, Maharashtra State Archives, General Department, 1853, vol. 48, comp. no. 231, 51–52.

13. For typologies of the lunatic asylum, see Scull, "A Convenient Place to Get Rid of Inconvenient People," 50–54. These types are based on Henry Burdett's survey titled *Hospitals and Asylums of the World*, which was published from 1891–93. He classified asylums on the basis of their plan. For the fourth type, the Corridor-Pavilion, see Taylor, *Hospital and Asylum Architecture in England 1840–1914*, 51–52.

14. Unlike hospitals in Western Europe where patients suffering from a variety of diseases had to share a common ward, the insane were housed in smaller rooms. See Thompson and Goldin, *The Hospital*, 41–45.

15. Ernst, *Mad Tales from the Raj*, 47–48.

16. Report on the Lunatic Asylum Colaba for the year ending 31 March 1852, by Dr. Campbell, Superintendent, Lunatic Asylum, Maharashtra State Archives, General Department, 1853, vol. 48, comp. no. 231, 57–62.

17. Ibid., 58–63.

18. Ernst, *Mad Tales from the Raj*, 49–51.

19. The upper class could utilize the central block's dining room as a day room and did not have to follow the "institutional diet." See Thompson and Goldin, *The Hospital*, 71–74.

20. Report on the Lunatic Asylum Colaba for the year ending 31 March 1852, by Dr. Campbell, Superintendent, Lunatic Asylum, Maharashtra State Archives, General Department, 1853, vol. 48, comp. no. 231, 93–94.

21. According to Campbell, the screen was "necessary to prevent the exposure of person and other indecencies to which unhappily, in many instances, the victims of mental disorder are but too prone." See ibid., 71.

22. Ibid., 69–70.

23. Ernst, *Mad Tales from the Raj*, 76–77.

24. For more on the subject of moral treatment in English insane asylums, see Thompson and Goldin, *The Hospital*, 71–76.

25. Ernst, *Mad Tales from the Raj*, 100.

26. Scull, "A Convenient Place to Get Rid of Inconvenient People," 45–48.

27. Report on the Lunatic Asylum Colaba for the year ending 31 March 1852, by

Dr. Campbell, Superintendent, Lunatic Asylum, Maharashtra State Archives, General Department, 1853, vol. 48, comp. no. 231, 75. The "largest class" was that of native patients.

28. Ibid., 73.

29. On the ground floor, one section was now the dispensary (A) and the other was occupied by the Matron or Head Female Keeper (B), while the part above was occupied by patients of the higher class (C, D). Also see ibid., 57, 59.

30. Ibid., 74.

31. Taylor, *Hospital and Asylum Architecture in England,* 172.

32. Letter from Surgeon-General W. McConaghy, M.D., I.M.S., Surgeon-General with the Government of Bombay, to the Secretary to Government, General Department, Bombay, no. 12114, 5 November 1904, in draft of Accompaniments to Government Resolution No. (no number), dated (no day) November 1904, Maharashtra State Archives, General Department, 1905, vol. 54, comp. no. 490, 243.

33. Ibid., 243.

34. *The Gazetteer of Bombay City and Island,* 3 vols., compiled by S. M. Edwardes, (Bombay: Times Press, 1909–10), 3:194–95.

35. See appendix A, in appendices referred to in the letter from the Superintendent, Lunatic Asylum, Colaba, no. 425, 17 May 1899, Maharashtra State Archives, General Department, 1900, vol. 62, comp. no. 378, 464.

36. Letter from Lieut.-Colonel J. P. Barry, Superintendent, Lunatic Asylum, Colaba, to the Personal Assistant to the Surgeon General with the Government of Bombay, no. 549, 25 June 1904 in draft of Accompaniments to Government Resolution No. (no number), dated (no day) November 1904, Maharashtra State Archives, General Department, 1905, vol. 54, comp. no. 490, 248.

37. Ibid., 249.

38. Scull, "A Convenient Place to Get Rid of Inconvenient People," 38.

39. See Thompson and Goldin, *The Hospital,* 83.

40. See ibid., p 84; Forty, "The Modern Hospital in England and France," 66–69.

41. For a description, drawings, and account of the European General Hospital, I have relied upon the following account, Capt. H. St. Clair Wilkins, "European General Hospital, Bombay," 406–10.

42. Ibid., 407–8.

43. Forty, "The Modern Hospital in England and France," 84–85.

44. Government Resolution no. 4691 of 1913, General Department, 24 June 1913, Maharashtra State Archives, General Department, 1913, vol. 75, comp. no. 274, 337–39.

45. Completed in 1764–65, the Royal Naval Hospital at Stonehouse near Plymouth in England accommodated 1,250 male patients who were sailors and is a prominent example of an institution for a specific group of the population. For more on this hospital, see Thompson and Goldin, *The Hospital,* 142–46.

46. *Gazetteer of Bombay City and Island,* 3:188–90.

47. Sir Jamsetjee Jeejeebhoy to the Senior Medical Officer in charge of J. J. Hospital, 3 November 1904, Maharashtra State Archives, General Department, 1905, vol. 44, comp. no. 398, 391.

48. Paragraphs 7 and 12 of Government letter to the committee appointed to arrange for the establishment of a medical college combined with a native hospital, no. 3850, 11 November 1840, in ibid., 403–4.

49. Paragraph 1 of Government letter to the Medical Board, no. 751, 7 March 1845, in ibid., 404–5.

50. Extract from the *Bombay Times and Journal of Commerce,* 21 May 1845, in ibid., 405.

51. Report of Balwant Mahadev, Record Keeper, no. 30 of 1905, in ibid., 398–99.

52. *Handbook of the Bombay Presidency with an Account of Bombay City,* 136.

53. Letter from W. McConaghy, Surgeon General with the Government of Bombay to the Secretary to Government, General Department, no. 12892 of 1904, 30 November 1904, in ibid., 389–90.

54. My field research notes, 1998–99, 2007.

55. Kulke, *The Parsees in India,* 129–30. For the term "purely white race," he referred to *Parsi* 1, no. 11 (1905): 533.

56. Postans, *Western India in 1838,* 1:132–33.

57. Kulke, *Parsees in India,* 23–27, 139–40.

58. *Gazetteer of Bombay City and Island,* 3:191–94.

59. Government Resolution no. 1187, General Department, 1 April 1886, relating to letter from Miss Edith Pechey to Secretary to Government, 23 March 1886, Maharashtra State Archives, General Department, 1886, vol. 47, comp. no. 105, pt. 1, 83, 84.

60. Opinion submitted to file referring to Cama Hospital, no. 1863 GL, in ibid., 70–72.

61. For biographical information, see Houston, *Representative Men of the Bombay Presidency,* 225–26.

62. Letter from Harkisandas Narotumdas to Brigade-Surgeon, Henry Cook, M.D., Principal, Grant Medical College, 27 April 1885, Maharashtra State Archives, General Department, 1885, vol. 70, comp. no. 789, 25–27.

63. Letter from the Surgeon General with the Government of Bombay to the Secretary to Government, General Department, no. 2922 of 1885, 19 May 1885, in ibid., 3–15. This information is from pp. 11–13.

64. Adams, *Medicine by Design,* 27.

65. For pavilion wards, see Thompson and Goldin, *The Hospital,* 130.

66. Taylor, *The Architect and the Pavilion Hospital,* vii.

67. Letter from Dr. James Arnott, Obstetric Physician, J. J. Hospital to the First Physician, J. J. Hospital, 22 June 1885; and letter from Khan Bahadur Muncherji Murzban, Executive Engineer, Bombay, to the Surgeon General with the Government of Bombay, no. 2875 of 1885, 8 July 1885, Maharashtra State Archives, General Department, 1885, vol. 70, comp. no. 789, 113–29.

68. Forty, "The Modern Hospital in England and France," 78–79.

69. Government Resolution no. 3036, 12 August 1885, Maharashtra State Archives, General Department, 1885, vol. 70, comp. no. 789, 141.

70. For biographical information on Bai Motlibai Jehangir Wadia, see Daruk-hanawala, *Parsi Lustre on Indian Soil,* 108, 126.

71. Her offer was accepted by the Government Resolution no. 741, 23 April 1888, referred to in Government Memorandum no. M/19 of 1888, Public Works Department, 2 June 1888, Maharashtra State Archives, General Department, 1889, vol. 79, comp. no. 726, 103–9.

72. See letter from W. F. Sinclair, Collector of Thana, no. 6331, 6 September 1893 submitting copies of the proceedings of the Committee appointed by Government Resolution, Public Works Department, no. 168, C.W. 641, 24 April 1893, to inspect and report on the site of the proposed lunatic asylum at Nowpada at Thana, in Maharashtra State Archives, General Department, 1894, vol. 82, comp. no. 378, 89r–90r; Government Resolution no. 2399, General Department, 26 June 1894, in ibid., 199r–200v.

73. Government Resolution no. 2399, General Department, 26 June 1894, referring to a memorandum by Surgeon-Major Clarkson, Acting Sanitary Commissioner for the Government of Bombay, attached to the proceedings of the Committee appointed by Government Resolution, Public Works Department, No. 168, C.W. 641, 24 April 1893, to inspect and report on the site of the proposed lunatic asylum at Nowpada at Thana, in ibid., 199r-200v.

74. Letter from the Surgeon General with the Government of Bombay to Secretary to Government, General Department, no. 7901, 13 November 1893, in ibid., 104r-106r.

75. Government Resolution No. 2399, General Department, 26 June 1894, in ibid., 199r-200v.

76. Government Resolution no. 215, General Department, 18 January 1895, Maharashtra State Archives, General Department, 1895, vol. 77, comp. no. 378, 141r-142r.

77. Government Resolution no. 2382, General Department, 10 June 1895, which also refers to letter from Dinsha Bamanji Pestanji Master, L.M. & S., Honorary Physician, the Nasarvanji Manekji Petit Charity Fund for destitute, insane Parsis, dated 5 February 1894, Maharashtra State Archives, General Department, 1895, vol. 77, comp. no. 378, 189r, 189v.

78. Letter from Dinsha Bamanji Pestanji Master, Honorary Physician, the Nasarvanji Manekji Petit Charity Fund for destitute insane Parsis, 28 June 1895, in Government Resolution no. 2522, General Department, 12 May 1900, Maharashtra State Archives, General Department, 1900, vol. 62, comp. no. 378, 449.

79. Ibid., 449.

80. See memo from Public Works Department, no. B-692, 13 December 1897 in Government Resolution no. 2522, General Department, 12 May 1900, Maharashtra State Archives, General Department, 1900, vol. 62, comp. no. 378, 452.

81. Letter from A. H. L. Fraser, Esq., C.S.I., Officiating Secretary to the Government of India, to the Secretary to the Government of Bombay, General Department, no. 1258, 16 September 1898, Maharashtra State Archives, General Department, 1898, vol. 55, comp. no. 379, 435–37.

82. Letter from the Superintendent, Lunatic Asylum, Colaba, to the Personal Assistant to the Surgeon General with the Government of Bombay, no. 425, 17 May 1899, in Government Resolution no. 2522, General Department, 12 May 1900, Maharashtra State Archives, General Department, 1900, vol. 62, comp. no. 378, 457.

83. Memorandum from the Accountant General, no. P.A.-756, 9 August 1899, referring to letter from D. B. Master, 24 November 1898 in Government Resolution no. 2522, General Department, 12 May 1900, in ibid., 458.

84. Letter from Dinsha Bamanji Pestanji Master, 28 August 1899 in Government Resolution no. 2522, General Department, 12 May 1900, in ibid., 460.

85. *Gazetteer of Bombay City and Island,* 3:207.

86. Mehta and Jhabvala, "Our Hospital," 1–7.

87. These were the Bhatia Hospital for the Bhatia community, the Aly Khan Hospital for Khojas, the Noor Hospital for Memons, and the Saifee Hospital for Bohras.

88. See J. R. B. Jejeebhoy, *The Muncherjee Khareghat Memorial Volume* (Bombay, 1953) 305, quoted in Mody, *Jamsetjee Jejeebhoy,* 61. For Sikh case, see Oberoi, "A New Social Imagination: The Making of the Tat Khalsa," chapter 6 in *Construction of Religious Boundaries,* 305–77.

89. For this interpretation of the role of the census, see Cohn, "The Census, Social Structure, and Objectification in South Asia," 225–54. Also see Oberoi, "Introduction," in *Construction of Religious Boundaries,* 1–35.

90. See Fergusson, *History of Indian and Eastern Architecture* as an example of such writing. For analysis of British writing in colonial era on South Asia's architecture, see Metcalf, *An Imperial Vision: Indian Architecture and Britain's Raj;* Flood, "Signs of Violence," 20–51. I am grateful to Finbarr Flood for this reference.

91. Letter from Harkisandas Narotumdas, 24 June 1896, with accompanying memorandum, Maharashtra State Archives, General Department, 1896, vol. 81, comp. no. 379, 124–27.

92. Letter from Acting Secretary to Government, to Harkisandas Narotumdas, Esquire, J.P, no. 2920, General Department, 6 July 1896, in ibid., 131r, 131v.

93. Letter from Harkisandas Narotumdas to Secretary to Government, General Department, 6 August 1896, in ibid., 81:132–36.

94. Minute by government official, 8 August 1896 (dated "8/8"), in ibid., 137v.

95. Minute by the Governor, 26 May 1896, in ibid., 140v, 141r.

96. Minute by the Hon'ble I. Nugent, 27 August 1896, in ibid., 141r, 141v.

97. Government Resolution no. 4067, General Department, 12 September 1896, in ibid., 143.

98. Government Resolution no. 2438, 5 May 1897, Maharashtra State Archives, General Department, 1897, vol. 69, comp. no. 379, 219.

99. See Thompson and Goldin, *The Hospital,* particularly chapter 2, "The Open Ward," 15–40, 128.

100. For more on chapels for hospitals. see Taylor, *Hospital and Asylum Architecture,* 161–66.

101. See ibid., 166–69.

102. Fozdar, "Constructing the 'Brother,'" 295. The association of state and Freemasonry continued. On 25 September 1906 the foundation stone of the Sir William Moore Operation Theatre, located in the J. J. Hospital, "was laid with Masonic rites" by the governor of Bombay, Lord Lamington, who was also the Grand Master of All Scottish Freemasonry at that time. See Wadia, *History of Lodge Rising Star of Western India*, 324. For Masonic rites at hospitals in the United States, see Thompson and Goldin, *The Hospital*, 96–105.

103. The *Bombay Times and Journal of Commerce*, January 4, 1843, 4 (italics Fozdar's), quoted in Fozdar, Constructing the "'Brother,'" 296–97.

5. AN UNFORESEEN LANDSCAPE OF CONTRADICTIONS

1. *The Gazetteer of Bombay City and Island*, 3:195.

2. Stoler, "Sexual Affronts and Racial Frontiers," 198–237.

3. Malabari, "The Parsi Girl of the Period," 141–43.

4. Ballhatchet, *Race, Sex, and Class under the Raj*, 4.

5. Government Resolution no. 1187, General Department, 1 April 1886, in response to letter from Miss Edith Pechey, 23 March 1886, in Maharashtra State Archives, General Department, 1886, vol. 47, comp. no. 105 pt. 1, 83–84.

6. Letter from John Peet, Principal, Grant Medical College, to the Secretary to the Principal Inspector General, Medical Department, 16 May 1863, Maharashtra State Archives, General Department, 1862–64, vol. 14, comp. no. 297 of 1863, 240–42.

7. The numbers reflected these changes in attitude: in 1855, medical aid was given to 19 parturient women; in 1862 to 68; in 1872 to 90; and in 1881 to 150. Women also came to get treatment for other female-related diseases, and the numbers under all categories had increased by 1885 leading to overcrowding of the available facilities. See letter from the Surgeon General with the Government of Bombay to the Secretary to Government, General Department, no. 2922 of 1885, 19 May 1885, Maharashtra State Archives, General Department, 1885, vol. 70, comp. no. 789, 3–6.

8. Para 2 of Government Resolution no. 96, C.W. 217, 17 February 1883, Public Works Department, in ibid., 5–6.

9. Government Resolution no. 2262, General Department, 13 April 1911, referring to letter from Messrs. Stanley Reed and Fazulbhoy Currimbhoy to the Private Secretary to the Governor, 12 August 1910, Maharashtra State Archives, General Department, 1911, vol. 48, comp. no. 780, 21.

10. *Gazetteer of Bombay City and Island*, 3:210–11.

11. Letter forwarded by the Surgeon General with the Government of Bombay to the Secretary to Government from the President, Majlise Taide Amvat Lavarisie Islamie, dated 28 August 1894, Maharashtra State Archives, General Department, 1894, vol. 64, comp. no. 815, 12–14.

12. Government Resolution no. 199 C. W.-1380 of 1896, Public Works Department, 1 October 1896, Maharashtra State Archives, General Department, 1896, vol. 62, comp. no. 398, 104r, 104v.

13. Letter from Jamsetjee Jeejeebhoy, Rustomjee Jamsetjee Jeejeebhoy, and Sorabjee Jamsetjee Jeejeebhoy to the Governor, Sir H. B. E. Frere, 24 April 1863, 1862–64, vol. 14, comp. no. 297 of 1863, 239.

14. Letter from John Peet, Principal, Grant Medical College, to the Secretary to the Principal Inspector General, Medical Department, 16 May 1863, Maharashtra State Archives, General Department, 1862–64, vol. 14, comp. no. 297 of 1863, 240–42.

15. Ibid., 240–42.

16. Letter from A. D. Robertson, Secretary to Government to Sir Jamsetjee Jeejeebhoy, Baronet, the Honorable Rustomjee Jamsetjee Jeejeebhoy, Esq. and Sorabjee Jamsetjee Jeejeebhoy, Esq., 5 June 1863, in ibid., 242–43.

17. See Thompson and Goldin, *The Hospital,* 79, 91.

18. Taylor, *The Architect and the Pavilion Hospital.*

19. *Indian Spectator,* 6 July 1890, in *Report on Native Papers Published in the Bombay Presidency* for the week ending 12 July 1890, 12.

20. *Bombay Samachar,* 12 September 1890, in *Report on Native Papers Published in the Bombay Presidency* for the week ending 13 September 1890, 13–14.

21. Newell, *Bombay (The Gate of India),* 24.

22. See Bagchi, "European and Indian Entrepreneurship in India, 1900–30," 245.

23. Karaka, *History of the Parsis,* 2:273.

24. Kulke, *The Parsees in India,* 32–34; Karaka, *History of the Parsis,* 2:8–9, 244.

25. Karaka, *History of the Parsis,* 1:xvii.

26. Kulke, *The Parsees in India,* 35.

27. Low, *A Vision of India,* 44–45.

28. Kulke, *The Parsees in India,* 72–73.

29. Caine, *Picturesque India,* 14.

30. My summary is of a quote from *Rast Goftar,* 16 November 1862, in Kulke, *The Parsees in India,* 73–74.

31. Karaka, *History of the Parsis,* 2:271.

32. Hinnells, "The Flowering of Zoroastrian Benevolence," 276, 308–14.

33. *Gazetteer of Bombay City and Island,* 3:180–84.

34. Background information on European General Hospital from *Gazetteer of Bombay City and Island,* 3:180–88; Maclean, *A Guide to Bombay* (1906), 245.

35. The information of Charles Henry Couzens recalled and reexamined on 15 September, was taken during the proceedings of a coroner's inquest held on the body of Margaret Louisa Couzens, who died of tetanus at the Cama Hospital on 13 September 1886, Maharashtra State Archives, General Department, 1886, vol. 47, comp. no. 105, pt. 1, 403–10.

36. Newspaper cuttings from the *Times of India,* 8 April 1913, in Maharashtra State Archives, General Department, 1913, vol. 75, comp. no. 274, 209–13; Dobbin

defines *mofussil* as "lit. suburban or provincial; the rural areas of a district or region distinct from the capital." See Dobbin, *Urban Leadership in Western India*, 288.

37. Newspaper cuttings from the *Times of India*, 8 April 1913, in Maharashtra State Archives, GS, 1913, vol. 75, comp. no. 274, 209–13.

38. *Gujaráti*, 20 April 1913, in *Report on Native Papers Published in the Bombay Presidency* for the week ending 19 April 1913, 28.

39. *Administration and Progress Report on the Civil Medical Institutions in the City of Bombay for the Year 1892*, 10–11.

40. Government Resolution no. 4691 of 1913, General Department, 24 June 1913, Maharashtra State Archives, General Department, 1913, vol. 75, comp. no. 274, 337–39.

41. Government Resolution no. 4866, 16 August 1906, Maharashtra State Archives, General Department, 1906, vol. 48, comp. no. 432, 269–71.

42. *Briton*, 23 June 1912, in *Report on Native Papers Published in the Bombay Presidency* for the week ending 29 June 1912, 35.

43. *Briton*, 25 August 1912, in *Report on Native Papers Published in the Bombay Presidency* for the week ending 31 August 1912, 20, 21.

44. *Parsi*, 21 June 1912, in *Report on Native Papers Published in the Bombay Presidency* for the week ending 22 June 1912, 35.

45. *Rast Goftar*, 13 October 1912; *Bombay Samachar*, 12 October 1912; *Parsi*, 12 October 1912; in *Report on Native Papers Published in the Bombay Presidency* for the week ending 12 October 1912, 33, 34.

46. Maclean, *A Guide to Bombay* (1906), 188–89.

47. *Dnyan Prakash*, 21 March 1870; *Arunodaya*, 20 March 1870; *Bombay Samachar*, 23 March 1870; in *Report on Native Papers Published in the Bombay Presidency* for the week ending 26 March 1870.

48. Morris, *The Emergence of an Industrial Labour Force in India*, 62–65.

49. Demi-official report, General Department, 1264B, (no day) April 1900, Maharashtra State Archives, General Department, 1900, vol. 53, comp. no. 1110, 69–74.

50. Letter from the President, Municipal Corporation, Bombay, to Government, no. 14107, 26 March 1900, in Government Resolution no. 3012, General Department, 13 June 1900, in ibid., 77.

51. Petition from Mrs. Lily Doughty Wylie to Mr. L. Robertson, 5 January 1909, Maharashtra State Archives, General Department, 1909, vol. 55, comp. no. 476, 263–69.

52. Sheppard, *Bombay*, 109. Dates when buildings were completed from my field research notes, 1998–99.

53. Rutnagur, *Bombay Industries*, 507–11.

54. Chaudhari, *History of Bombay*, 116–18.

55. Rutnagur, *Bombay Industries*, 511.

56. Wolpert, *A New History of India*, 250–74.

57. Harris, *Jamsetji Nusserwanji Tata*, 123–26.

58. See Harris, "The Institute of Science: Inception," and "The Institute of Science: Completion," chapters 6 and 7 of *Jamsetji Nusserwanji Tata*, 120–54.

59. Ibid., 133–35.

60. *Mahratta,* 11 September 1904; *Kathiawar Times,* 25 September 1904; *Kesari,* 13 September 1904; *Indian Spectator,* 17 September 1904; in *Report on Native Papers Published in the Bombay Presidency* for the week ending 17 September 1904, 32, 33.

61. *Jam-e-Jamshed,* 17 July 1913; in *Report on Native Papers Published in the Bombay Presidency* for the week ending 19 July 1913, 45, 46.

62. *Jam-e-Jamshed,* 7 October 1914; in *Report on Native Papers Published in the Bombay Presidency* for the week ending 10 October 1914, 32, 33.

63. Ramanna, *Western Medicine,* 19.

64. Reba Lewis, *Three Faces Has Bombay,* 81–82.

65. Ramanna, *Western Medicine,* 19.

66. Lewis, *Three Faces,* 82–83. A plaque at K. E. M. Hospital says that Dr. Habib Ismail Janmahomed donated Rs. 30,000 toward the hospital, while Lewis states the sum to be Rs. 50,000. The smaller figure is likely to be more accurate.

67. Anderson, *Imagined Communities.*

68. Maclean, *Recollections of Westminister and India,* 25.

6. OF GODS AND MORTAL HEROES

1. Gerald Aungier is considered by many to be the "real founder of Bombay." He was governor of Bombay from 1669 to 1677. Bombay formed part of the royal dower of Infanta Catherine of Braganza, sister of King Alphonso VI of Portugal, on her marriage to Charles II of England. In 1668, Bombay was transferred to the East India Company. See Sheppard, *Bombay,* 8, 17, 20; Masselos, *Towards Nationalism,* 8–9.

2. Kosambi, *Bombay in Transition,* 32.

3. Sheppard notes that the original Walkeshwar temple "was later destroyed, either by Mahomedans or Portuguese." See Sheppard, *Bombay,* 1. Bombay was ceded to the Portuguese by Sultan Bahadur of Gujarat in 1534. See Masselos, *Towards Nationalism,* 7.

4. See Sheppard, *Bombay Place-Names and Street-Names,* 104–5; *The Gazetteer of Bombay City and Island,* 1:38. According to Sheppard, Mumbadevi temple was moved in 1737; according to the *Gazetteer,* which is more likely to be correct, this happened in 1766; da Cunha, *The Origin of Bombay,* 201–3.

5. *Gazetteer of Bombay City and Island,* 3:356–57.

6. Davis, *Lives of Indian Images,* 7.

7. *Gazetteer of Bombay City and Island,* 3:287–28.

8. Davies, *The Penguin Guide to the Monuments of India,* 2:449.

9. S. M. Edwardes, *Census of India—1901,* vol. 10, pt. 4, 8.

10. *Gazetteer of Bombay City and Island,* 3:361.

11. Nora, "Between Memory and History," 8.

12. Nora says, "These *lieux de mémoire* are fundamentally remains, the ultimate embodiments of a memorial consciousness that has barely survived in a historical age that calls out for memory because it has abandoned it. . . . *Lieux de mémoire* originate

with the sense that there is no spontaneous memory, that we must deliberately create archives, maintain anniversaries, organize celebrations, pronounce eulogies, and notarize bills because such activities no longer occur naturally." See ibid., 12.

13. Other prominent cave sites in Bombay's vicinity were the Jogeshwari caves, the Kanheri caves, and the Mandapeshwar caves.

14. Europeans may have discovered Elephanta in the fifteenth century, but there is written evidence of this encounter in the sixteenth century. See Mitter, *Much Maligned Monsters,* 35.

15. In the sixteenth century João do Castro measured the temple, thus marking the first attempt to document an Indian monument. See ibid., 36.

16. Ibid., 105–6.

17. Ibid., 105–6, 120–40.

18. Metcalf, *An Imperial Vision,* 25.

19. See Guha-Thakurta, *The Making of a New 'Indian' Art,* 118–24, particularly p. 121 for debate with Fergusson. Ram Raz wrote *Essays on the Architecture of the Hindus* (London, 1834), while Rajendralal Mitra's writings include *The Antiquities of Orissa,* vol. 1 (Calcutta, 1875) and vol. 2 (Calcutta, 1880), and *Indo Aryans: Contributions towards the Elucidation of Their Ancient and Medieval History,* 2 vols. (London/Calcutta, 1881).

20. Mitter, *Much Maligned,* 140, 171. Surveyors also played an important early role in collecting information, sketching, and drawing architectural sites, temples, reliefs, and sculptures of temples and other monuments. For the role of Colin Mackenzie, who became surveyor-general of India, as a collector of information, see Dirks, "Guiltless Spoliations," 211–32.

21. Anonymous, *Life in Bombay,* 214.

22. Ibid., 218–19.

23. Mitter, *Much Maligned,* 253.

24. See Anonymous, *Life in Bombay,* 211; Government Resolution No. A.–2099 of 1903, Public Works Department, dated 29 August 1903, in 1903, General Department, vol. 19, comp. no. 138, 137.

25. da Cunha, *Origin of Bombay,* 129–30; Mitter, *Much Maligned,* 34.

26. Guha-Thakurta, *Monuments, Objects, Histories,* 295, quoting from the "Ancient Monuments Preservation Bill, 1900–1901," in Curzon Collection Papers, Oriental and India Office Collections, London, on "Indian Archaeology, 1889–1905," 14.

27. Archer, "Artists and Patrons in 'Residency' Delhi, 1803–1858," 164.

28. Cohn, "Representing Authority in Victorian India," 209.

29. Government Resolution No. A.–2099 of 1903, Public Works Department, dated 29 August 1903, in 1903, General Department, vol. 19, comp. no. 138, 137–39.

30. Gell, *Art and Agency,* 97.

31. Ibid.

32. Guha-Thakurta, *Monuments, Objects, Histories,* 55–63.

33. Ibid., 61.

34. Bellah, *The Broken Covenant,* 3.

35. Bellah, *Beyond Belief,* 168.

36. Ibid., 178–79.

37. Bellah, *The Broken Covenant*, 3.

38. Metcalf and Metcalf, *A Concise History of India*, 92–93.

39. Ibid., 106.

40. *Handbook of the Bombay Presidency* (1881), 124.

41. Ibid., 123–26.

42. For a discussion of the attempts of the British to prove the essential difference between them and Indians, see chapter 3, "The Creation of Difference," and chapter 4, "The Ordering of Difference," in Metcalf, *Ideologies of the Raj*, 66–159.

43. Wacha thinks the statue of Cornwallis was raised in 1805; see Sir Dinshaw Wacha, *Shells from the Sands of Bombay*, 150.

44. Nilsson, *European Architecture in India 1750–1850*, 132–34.

45. Ibid., 109.

46. Cannadine, "The Context, Performance, and Meaning of Ritual," 116.

47. Metcalf, *An Imperial Vision*, 2.

48. Ibid., 3. Gilbert Scott was chosen to design the Foreign Office in 1859 and a detail of the India Office appeared in the *Builder* in 1867.

49. For the status of monarchy in Britain, see Cannadine, "The Context, Performance, and Meaning of Ritual," 120–26.

50. Cohn, "Representing Authority in Victorian India," 190.

51. Ibid., 179–95.

52. For a brief discussion of comments by Parsis on photographs of British royalty, see Luhrmann, *The Good Parsi*, 48–51.

53. Kulke, *The Parsees in India*, 72–73.

54. My summary is of a quote from the Parsi newspaper *Rast Goftar*, 16 November 1862, in ibid., 73–74.

55. Mistry, *Doongaji House*, 26. *Doongaji House* was written when Cyrus Mistry was twenty-one, probably in 1977 (since he wrote his first short story in 1976 at the age of twenty), and he won the Sultan Padamsee Award for it in 1978. Its first theatrical production was in Bombay in 1990, and it is set in Bombay in the late 1960s. "Hormusji *(disagrees):* 'The old acquisitive instinct, Darabshaa . . . Snatch, snatch! Maharashtra for Maharashtrians. Indeed! After we Parsis have built the whole city! . . . Now if the British were here, they would have just flogged one or two of them in a public place'" (26).

56. Low, *A Vision of India*, 44–45.

57. Wacha, *Shells from the Sands of Bombay*, 143. Cowasji Jehangir also contributed Rs. 7,500 toward the Afghan Memorial Church, which was the largest individual contribution.

58. Ibid., 143.

59. Jacobs, *Edge of Empire*, 113.

60. *Govind Narayan's Mumbai*, 129.

61. Ibid., 128. For other examples, see Groseclose, *British Sculpture and the Company Raj*, 23–24. For discussion of native reaction to sculptures of Europeans in Bombay's public spaces, see *Govind Narayan's Mumbai*, 128–30. Written in Marathi, under

the title of *Mumbaiche Varnan,* this was the first comprehensive account of Bombay that preceded other urban biographies of the city written in other languages.

62. Douglas, *Glimpses of Old Bombay and Western India,* 16.

63. Also see Groseclose, *British Sculpture and the Company Raj,* 23.

64. Tindall, *City of Gold,* 78.

65. *Govind Narayan's Mumbai,* 128–29.

66. Rafael, *Contracting Colonialism,* 1–12. The term "fish out" is from p. 2.

67. The Timucua Indians on the coast of Florida thought the monumental stone pillar the French had left as a marker of possession was a sacred object and treated it as such. Seed points out that "the Timucuas assimilated the 'important' object into their own categories of importance, not the Frenchmen's" (59). See Seed, *Ceremonies of Possession,* 57–59.

68. Davis, *Lives of Indian Images,* 5–6; the terms "cult value" and "exhibition value" are taken from Benjamin, "The Work of Art in the Age of Mechanical Reproduction," 224.

69. Benjamin, "The Work of Art in the Age of Mechanical Reproduction," 217–51.

70. Letter from Ollivant, Chairman of the Committee, to John Nugent, Secretary to Government, 9 March 1886, Maharashtra State Archives, General Department, 1886, vol. 116, comp. no. 816, 87–90.

71. Maclean, *A Guide to Bombay* (1906), 224–25.

72. Guha-Thakurta, *Monuments, Objects, Histories,* 49–50.

73. Ibid., 255–56.

74. *Gazetteer of Bombay City and Island,* 3:377.

75. Roth, *The Sassoon Dynasty,* 66–67.

76. *Gazetteer of Bombay City and Island,* 3:377–78; Roth, *Sassoon Dynasty,* 66.

77. With the permission of the government, Dr. George Birdwood had ordered the bust for the museum from England, which he received at the end of Sir Bartle Frere's administration around March 1867. See memo by W. Lee Warner, Private Secretary, 15 July 1872, Maharashtra State Archives, General Department, 1872, vol. 70, comp. no. 589, 133.

78. *Gazetteer of Bombay City and Island,* 3:377n.

79. Ibid. 3:377–79.

80. Maclean, *A Guide to Bombay* (1906), 224.

81. *Gazetteer of Bombay City and Island,* 3:377. This volume was published in 1910. While no specific date for the defacement of Lady Frere's bust is given, the act took place "several years" before.

82. Duncan, *Civilizing Rituals,* 8–20. While Duncan is referring to art museums, I believe this argument holds for all museums, including the Victoria and Albert Museum in Bombay that was not only an art museum.

83. Guha-Thakurta, *Monuments, Objects, Histories,* 80, quoting Edgar Thurston, superintendent of the Madras Museum; Duncan, *Civilizing Rituals,* 10.

84. Letter from E. W. Ravenscroft, Acting Municipal Commissioner, to the Chief Secretary to Government, General Department, no. 48970 of 1874, 28 September 1874, Maharashtra State Archives, General Department, 1875, vol. 34, comp. no. 67, 19–22.

85. Letter from the Town Council, no. 925, dated 8 September 1874, to the Municipal Commissioner, in ibid., 47–48.

86. Memo: "Relating to the mosque and tank lately completed in the Victoria Gardens," by E. W. Ravenscroft, dated 30 June 1874, attached to Ravenscroft's letter no. 48970 of 1874, dated 28 September 1874, to the Chief Secretary to Government, in ibid., 23.

87. Edwardes, *By-Ways of Bombay,* 74.

88. Ibid., 74–75.

89. de Certeau, *The Practice of Everyday Life,* 24–28.

90. Chatterjee, *The Nation and Its Fragments,* 6.

Bibliography

RECORDS

Maharashtra State Archives (Government of Maharashtra Secretariat Record Office),
    Elphinstone College Building, Bombay:
        General Department
        Judicial Department
        Public Works Department
        Revenue Department

PRIVATE PAPERS

Papers of Sir Pherozeshah Mehta, Nehru Memorial Museum and Library, New Delhi
Papers of Sir George Christopher Molesworth Birdwood (MSS Eur F 216), Oriental
    and India Office Collections (OIOCs), British Library, London.

OFFICIAL PUBLICATIONS

*Administration and Progress Report on the Civil Medical Institutions in the City of Bombay
    for the Year 1892.* Bombay: Government Central Press, 1893.
Administration Report of the Municipal Commissioner for the City of Bombay, 1865/
    66–1919/20 (annually).
Annual Administration Report of the City of Bombay Improvement Trust, 1898/99–1919/20.
Bombay 1921–22, a Review of the Administration of the Presidency.
Campbell, Sir James McNabb (Chairman). *Report of the Plague Commission Appointed
    by Government Resolution No. 1204/720P, on the Plague in Bombay, for the Period*

Extending from 1 July 1897 to the 30 April 1898. Bombay: Times of India Steam Press, 1898.

Census of India 1871/72. Taken on 21 February 1872. Bombay City.

Census of India 1881: Census of City and Island of Bombay. By T. S. Weir. Bombay, 1883.

Chaudhari, K. K. *History of Bombay: Modern Period.* Maharashtra State Gazetteers. Bombay: Government of Maharashtra, 1987.

Correspondence Relative to the "Sir Jamsetjee Jejeebhoy Dhurrumsalla," built by Sir Jamsetjee Jejeebhoy, Knight, and Made Over to Him by Government, for the District Benevolent Society of Bombay. Bombay: Times Press, 1851.

Edwardes, S. M. *Census of India—1901.* Vol. 10, *Bombay (Town & Island),* pt. 4, *History.* Bombay: Times of India Press, 1901.

———. *Census of India—1901.* Vol. 11, *Bombay (Town & Island),* pt, 5, *Report.* Bombay: Times of India Press, 1901.

———. *Kharshedji Rustamji Cama, 1831–1909: A Memoir* (Oxford: Oxford University Press, 1923), 50–53.

Gatacre, Brigadier-General W. F., Chairman of the Plague Committee. *Report on the Bubonic Plague in Bombay 1896–97.* Bombay: Times of India Steam Press, 1897.

The Gazetteer of Bombay City and Island. 3 vols. Compiled by S. M. Edwardes. Bombay: Times Press, 1909–10.

Gazetteer of the Bombay Presidency. Vol. 9, pt. 2, *Gujarat Population: Musalmans and Parsis.* Bombay: Government Central Press, 1899.

Mead, P. J., and G. Laird Macgregor. *Census of India, 1911.* Vol. 8, *Bombay (Town and Island),* pts. 1–& 2, *Report and Tables.* Bombay: Government Central Press, 1912.

Report on Native Papers Published in the Bombay Presidency, 1868–1918.

Report of the Bombay Plague Committee, Appointed by Government Resolution No. 1204/720P, on the Plague in Bombay, for the Period Extending from the 1st July 1897 to the 30th April 1898. Under the Chairmanship of Sir James MacNabb Campbell, examined by Captain the Hon. R. Mostyn, Extra Secretary, Bombay Plague Committee. Bombay: Times of India Press, 1898.

Report on the Development Plan for Greater Bombay 1964. Bombay: Government Central Press, 1964.

Selections from the Bombay Corporation's Proceedings and Debate on the City of Bombay Improvement Trust's Sandhurst Road to Crawford Market Street Scheme. Bombay: Times Press, 1911.

BOOKS AND ARTICLES

Abu-Lughod, Janet L. *Cairo: 1001 Years of the City Victorious.* Princeton, N.J.: Princeton University Press, 1971.

———. *Rabat: Urban Apartheid in Morocco.* Princeton Studies on the Near East. Princeton, N.J.: Princeton University Press, 1980.

Acarya, Balakrishna Bapu, and Moro Vinayak Shingne. *Mumbaicha Vrittanta* (A Descriptive Account of Bombay, Being an Outline of Events Both Past and Present, with Maps). Edited by Bapurao Naik. 1889. Reprint, Mumbai: Maharashtra Rajya Sahitya Sanskriti Mandal, 1980.

Adam, Thomas. "Transatlantic Trading: The Transfer of Philanthropic Models between European and North American Cities during the Nineteenth and Early Twentieth Centuries." *Journal of Urban History* 28, no. 3 (March 2002): 328–51.

Adams, Annmarie. *Medicine by Design: The Architect and the Modern Hospital, 1893–1943.* Minneapolis: University of Minnesota Press, 2008.

Albuquerque, Teresa. *Urbs Prima in Indis: An Epoch in the History of Bombay, 1840–1865.* New Delhi: Promilla & Company, 1985.

AlSayyad, Nezar, ed. *Forms of Dominance: On the Architecture and Urbanism of the Colonial Experience.* Aldershot: Avebury, 1992.

Ahmed, Aijaz. *In Theory: Classes, Nations, Literatures.* Delhi: Oxford University Press; London: Verso, 1992.

Anderson, Benedict. *Imagined Communities: Reflections on the Origin and Spread of Nationalism.* London: Verso, 1991.

Anonymous. "Anglo-Indian Architecture." *Builder* 55 (3 November 1888): 313–15.

———. "Architecture in the Reign of Queen Victoria." *Builder* 53 (25 June 1887): 927–29.

———. "The Civic Decorations of Bombay, On the Occasion of the Royal Visit to India: George Wittet, Architect," *Architectural Review* (Boston) 18: 137–38.

———. "The High Court, Calcutta: Public Works of India." *Builder* 27 (30 October 1869): 857–58.

———. "Khan Bahadur Muncherjee Murzban (Notice of Deceased)." *Journal of the Royal Institute of British Architects* 25 (May 1918): 121, 168.

———. *Life in Bombay, and the Neighbouring Out-Stations.* London: Richard Bentley, 1852.

———. "On the Public Works Department of India." *Builder* 27 (18 December 1869): 1009–10.

———. "Pay in the Public Works Department, India." *Builder* 26 (12 September 1868): 679–80.

Appadurai, Arjun. *Worship and Conflict under Colonial Rule: A South Indian Case.* Cambridge: Cambridge University Press, 1981.

Archer, Mildred. "Artists and Patrons in 'Residency' Delhi, 1803–1858." In *Delhi Through the Ages: Selected Essays in Urban History, Culture and Society,* edited by R. E. Frykenberg, 157–64. Delhi: Oxford University Press, 1993.

Arnold, David. *Colonizing the Body: State Medicine and Epidemic Disease in Nineteenth-Century India.* Berkeley: University of California Press, 1996.

———. *Science, Technology and Medicine in Colonial India.* New Cambridge History of India III.5. Cambridge: Cambridge University Press, 2000.

———. "Touching the Body: Perspectives on the Indian Plague, 1896–1900." In *Subaltern Studies V: Writings on South Asian History and Society,* edited by Ranajit Guha, 55–90. Delhi: Oxford University Press, 1987.

Arnold, Edwin. *India Revisited.* London: Trubner & Company, 1886.

Ashcroft, Bill, Gareth Griffiths, and Helen Tiffin. *Key Concepts in Post-Colonial Studies.* London: Routledge, 1998.

Bagchi, Amiya Kumar. "European and Indian Entrepreneurship in India, 1900–30." In *Elites in South Asia,* edited by Edmund Leach and S. N. Mukherjee. Cambridge: Cambridge University Press, 1970.

Ballhatchet, Kenneth. *Race, Sex, and Class under the Raj: Imperial Attitudes and Policies and Their Critics, 1793–1905.* New York: St. Martin's Press, 1980.

———. *Social Policy and Social Change in Western India, 1817–1830.* London Oriental Series, vol. 5. London: Oxford University Press, 1957.

Barker, Paul. "Charitable Architecture: The Prophetic Eye: The Life and Work of George Peabody, 1795–1869." Exhibition Review. *RSA Journal* 143, no. 5460 (1995): 64–66.

Basu, Dilip K., ed. *The Rise and Growth of the Colonial Port Cities in Asia.* London: University Press of America, 1985.

Batley, Claude. *Bombay's Houses and Homes.* Bombay Citizenship Series, edited by Dr. H. F. Bulsara. Bombay: National Information & Publications Ltd., 1949.

Baucom, Ian. *Out of Place: Englishness, Empire, and the Locations of Identity.* Princeton, N.J.: Princeton University Press, 1999.

Begg, John. "The Architect in India." *Architect and Contract Reporter* (May 19, 1911): 310–14.

———. "Architecture in India." *Journal of the Royal Institute of British Architects* 27 (1920): 333–49.

———. "The Work of George Wittet." *Journal of the Royal Institute of British Architects* 36 (1929): 539–48.

Bellah, Robert N. *Beyond Belief: Essays on Religion in a Post-Traditional World.* New York: Harper & Row, 1970; paperback edition published in 1976.

———. *The Broken Covenant: American Civil Religion in Time of Trial.* 2nd ed. Chicago: University of Chicago Press, 1992.

Benjamin, Walter. "The Work of Art in the Age of Mechanical Reproduction." In *Illuminations: Essays and Reflections,* edited and with an introduction by Hannah Arendt, 217–51. New York: Schocken Books, 1968.

Bhabha, Homi. *The Location of Culture.* London: Routledge, 1994.

———. "Of Mimicry and Man: The Ambivalence of Colonial Discourse." *October* 28 (Spring 1984): 125–33.

Berman, Marshall. *All That Is Solid Melts into Air: The Experience of Modernity.* New York: Viking Penguin, 1982.

Blake, Stephen P. "Cityscape of an Imperial Capital: Shahjahanabad in 1739." In *Delhi through the Ages: Selected Essays in Urban History, Culture and Society,* edited by R. E. Frykenberg, 66–105. Delhi: Oxford University Press, 1986; Oxford India Paperback, 1993.

———. *Shahjahanabad: The Sovereign City in Mughal India, 1639–1739.* Cambridge South Asia Studies, 49. Cambridge: Cambridge University Press, 1991.

Bloom, Harold. *The American Religion: The Emergence of the Post-Christian Nation.* New York: Simon & Schuster, 1992.

The Bombay Guide and Directory. 2nd ed. Bombay: Bombay Publishing Company, 1938.

Bose, Sugata, and Ayesha Jalal. *Modern South Asia: History, Culture, Political Economy.* London: Routledge, 1998. First published: Delhi: Oxford University Press, 1997.

Bourdieu, Pierre. *Distinction: A Social Critique of the Judgement of Taste.* Translated by Richard Nice. Cambridge, Mass.: Harvard University Press, 1984.

Brown, Kenneth. L. *People of Sale: Tradition and Change in a Moroccan City, 1830–1930.* Cambridge, Mass.: Harvard University Press, 1976.

Bulsara, Dr. Jal F. "Parsis, the Most Urbanised Community on Earth." In *The B. D. Petit Parsee General Hospital, 1912–1972,* edited by M. D. Petit et al. Bombay: Editorial Board of the B. D. Petit Parsi General Hospital Executive Committee, 1973.

Burnell, John. *Bombay in the Days of Queen Anne: Being an Account of the Settlement.* Works issued by the Hakluyt Society, 2nd ser., no. 72. London: printed for the Hakluyt Society, 1933.

Burnett-Hurst, A. R. *Labour and Housing in Bombay: A Study in the Economic Conditions of the Wage-Earning Classes in Bombay.* London: P. S. King & Son, 1925.

Caine, W. S. *Picturesque India: A Handbook for European Travellers.* London: George Routledge & Sons Ltd., 1890.

Calhoun, Craig, ed. *Habermas and the Public Sphere.* Cambridge, Mass.: MIT Press, 1992.

Cannadine, David. "The Context, Performance, and Meaning of Ritual: The British Monarchy and the 'Invention of Tradition,' c. 1820–1977." In *The Invention of Tradition,* edited by Eric Hobsbawm and Terence Ranger, 101–64. Cambridge: Cambridge University Press, 1983; Canto ed., 1992.

Carter, Paul. *The Road to Botany Bay: An Exploration of Landscape and History.* Chicago: University of Chicago Press, 1989.

Chandavarkar, Rajnarayan. *The Origins of Industrial Capitalism in India: Business Strategies and the Working Classes in Bombay, 1900–1940.* Cambridge: Cambridge University Press, 1994.

Chatterjee, Partha. *Nationalist Thought and the Colonial World: A Derivative Discourse.* Minneapolis: University of Minnesota Press, 1986.

———. *The Nation and Its Fragments: Colonial and Postcolonial Histories.* Princeton, N.J.: Princeton University Press, 1993.

Chattopadhyay, Swati. "Blurring Boundaries: The Limits of 'White Town' in Colonial Calcutta." *Journal of the Society of Architectural Historians* 59, no. 2 (June 2000): 154–79.

———. *Representing Calcutta: Modernity, Nationalism, and the Colonial Uncanny.* London: Routledge, 2005.

Cherry, Gordon E. "Introduction: Aspects of Twentieth-Century Planning." In *Shaping an Urban World: Planning in the Twentieth Century,* edited by Gordon E. Cherry, 1–21. New York: St. Martin's Press, 1977.

Chopra, Preeti. "The City and Its Fragments: Colonial Bombay 1854–1918." PhD diss., University of California, Berkeley, 2003.

———. "Imagining the City: The Naming of Colonial Bombay's City Divisions." In *Mumbai Reader,* International Architecture Exhibition for la Biennale di Venezia 2006,

70–87. Mumbai: Urban Design Research Institute, 2006. Originally published in *Divisions de la ville,* edited by Christian Topalov. Paris: Editions UNESCO: Editions de la Maison des sciences de l'hommes, 2002.

———. "Refiguring the Colonial City: Recovering the Role of Local Inhabitants in the Construction of Colonial Bombay." *Buildings and Landscapes* (Journal of the Vernacular Architecture Forum) 14 (Fall 2007): 109–25.

———. "La ville imaginee: Nommer les divisions de Bombay coloniale (1800–1918)." In *Divisions de la ville,* edited by Christian Topalov, 125–56. Paris: Editions UNESCO: Editions de la Maison des sciences de l'hommes, 2002.

Clark, T. J. *The Painting of Modern Life: Paris in the Art of Manet and His Followers.* New York: Alfred A. Knopf, 1985.

Cohn, Bernard S. "The Census, Social Structure, and Objectification in South Asia." *Folk* 26 (1984): 225–54.

———. "Cloth, Clothes, and Colonialism in India." In *Cloth and Human Experience,* edited by Annette B. Weiner and Jane Schneider, 303–53. Washington D.C.: Smithsonian Institution Press, 1989.

———. "Representing Authority in Victorian India." In *The Invention of Tradition,* edited by Eric Hobsbawm and Terence Ranger, 165–209. Cambridge: Cambridge University Press, 1983; Canto ed., 1992.

Conlon, Frank F. *A Caste in a Changing World: The Chitrapur Saraswat Brahmans, 1700–1935.* Berkeley: University of California Press, 1977.

———. "Dining Out in Bombay." In *Consuming Modernity: Public Culture in a South Asian World,* edited by Carol A. Breckenridge, 90–127. Minneapolis: University of Minnesota Press, 1998.

———. "Industrialization and the Housing Problem in Bombay, 1850–1940." In *Changing South Asia: Economy and Society,* vol. 4, edited by Kenneth Ballhatchet and David Taylor, 153–68. London: Centre of South Asian Studies, SOAS, 1984.

Cooper, Frederick, and Ann Laura Stoler. "Between Metropole and Colony: Rethinking a Research Agenda." In *Tensions of Empire: Colonial Cultures in a Bourgeois World,* edited by Frederick Cooper and Ann Laura Stoler, 1–56. Berkeley: University of California Press, 1997.

———, eds. 1997. *Tensions of Empire: Colonial Cultures in a Bourgeois World.* Berkeley: University of California Press.

Crinson, Mark. *Empire Building: Orientalism and Victorian Architecture.* London: Routledge, 1996.

Curl, James Steven. *Victorian Architecture.* Newton Abbot: David & Charles, 1990.

da Cunha, Dr. J. Gerson. *The Origin of Bombay.* 1900. Reprint, New Delhi: Asian Educational Services, 1993.

———. "Words and Places in and about Bombay." *Indian Antiquary* 3 (1874): 247–49, 292–95.

———. "Words and Places in and about Bombay (continued from vol. 3)." *Indian Antiquary* 4 (1875): 358–61.

Dahejia, Vidya. *Indian Art.* Art & Ideas Series. London: Phaidon Press Ltd., 1997.

Darukhanawala, H. D. *Parsi Lustre on Indian Soil.* Vol. 1. Bombay: G. Claridge & Company, 1939.

———. *Parsis and Sports and Kindred Subjects.* With a foreword by the Hon. Sir H. M. Mehta. n.p., 1935.

Das Gupta, Ashin. "The Merchants of Surat, c. 1700–50." In *Elites in South Asia,* edited by Edmund Leach and S. N. Mukherjee. Cambridge: Cambridge University Press, 1970.

Davies, Philip. *The Penguin Guide to the Monuments of India.* Vol. 2, *Islamic, Rajput, European.* London: Viking, 1989.

———. *Splendours of the Raj: British Architecture in India 1660–1947.* Harmondsworth: Penguin Books, 1985.

Davis, Richard H. *Lives of Indian Images.* Princeton, N.J.: Princeton University Press, 1997.

de Certeau, Michel. *The Practice of Everyday Life.* Translated by Steven Rendall. Berkeley: University of California Press, 1984.

Diqui, Ben. *A Visit to Bombay.* London: Watts & Company, 1927.

Dirks, Nicholas B. "Guiltless Spoliations: Picturesque Beauty, Colonial Knowledge, and Colin Mackenzie's Survey of India." In *Perceptions of South Asia's Visual Past,* edited by Catherine B. Asher and Thomas R. Metcalf, 211–32. New Delhi: Oxford & IBH Publishing Company, 1994.

Dobbin, Christine. "Competing Elites in Bombay City Politics in the Mid-Nineteenth Century (1852–83)." In *Elites in South Asia,* edited by Edmund Leach and S. N. Mukherjee. Cambridge: Cambridge University Press, 1970.

———. *Urban Leadership in Western India: Politics and Communities in Bombay, 1840–1885.* London: Oxford University Press, 1972.

Dossal, Mariam. *Imperial Designs and Indian Realities: The Planning of Bombay City, 1845–1875.* Bombay: Oxford University Press, 1991.

Douglas, James. *A Book of Bombay.* Bombay: Bombay Gazette Steam Press, 1883.

———. *Glimpses of Old Bombay and Western India.* London: Sampson Low, Marston and Company, 1900.

———. *Round about Bombay.* Bombay: Bombay Gazette Steam Press, 1886.

Douglas, Mary. *Thought Styles: Critical Essays on Good Taste.* London: Sage Publications, 1996.

Duncan, Carol. *Civilizing Rituals: Inside Public Museums.* London: Routledge, 1995.

Dwivedi, Sharada and Rahul Mehrotra. *Banganga: Sacred Tank.* Bombay: Eminence, 1996.

———. *Bombay: The Cities Within.* Bombay: India Book House Pvt. Ltd., 1995.

———. *Fort Walks: Around Bombay's Fort Area.* Bombay: Eminence Designs Pvt. Ltd., 1999.

Edney, Matthew H. "Defining a Unique City: Surveying and Mapping Bombay After 1800." *Marg* 48, no. 4: 28–45.

Edwardes, S. M. *By-Ways of Bombay.* Bombay: D. B. Taraporevala Sons & Company, 1912.

———. *The Bombay City Police: A Historical Sketch, 1672–1916.* London: Oxford University Press, 1923.

———. *Kharshedji Rustamji Cama, 1831–1909: A Memoir.* Oxford: Oxford University Press, 1923.

———. *The Population of the City of Bombay: A Few Remarks concerning Its Origin and Growth.* Bombay: British India Press, 1926. Pamphlet.

———. *The Rise of Bombay.* Bombay: Times of India Press, 1902.

Ernst, Waltraud. *Mad Tales from the Raj: The European Insane in British India, 1800–1858.* London: Routledge, 1991.

Evenson, Norma. *The Indian Metropolis: A View Toward the West.* New Haven, Conn.: Yale University Press, 1989.

Falkland, Viscountess. *Chow Chow: Being Selections from a Journal Kept in India, Egypt, and Syria.* 2 vols. London: Hurst and Blakett, 1857.

Fergusson, James. *History of Indian and Eastern Architecture.* London: J. Murray 1876.

Flood, Finbarr Barry. "Signs of Violence: Colonial Ethnographies and Indo-Islamic Monuments." *Australian and New Zealand Journal of Art* 5, no. 2 (2004): 20–51.

Forty, Adrian. "The Modern Hospital in England and France: The Social and Medical Uses of Architecture." In *Buildings and Society: Essays on the Social Development of the Built Environment,* edited by Anthony D. King, 61–93. London: Routledge & Kegan Paul, 1980.

Foucault, Michel. *Discipline and Punish: The Birth of a Prison.* Translated from the French by Alan Sheridan. New York: Vintage Books, 1977.

———. *Madness and Civilization: A History of Insanity in the Age of Reason.* Translated from the French by Richard Howard. New York: Pantheon Books, 1965.

Fozdar, Vahid Jalil. "Constructing the 'Brother': Freemasonry, Empire, and Nationalism in India, 1840–1925." PhD diss., University of California, Berkeley, 2001 (copyright 2002).

Fraser, Nancy. "Rethinking the Public Sphere: A Contribution to the Critique of Actually Existing Democracy." In *The Phantom Public Sphere,* edited by Bruce Robbins, 109–42. Minneapolis: University of Minnesota Press, 1993.

Freitag, Sandria. *Collective Action and Community: Public Arenas and the Emergence of Communalism in North India.* Berkeley: University of California Press, 1989.

———. "State and Community: Symbolic Popular Protest in Banaras's Public Arenas." In *Culture and Power in Banaras: Community, Performance, and Environment, 1800–1980,* edited by Sandria Freitag, 203–28. Berkeley: University of California Press, 1989.

Frere, Sir Bartle. "Modern Architecture in Western India." *The Building News and Engineering Journal* 18 (3 June 1870): 421–22.

Furneaux, J. H., ed. *Glimpses of India: A Grand Photographic History of the Land of Antiquity, the Vast Empire of the East.* Bombay: C. B. Burrows, 1895.

Gell, Alfred. *Art and Agency: An Anthropological Theory.* Oxford: Clarendon Press, 1998.

Giedion, Sigfried. *Space, Time, and Architecture: The Growth of a New Tradition.* 5th ed. Cambridge, Mass.: Harvard University Press, 1967.

Gillion, Kenneth L. *Ahmedabad: A Study in Indian Urban History.* Berkeley: University of California Press, 1968.

Glover, William J. "Ethnology, Engineering, and Modern Architecture in India, or Ganga Ram Goes to England." Talk delivered to the South Asia Center, University of Wisconsin, Madison, March 2, 2006.

———. "'A Feeling of Absence from Old England:' The Colonial Bungalow." *Home Cultures* 1, no. 1 (2004): 61–82.

———. *Making Lahore Modern: Constructing and Imagining a Colonial City.* Minneapolis: University of Minnesota Press, 2007.

———. "Objects, Models, and Exemplary Works: Educating Sentiment in Colonial India." *Journal of Asian Studies* 64, no. 3 (August 2005): 539–66.

Gordon, A. D. D. *Businessmen and Politics: Rising Nationalism and a Modernising Economy in Bombay, 1918–1933.* Australian National University Monographs on South Asia No. 3. New Delhi: Manohar, 1978.

Govind Narayan's Mumbai: An Urban Biography from 1863. Edited and translated by Murali Ranganathan. Foreword by Gyan Prakash. London: Anthem Press, 2008.

Groseclose, Barbara. *British Sculpture and the Company Raj: Church Monuments and Public Statuary in Madras, Calcutta, and Bombay to 1858.* Newark, N.J.: University of Delaware Press; London: Associated University Presses, 1995.

Guha-Thakurta, Tapati. *The Making of a New 'Indian' Art: Artists, Aesthetics, and Nationalism in Bengal, c. 1850–1920.* Cambridge: Cambridge University Press, 1992.

———. *Monuments, Objects, Histories: Institutions of Art in Colonial and Postcolonial India.* Delhi: Permanent Black, 2004.

Gupta, Narayani. *Delhi between Two Empires, 1803–1931: Society, Government, and Urban Growth.* Delhi: Oxford University Press, 1981.

Habermas, Jürgen. *The Structural Transformation of the Public Sphere: An Inquiry into a Category of Bourgeois Society.* Translated by Thomas Burger with the assistance of Frederick Lawrence. Cambridge, Mass.: MIT Press, 1989.

A Handbook for Travellers in India, and Pakistan, Burma, and Ceylon. 16th ed. London: John Murray, 1949.

Handbook of the Bombay Presidency with an Account of Bombay City. 2nd ed. London: John Murray, 1881.

Harris, F. R. *Jamsetji Nusserwanji Tata: A Chronicle of His Life.* London: Oxford University Press, 1925.

Harrison, John, and Kenneth Ballhatchet, eds. *The City in South Asia: Pre-Modern and Modern.* London: Curzon Press, 1980.

Haynes, Douglas E. *Rhetoric and Ritual in Colonial India: The Shaping of a Public Culture in Surat City 1852–1928.* Berkeley: University of California Press, 1991.

Hazareesingh, Sandip. *The Colonial City and the Challenge of Modernity: Urban Hegemonies and Civic Confrontations in Bombay 1900–1925.* Delhi: Orient Longman, 2007.

———. "Colonial Modernism and the Flawed Paradigms of Urban Renewal: The Uneven Development of Bombay City, 1900–1925." *Urban History* 28, no. 2 (2001): 235–55.

————. "The Quest for Urban Citizenship: Civic Rights, Public Opinion, and Colonial Resistance in Early Twentieth-Century Bombay." *Modern Asian Studies* 34, no. 4 (2000): 797–829.

Hesilrige, Arthur G. M., ed. *Debrett's Peerage, Baronetage, Knightage, and Companionage*. London: Dean & Son, Ltd., 1915.

Hinnells, John R. "The Flowering of Zoroastrian Benevolence." In *Papers in Honour of Professor Mary Boyce, Hommages et Opera Minora*, 10:261–326. Leiden: E. J. Brill, 1985.

Hosagrahar, Jyoti. "City as Durbar: Theater and Power in Imperial Delhi." In *Forms of Dominance: On the Architecture and Urbanism of the Colonial Enterprise*, edited by Nezar AlSayyad, 83–106. Aldershot: Avebury, 1992.

————. *Indigenous Modernities: Negotiating Architecture and Urbanism*. London: Routledge, 2005.

Houston, John. *Representative Men of the Bombay Presidency*. Bombay and London: C. B. Burrows, 1897.

Irving, Robert G. *Indian Summer: Lutyens, Baker, and Imperial Delhi*. New Haven, Conn.: Yale University Press, 1981.

Irwin, John. "'Ashok' Pillars: A Reassessment of the Evidence." Pts. 1–4. *Burlington Magazine* (November 1973): 706–20; (December 1974): 712–27; (October 1975): 631–43; (November 1976): 734–53.

Jackson, Stanley. *The Sassoons*. London: Heinemann, 1968.

Jacobs, Jane M. *Edge of Empire: Postcolonialism and the City*. London: Routledge, 1996.

Jalbhoy, R. H. *The Portrait Gallery of Western India*. Bombay: Education Society's Press, 1886.

Karageorgevitch, Prince Bojidar. *Enchanted India*. New York: Harper and Brothers, 1899.

Karaka, Dosabhai Framji. *History of the Parsis, including Their Manners, Customs, Religion, and Present Position*. 2 vols. 1884. Reprint. Delhi: Discovery Publishing House, 1986.

Karkaria, R. P., ed. *The Charm of Bombay: An Anthology of Writings in Praise of the First City in India*. Bombay: D. B. Taraporevala, Sons & Company, 1915.

Khan, Aga. *The Memoirs of Aga Khan: World Enough and Time*. New York: Simon and Schuster, 1954.

Khote, Durga. *I, Durga Khote: An Autobiography*. Translated from Marathi by Shanta Gokhale. New Delhi: Oxford University Press, 2006.

Kidambi, Prashant. "Housing the Poor in a Colonial City: The Bombay Improvement Trust, 1898–1918." *Studies in History*, n.s., 17, no. 1 (2001): 65.

————. *The Making of an Indian Metropolis: Colonial Governance and Public Culture in Bombay, 1890–1920*. Aldershot, England: Ashgate, 2007.

King, Anthony D. *The Bungalow: The Production of a Global Culture*. New York: Oxford University Press, 1984.

————. "Colonial Cities: Global Pivots of Change." In *Colonial Cities: Essays on Urbanism in a Colonial Context*, edited by Robert J. Ross & Gerard J. Telkamp. Comparative Studies in Overseas History, vol. 5. Dordrecht, Netherlands; Boston: Martinus Nijhoff Publishers, 1985.

—————. *Colonial Urban Development: Culture, Social Power, and Environment.* London: Routledge and Kegan Paul, 1976.

—————. *Global Cities: Post-Imperialism and the Internationalization of London.* London: Routledge, 1990.

—————. "Exporting Planning: The Colonial and Neo-Colonial Experience." In *Shaping an Urban World: Planning in the Twentieth Century,* edited by Gordon E. Cherry, 203–26. New York: St. Martin's Press, 1977.

—————. *Urbanism, Colonialism, and the World Economy: Cultural and Spatial Foundations of the World Urban System.* London: Routledge, 1990.

—————. "Writing Colonial Space. A Review Article." *Comparative Study of Society and History* 37, no. 3 (July 1995): 541–54.

Kipling, John Lockwood. "Indian Architecture of Today." *Journal of Indian Art* [later called *Journal of Indian Art and Industry*] 1, no. 3 (1884–86, n.d.): 1–5.

Koenigsmarck, Count Hans Von. *A German Staff Officer in India: Being the Impressions of an Officer of the German General Staff of His Travels through the Peninsula; With an Epilogue Specially Written for the English Edition.* Translated by P. H. Oakley Williams. London: Kegan Paul, Trench, Trübner & Company, 1910.

Kosambi, Meera. *Bombay in Transition: The Growth and Social Ecology of a Colonial City, 1880–1980.* Stockholm: Almqvist & Wiksell International, 1986.

Kulke, Eckehard. *The Parsees in India: A Minority as Agent of Social Change.* Munich: Weltforum Verlag, 1974.

Kumar, Anil. *Medicine and the Raj: British Medical Policy in India, 1835–1911.* Walnut Creek, Calif.: Altamira Press (division of Sage Publications), 1998.

Kusno, Abidin. *Behind the Postcolonial: Architecture, Urban Space, and Political Cultures in Indonesia.* London: Routledge, 2000.

Legg, Stephen. *Spaces of Colonialism: Delhi's Urban Governmentalities.* Malden, Mass.: Blackwell Publishing, 2007.

Lewis, Reba. *Three Faces Has Bombay.* Bombay: Popular Book Depot, 1957.

Liechty, Mark. *Suitably Modern: Making Middle-Class Culture in a New Consumer Society.* Princeton: Princeton University Press, 2003.

List of Statues and Busts in the Town and Island of Bombay (n.p., n.d.), in the Oriental and India Office Collections, British Library, London.

Llewellyn-Jones, Rosie. *A Fatal Friendship: The Nawabs, the British, and the City of Lucknow.* Delhi: Oxford University Press, 1985.

London, Christopher W. *Bombay Gothic.* Mumbai: India Book House Pvt. Ltd., 2002.

Low, Sidney. *A Vision of India: As Seen during the Tour of the Prince and Princess of Wales.* London: Smith, Elder, & Company, 1907.

Luhrmann, T. M. *The Good Parsi: The Fate of a Colonial Elite in a Postcolonial Society.* Delhi: Oxford University Press, 1996.

Maclean, James Mackenzie. *A Guide to Bombay: Historical, Statistical, and Descriptive.* 5th ed. 1880; 31st ed. Bombay: Bombay Gazette Steam Press, 1906.

————. *Recollections of Westminister and India.* Manchester: Sherratt & Hughes, n.d. prob. 1901.

Madan, T. N. "Secularism in Its Place." *Journal of Asian Studies* 46, no. 4 (November 1987): 747–59.

Madgavkar, Govind Narayan. *Mumbaiche Varnan* (Bombay Past and Present; An Historical Sketch in Marathi, with Maps and Glossary). Edited by Professor Narhar Raghunath Phatak. 2nd ed. 1863; reprint, with a foreword by Professor N. R. Phatak, Mumbai: Mumbai Marathi Grantha-Sangrahalaya, 1961.

Majmudar, M. R. *Cultural History of Gujarat.* Bombay: Popular Prakashan, 1965.

Malabari, Behramji M. "The Parsi Girl of the Period—An Argument in Favour of Infant Marriage." In *The Life and Life-Work of Behramji M. Malabari,* edited by Dayaram Gidumal. Bombay: Education Society's Press, 1888.

Malabari, Phiroze B. M. *Bombay in the Making: Being Mainly a History of the Origin and Growth of Judicial Institutions in the Western Presidency, 1661–1726.* London: T. Fisher Unwin, 1910.

Masani, R. P. *Evolution of Local Self-Government in Bombay.* London: Oxford University Press, 1929.

Masselos, Jim C. "Change and Custom in the Format of the Bombay Mohurrum during the Nineteenth and Twentieth Centuries." *South Asia,* n.s., 5, no. 2 (December 1982): 47–67.

————. "The Khojas of Bombay: The Defining of Formal Membership Criteria during the Nineteenth Century." In *Caste and Social Stratification among Muslims in India,* edited by Imtiaz Ahmad, 97–116. 2nd. ed. New Delhi: Manohar, 1978.

————. "Power in the Bombay 'Moholla,' 1904–14: An Initial Exploration into the World of the Indian Urban Muslim." *South Asia,* no. 6 (December 1976): 75–95.

————. "Spare Time and Recreation: Changing Behaviour Patterns in Bombay at the Turn of the Nineteenth Century." *South Asia,* n.s., 7, no. 1 (June 1984): 34–57.

————. *Towards Nationalism: Group Affiliations and the Politics of Public Associations in Nineteenth Century Western India.* Bombay: Popular Prakashan, 1974.

Medley, Major J. G. "Anglo-Indian Architecture." *Professional Papers in Indian Engineering* I (1863–64): 201–6.

Mehta, Dr. H. S., and P. S. Jhabvala. "Our Hospital." In *The B. D. Petit Parsee General Hospital, 1912–1972,* edited by the Editorial Board of the B. D. Petit Parsi General Hospital Executive Committee, 1–7. Bombay: Editorial Board of the B. D. Petit Parsi General Hospital Executive Committee, 1973.

Mehta, Uday. "Liberal Strategies of Exclusion." In *Tensions of Empire: Colonial Cultures in a Bourgeois World,* edited by Frederick Cooper and Ann Laura Stoler, 59–86. Berkeley: University of California Press, 1997.

Menant, Delphine. *The Parsis.* 3 vols. Translated from the French by Anthony D. Mango. Bombay: Danai, 1996. Originally published in French, 1917.

Metcalf, Barbara D., and Thomas R. Metcalf. *A Concise History of India.* Cambridge: Cambridge University Press, 2002.

Metcalf, Thomas R. *Ideologies of the Raj.* New Cambridge History of India, pt. 3, vol. 4. Cambridge: Cambridge University Press, 1994.

———. *An Imperial Vision: Indian Architecture and the British Raj.* Berkeley: University of California Press, 1989.

Mistry, Cyrus. *Doongaji House: A Play in Five Acts.* Bombay: Xal-Praxis, 1991.

Mistry, Rohinton. *Family Matters.* New York: Alfred A. Knopf, 2002.

Mitchell, Timothy. *Colonising Egypt.* Berkeley: University of California Press, 1987.

Mitter, Partha. *Art and Nationalism in Colonial India, 1850–1922.* Cambridge: Cambridge University Press, 1994.

———. *Indian Art.* Oxford History of Art Series. Oxford: Oxford University Press, 2001.

———. *Much Maligned Monsters: A History of European Reactions to Indian Art.* 1977; Chicago: University of Chicago Press, 1992.

Mody, Jehangir R. P. *Jamsetjee Jejeebhoy: The First Knight and Baronet (1783–1859).* Bombay: Jehangir R. P. Mody, 1959.

Morris, Jan, with Simon Winchester. *Stones of Empire: The Buildings of the Raj.* Oxford: Oxford University Press, 1983.

Morris, Morris David. *The Emergence of an Industrial Labor Force in India: A Study of the Bombay Cotton Mills, 1854–1947.* Berkeley: University of California Press, 1965.

Murzban, Murzban Muncherji. *Leaves from the Life of Khan Bahadur Muncherji Cowasji Murzban, C.I.E.: With an Introduction Containing a Life-Sketch of Fardunji Murzbanji.* Bombay: Printed for author by Furdoonji Byramji Marzban, 1915.

Myers, Garth Andrew. *Verandahs of Power: Colonialism and Space in Urban Africa.* Syracuse, N.Y.: Syracuse University Press, 2003.

Napier, Lord William. "Architecture for India" (quoting from Lord Napier's Lecture on Architecture). *Builder* 28 (August 27 and September 10, 1870): 680–82, 722–23.

Neild, Susan M. "Colonial Urbanism: The Development of Madras City in the Eighteenth and Nineteenth Centuries." *Modern Asian Studies* 13, no. 2 (1979): 217–46.

Newell, Lt. Col. H. A. *Bombay (The Gate of India): A Guide to Places of Interest with Map.* 2nd ed. n.p., 1920.

Nightingale, Pamela. *Trade and Empire in Western India, 1784–1806.* London: Cambridge University Press, 1970.

Nilsson, Sten. *European Architecture in India 1750–1850.* London: Faber and Faber, 1968.

Nora, Pierre. "Between Memory and History: *Les Lieux de Mémoire.*" *Representations,* no. 26 (Spring 1989): 7–24.

Oberoi, Harjot. *The Construction of Religious Boundaries: Culture, Identity, and Diversity in the Sikh Tradition.* Chicago: University of Chicago Press, 1994.

Oldenburg, Veena Talwar. *The Making of Colonial Lucknow, 1856–1877.* Princeton, N.J.: Princeton University Press, 1984.

Owen, David. *English Philanthropy 1660–1960.* Cambridge, Mass.: Belknap Press of Harvard University Press, 1964.

Palsetia, Jesse S. *The Parsis of India: Preservation of Identity in Bombay City.* Leiden: Brill, 2001.

Pandey, Gyanendra. "In Defense of the Fragment: Writing about Hindu-Muslim Riots in India Today." *Representations,* no. 37 (Winter 1992): 27–55.

Patel, Sujata, and Alice Thorner, eds. *Bombay: Metaphor for Modern India.* Bombay: Oxford University Press, 1996.

———. *Bombay: Mosaic of Modern Culture.* Bombay: Oxford University Press, 1996.

Postans, Mrs. [Marianne Young, second name]. *Western India in 1838.* 2 vols. London: Saunders and Otley, 1839.

Prakash, Gyan, and Douglas Haynes. "Introduction: The Entanglement of Power and Resistance." In *Contesting Power: Resistance and Everyday Social Relations in South Asia,* edited by Douglas Haynes and Gyan Prakash, 1–22. Berkeley: University of California Press, 1991.

Prakash, Vikramaditya, and Peter Scriver, eds. *Modernities: Building, Dwelling, and Architecture in British India and Ceylon.* London: Routledge, 2007.

Pred, Allan. "Power, Everyday Practice, and the Discipline of Human Geography." Reprint no. 189. Berkeley: University of California, Berkeley, Institute of Urban and Regional Development, 1981.

Rabinow, Paul. *French Modern: Norms and Forms of the Social Environment.* Cambridge, Mass.: MIT Press, 1989.

———. "Introduction." In *The Foucault Reader,* edited by Paul Rabinow. New York: Pantheon Books, 1984.

Rafael, Vincente L. *Contracting Colonialism: Translation and Christian Conversion in Tagalog Society under Early Spanish Rule.* Ithaca, N.Y.: Cornell University Press, 1988.

Raghunathji, K. *The Hindu Temples of Bombay.* Bombay: Fort Printing Press, 1900.

Ramanna, Mridula. *Western Medicine and Public Health in Colonial Bombay, 1845–1895* (Hyderabad: Orient Longman, 2002).

Ross, Robert, and Gerard J. Telkamp, eds. *Colonial Cities: Essays on Urbanism in a Colonial Context.* Comparative Studies in Overseas History, vol. 5. Dordrecht, Netherlands; Boston: Martinus Nijhoff Publishers, 1985.

Roth, Cecil. *The Sassoon Dynasty.* London: Robert Hale Ltd., 1941.

Rousselet, Louis. *India and its Native Princes: Travels in Central India and in the Presidencies of Bombay and Bengal.* Revised and edited by Lieut.-Col. Buckle, 1882. Reprint, Delhi: B. R. Publishing Corporation, 1975.

Rutnagur, Sorabji M., ed. *Bombay Industries: The Cotton Mills. A Review of the Progress of the Textile Industry in Bombay from 1850 to 1926 and the Present Constitution, Management, and Financial Position of the Spinning and Weaving Factories.* Bombay: Indian Textile Journal, 1927.

Said, Edward W. *Orientalism.* New York: Vintage Books, 1978.

Schapiro, Meyer. "Style." In *Anthropology Today: Selections,* edited by Sol Tax, 278–303. Chicago: University of Chicago Press, 1962.

Schorske, Carl E. *Fin-de-Siècle Vienna: Politics and Culture.* New York: Alfred A. Knopf, 1980; distributed in the United States by Random House.

Scriver, Peter. "Empire-Building and Thinking in the Public Works Department of British India." In *Modernities: Building, Dwelling, and Architecture in British India and Ceylon,* edited by Vikramaditya Prakash and Peter Scriver, 69–92. London: Routledge, 2007.

Scull, Andrew. "A Convenient Place to Get Rid of Inconvenient People: The Victorian Lunatic Asylum." In *Buildings and Society: Essays on the Social Development of the Built Environment,* edited by Anthony D. King, 37–60. London: Routledge & Kegan Paul, 1980.

Seaports of India and Ceylon: Historical and Descriptive Commercial and Industrial Facts, Figures, and Resources. Compiled and edited by Allister Macmillan. London: W. H. L. Collingridge, 1928.

Seed, Patricia. *Ceremonies of Possession in Europe's Conquest of the New World, 1492–1640.* Cambridge: Cambridge University Press, 1995.

Sheppard, Samuel T. *Bombay.* Bombay: Times of India Press, 1932.

———. *Bombay Place-Names and Street-Names: An Excursion into the By-Ways of the History of Bombay City.* Bombay: Times Press, 1917.

———. *The Byculla Club, 1833–1916: A History.* Bombay: Bennett, Coleman & Company, 1916.

Smith, T. Roger. "Architectural Art in India." *Journal of the Society of Arts* 21 (1873): 278–87.

———. "On Buildings for European Occupation in Tropical Climates, Especially India." *Builder* 26 (1868): 311–13, 348–50.

———. "On Buildings for European Occupation in Tropical Climates, Especially India." *Papers Read at the Royal Institute of British Architects, 1854–1874,* 1st series, 18 (1867/8): 197–208.

Spivak, Gayatri Chakravorty. "Can the Subaltern Speak?" In *Colonial Discourse and Post-Colonial Theory: A Reader,* edited by Patrick Williams and Laura Chrisman. New York: Columbia University Press, 1994.

Stamp, Gavin. "British Architecture in India, 1857–1947." *Journal of the Royal Society of Arts* 129 (1981): 357–79.

———. "Victorian Bombay: Urbs Prima in Indis." *Art and Archaeology Research Papers* (June 1977): 22–27.

Stein, Burton. "The Economic Function of a Medieval South Indian Temple." *Journal of Asian Studies* 19, no. 2 (February 1960): 163–76.

———. "Introduction." In *South Indian Temples: An Analytical Reconsideration,* edited by Burton Stein, 1–9. New Delhi: Vikas Publishing House, 1978.

Stoler, Ann Laura. "Sexual Affronts and Racial Frontiers: European Identities and the Cultural Politics of Exclusion in Colonial Southeast Asia," 198–237. In *Tensions of Empire: Colonial Cultures in a Bourgeois World,* edited by Frederick Cooper and Ann Laura Stoler. Berkeley: University of California Press, 1997.

Sulivan, Raymond J. F. *One Hundred Years of Bombay: History of the Bombay Chamber of Commerce, 1836–1936*. Bombay: Times of India Press, 1937.

Sutcliffe, Anthony. "Introduction: British Town Planning and the Historian." In *British Town Planning: The Formative Years*, edited by Anthony Sutcliffe, 2–14. Leicester: Leicester University Press, 1981.

Tarapor, Mahrukh. "Growse in Bulandshahr." *Architectural Review* 172 (September 1982): 44–52.

———. "John Lockwood Kipling and British Art in India." *Victorian Studies* 24 (1980): 53–81.

Tarlo, Emma. *Clothing Matters: Dress and Identity in India*. Chicago: University of Chicago Press, 1996.

Tarn, John Nelson. *Five Per Cent Philanthropy: An Account of Housing in Urban Areas between 1840 and 1914*. Cambridge: Cambridge University Press, 1973.

Taylor, Jeremy. *The Architect and the Pavilion Hospital: Dialogue and Design Creativity in England 1850–1914*. London: Leicester University Press, 1997.

———. *Hospital and Asylum Architecture in England 1840–1914: Building for Health Care*. London: Mansell Publishing Ltd., 1991.

Temple, Sir Richard. *Men and Events of My Time in India*. London: John Murray, 1882.

Thomas, Nicholas. *Colonialism's Culture: Anthropology, Travel, and Government*. Princeton, N.J.: Princeton University Press, 1994.

Thompson, John D. and Grace Goldin. *The Hospital: A Social and Architectural History*. New Haven, Conn.: Yale University Press, 1975.

Tillotson, G. H. R. *The Tradition of Indian Architecture: Continuity, Controversy, and Change since 1850*. New Haven, Conn.: Yale University Press, 1989.

Tindall, Gillian. *City of Gold: The Biography of Bombay*. 1982; reprint, with new introduction by the author, New Delhi: Penguin Books India, 1992.

Upton, Dell. "Architectural History or Landscape History." *Journal of Architectural Education* 44, no. 4 (1991): 195–99.

———. *Architecture in the United States*. Oxford History of Art series. Oxford: Oxford University Press, 1998.

———. "Form and User: Style, Mode, Fashion, and the Artifact," 156–69. In *Living in a Material World: Canadian and American Approaches to Material Culture*, edited by Gerald L. Pocius. Newfoundland: Institute of Social and Economic Research, 1991.

———. "Seen, Unseen, and Scene." In *Understanding Ordinary Landscapes*, edited by Todd W. Bressi and Paul Groth, 174–79. New Haven, Conn.: Yale University, 1997.

Wacha, Sir Dinshaw E. *A Financial Chapter in the History of Bombay City*. Bombay: Commercial Press, 1910.

———. *Rise and Growth of Bombay Municipal Government*. Madras: G. A. Natesan & Company, 1913.

———. *Shells from the Sands of Bombay: Being My Recollections and Reminiscences, 1860–1875*. Bombay: K. T. Anklesaria, 1920.

Wadia, D. F. *History of Lodge Rising Star of Western India, No. 342 S.C.* Bombay: British India Press, 1912.

Weber, Max. *Basic Concepts in Sociology.* Translated and with an introduction by H. P. Secher. Secaucus, N.J.: Citadel Press, 1980; copyright 1962, Philosophical Library.

————. *The Protestant Ethic and the Spirit of Capitalism.* Translated by Talcott Parsons, with a foreword by R. H. Tawney. New York: Charles Scribner's Sons, 1958.

White, Richard. *The Middle Ground: Indians, Empires, and Republics in the Great Lakes Region, 1650–1815.* New York: Cambridge University Press, 1991.

Wilkins, Capt. H. St. Clair. "European General Hospital, Bombay." Designed by Capt. H. St. Clair Wilkins. In *Professional Papers in Indian Engineering,* vol. 1, 1863–64, edited by Major J. G. Medley, 406–10. Roorkee: Thomason College Press, 1864.

Wilkinson, Catherine. "The New Professionalism in the Renaissance." In *The Architect: Chapters in the History of the Profession,* edited by Spiro Kostof, 124–60. With a new foreword and epilogue by Dana Cuff. Berkeley: University of California Press, 1977; foreword and epilogue copyright by Dana Cuff, 2000.

Williams, Raymond. *Keywords: A Vocabulary of Culture and Society.* Rev. ed. New York: Oxford University Press, 1983.

Wilson, William H. *The City Beautiful Movement.* Baltimore, Md.: Johns Hopkins University Press, 1989.

Wilton-Ely, John. "The Rise of the Professional Architect in England." In *The Architect: Chapters in the History of the Profession,* edited by Spiro Kostof, 180–208. With a new foreword and epilogue by Dana Cuff. Berkeley: University of California Press, 1977; foreword and epilogue copyright Dana Cuff, 2000.

Wohl, A. S. "The Housing of the Working Classes in London, 1815–1914." In *The History of Working-Class Housing: A Symposium,* edited by Stanley D. Chapman. Totowa, N.J: Rowman and Littlefield, 1971.

Wolpert, Stanley. *A New History of India.* 2nd ed. Oxford University Press: New York, 1982.

Wright, Gwendolyn. *The Politics of Design in French Colonial Urbanism.* Chicago: University of Chicago Press, 1991.

Yeoh, Brenda S. A. *Contesting Space: Power Relations and the Urban Built Environment in Colonial Singapore.* Kuala Lampur: Oxford University Press, 1996.

Index

Preeti Chopra is associate professor of visual culture studies and architectural and urban history at the University of Wisconsin–Madison. She has worked as an architect and landscape architect and has trained as a city and regional planner with a focus on urban design.